Contents

Acknowledgements

Charley Baker

I would like to thank the late Fran Biley, for everything. Thanks to Vida Guildford who, as ward manager of the inner-London adolescent unit I began working on at the age of 20, opened my eyes to a range of positive approaches towards people experiencing self-harm. I would like to thank my husband Simon, who, as a practising registered mental health nurse, both challenges and encourages me, and gave me the space and time I needed to pull this book together. Finally, and most importantly, I want to thank all those who were generous and brave in sharing their stories to create this book, and to acknowledge all those who are experiencing self-harm – your strength in struggle is inspiring.

Clare Shaw

I'd like to thank Lou Pembroke, Maggie Ross, Judi Chamberlin, David Webb, Debra Shulkes, Janet Frame, Andy Smith, and all those other men and women who walked bravely in dark places. For your words and for the conviction you gave me that words bring light and change lives, thank you. Anna, Kaety, Laura, Xoe, Lizzie, Rachel, Leanne, Denise, Judith, Dee Dee, and all those I met in the darkness … for those of us who made it, and those of us who didn't, I give very sincere thanks. And to Tamsin, Alice, Ria, Dona and Esther, and all my other sisters-in-arms – thanks, thanks, thanks for the love, the laughs, the fury and the friendship. Long may we continue.

Editors

Charley Baker

Charley Baker is a lecturer in Mental Health at the University of Nottingham. She has a BA and MA in literature and is working on her PhD on psychosis and postmodernism at Royal Holloway, University of London. During her studies, Charley worked in both community adult and inpatient adolescent mental health for the NHS. Charley is Associate Editor of the *Journal of Psychiatric and Mental Health Nursing*, has been awarded the title of Fellow of the Institute of Mental Health, and serves on the editorial board for the *Journal of Medical Humanities*. She has spoken internationally on issues of representations of mental illness in literature, and has interests around self-harm, suicide, 'personality disorders' and the therapeutic use of reading. She is lead author on the co-authored monograph *Madness in Post-1945 British and American Fiction* (Palgrave, 2010) and was invited contributor and literary advisor for the psychiatry textbook *Psychiatry PRN* (Oxford University Press, 2009). She has also written on rape in Angela Carter's fiction, and has published a range of peer-reviewed journal articles. Charley is co-founder of the Arts and Humanities Research Council-funded international Madness and Literature Network (www.madnessandliterature.org) and International Health Humanities Network (www.healthhumanities.org).

Clare Shaw

Clare Shaw (BA, MA) is a survivor-activist and educationalist who draws from personal, academic and professional experience of self-harm. A prominent figure in the UK self-harm movement, Clare was a founding member of several organisations, including the National Self-Harm Minimisation Group. From 2006 until 2013 Clare was also a director and lead trainer at harm-ed. As an independent freelance self-harm trainer and consultant (www.clareshawconsultancy.co.uk) Clare continues to influence practice across the UK and beyond. She has published a range of articles and chapters, and has spoken internationally on issues including self-harm, suicide, sexual abuse and borderline personality disorder. 2013 will see the publication of 'Minimising Harm, Maximising Hope', a special edition of *Asylum: The Magazine for Democratic Psychiatry* co-edited by Clare alongside Helen Spandler and Sam Warner; and *Otis Doesn't Scratch*, a groundbreaking storybook guide for children living with self-harm with an accompanying guide for the adults who support them, written by Clare with illustrations by Tamsin Walker. Clare is also an acclaimed poet and a popular performer of her own work. Described by the Arvon Foundation as 'one of Britain's most dynamic and powerful young poets', she is widely anthologised and has two collections published with Bloodaxe (www.clareshawpoetry.co.uk).

Fran Biley

The late Dr Francis C. Biley initially trained as a mental health and an adult nurse and, after holding a range of clinical and practice development posts, moved into undergraduate and postgraduate research and teaching. He co-edited *Our Encounters with Madness* (PCCS Books, 2011) with Alec Grant and Hannah Walker. He was Associate Professor in the Centre for Qualitative Research at Bournemouth University in the UK, Adjunct Professor of Nursing at Seton Hall University, New Jersey, in the USA, and a governor of a local Foundation Trust hospital.

Foreword

Helen Spandler

I was honoured to be asked to write a foreword to this book. As part of the 'Encounters' book series, it takes its place within an important tradition which foregrounds experiential knowledge. In the field of self-harm, the first anthology of survivor experiences was the now-legendary *Self-Harm: Perspectives from personal experience*, edited by Louise Pembroke in 1994. This came out of a ground-breaking conference in 1989 organised by activists – psychiatric survivors in Survivors Speak Out and feminists from the Bristol Crisis Service for Women. At this time, self-harm was as much of a taboo as sexual abuse had previously been, and self-harm was little researched (other than by clinicians). Self-harm, like sexual abuse, is no longer such a taboo, and we now have a much greater awareness about the various meanings and functions of self-harm.

This change would not have been possible without the determination of early activists like these. They were pioneers who courageously spoke out about their experiences, locating them in oppressive social structures and relations, and campaigned for better services and understanding. In this process, personal lives were transformed into public acts of witness and resistance. Some of these early activists continue their struggle; some have gone on to other things; others live quieter lives. Some paid a great price for their courage, and took their own lives. We owe them all a great deal. Through their actions they opened up a space behind them, for others – not just activists, but 'ordinary' people – to share their experiences. They paved the way for books like this.

Yet if things have changed so much for the better, if the subject of self-harm is no longer taboo, and if it is so well researched, why do we still need books like these? Unfortunately, and paradoxically, the growth in research and self-harm literature does not necessarily make it any easier for people to tell their own stories. Whilst there is a proliferation of research literature, survivors' voices still struggle to be heard. In order to keep open the spaces created for us, we must continue to occupy them.

At the same time, where once the issue of self-harm was silenced and hidden, there is now a danger of it being dismissed as last year's issue. Yet the profoundly disturbing and widespread reality of self-harm cannot be ignored. Neither can it be easily remedied by new clinical techniques, guidelines or pills. Self-harm is a powerful act and in naming it we recognise what it is like to feel this bad about ourselves. It is an indictment of our society, reminding us that many of us are, quite literally, tearing our own bodies apart.

When we listen to the experience of survivors we are taught not only about self-harm, but also about the nature of wider society, a society that generates the conditions in which people feel worthless, that often lacks compassion for the most vulnerable amongst us. The glib rejection of survivor stories as either 'anecdotal' or symptomatic of a 'victim culture' is done at our peril, for it denies our vulnerabilities (and our strengths) and perpetuates cultures which lack compassion.

Books like 'Encounters' and 'Perspectives' are rarely referenced by academics or clinicians, and rarely do they make their way into policy documents and clinical guidelines. However, they can still have a profound impact. As Clare Shaw explains, books and stories can save lives. I've seen many presentations at various academic, professional and political conferences and events. Two stand out in my mind, both delivered by self-harm survivor-activists. I first saw Louise Pembroke speak at a conference in the early 1990s. Her presentation challenged my own thinking on self-harm and massively influenced my work in this area. More recently, I was privileged to witness a presentation called 'Let Us Stand Up and Say that Evil has been Done to Us', by Clare Shaw and Debra Shulkes. This resulted in the audience being collectively moved to tears. Powerful stories affect us, and they can result in action and change.

Not everyone has the opportunity to hear such inspiring speakers and not everyone relates to them in the same way. In collating individual experiences, books like these enable others to be able to access, and benefit from, our individual learning. By giving voice to the diversity of experience, we increase the chances of us finding stories in which we can recognise ourselves. There is nothing quite like the feeling that accompanies seeing our own private struggles finally reflected back to us.

Therefore, this book offers an important contribution, not only to the growing literature on self-harm, but also to our understanding of how individuals experience and respond to suffering. It doesn't offer easy solutions or grand theories. Neither does it present straightforward 'recovery' stories. But it does illustrate the rich, often raw, complexities of self-harm. In so doing, it exemplifies the dilemmas involved for all of us. If we take these stories seriously, they warn us off too readily making assumptions about the causes and meanings of self-harm or jumping to any simple conclusions. Yet the wealth of accumulated experience presented here demonstrates that the early activists were right. They might not have been 'representative', but they did not just speak for themselves.

About the author

Helen Spandler is Reader in Mental Health at the University of Central Lancashire. She is the author of *Who's Hurting Who?: Young people self-harm and suicide* (42nd Street, 1996) and co-editor of *Beyond Fear and Control: Working with young people with who self-harm* (PCCS Books, 2007). She is also on the editorial collective of *Asylum: The Magazine for Democratic Psychiatry* (published by PCCS Books) and recently edited a special issue of the magazine on 'Self-Harm: Minimising harm, maximising hope' (2013; 20: 2).

Reference

Pembroke, L (1994) *Self-Harm: Perspectives from personal experience.* London: Survivors Speak Out.

Preface

Clare Shaw

There were six beds in the room: two rows of three, each separated by a chipboard locker (keys long lost) and a stiff grey and purple curtain. The rails were detachable. I was in the bed closest to the double doors, which led out onto the corridor – lightless, furthest from the windows. The flat roofs of the hospital's ground floor lay beneath us; the low houses of Toxteth stretched on towards to the river.

It's the light I remember – the lack of it. What light did seep into that place was yellow-grey, the colour of old water. The shadows were long; they wouldn't lift; the sun never reached my bed. I'd lie and shake, in a pain so acute that even now my stomach clenches when I remember it. Not just the quality and depth of pain, but the dirty tangle of thoughts that surrounded it. The confusion. The utter, utter hopelessness. The sound-smell of the ward; its squalor.

An absence of light and a darkness that grew and persisted. I was 22 and had lost everything: my family, my friends, my career, my hopes and ambitions; everything had fallen away. I was a psychiatric patient – long-term. Worse than that, I was personality disordered. I was never going to get better. The fault, as I had always suspected, lay inside me. I was all wrong and no one could help me.

What kept me going? Friends? Literature? I don't know. Lizzie brought me a shell in the shape of a unicorn's horn and a string of Russian classics in the belief that I wouldn't kill myself halfway through a good story. Good theory – I had always been a reader. I was hungry, not just for knowledge, not just for language, but for the food and fuel that it brought to the starving place I was in. My body was too thin; my spine, a line of bruises. My arms were gaping with wounds.

And into that place came light: Louise Pembroke's *Self-harm: Perspectives from personal experience*, Dorothy Rowe's *Depression: The way out of your prison*, and Judi Chamberlin's *On Our Own: Patient controlled alternatives to the mental health system*. I don't know which I read first but I do know – with total certainty – that these women saved my life. In the time that it took to read those books, I moved. I read and read, and my world changed. Even in the reality of ongoing struggles with distress, I continued – I continue – to move. From powerlessness to power. From hopelessness to hope. From numb interminable grief to passionate fury. From bewildered passivity to action, action, action.

Action on my own behalf – rejecting the labels and the treatments that had not worked for me. Reclaiming the territory of my own mind, my own body, my own small world. I can decide who I am and how I am going to live. And realising within that I am not alone. Action with others, for others.

It is now almost 20 years since *Perspectives* was first published, but its importance still resonates through my life. So when I was approached by Fran Biley and Charley Baker and asked if I would co-edit a book which would, in many ways, act as an updated version, it was an easy decision to make.

Action does not have to mean setting up groups, or producing newsletters, or attending rallies, or running for election. One of the most important actions we can ever take is telling our stories. For ourselves, to ourselves. Acknowledging and meeting the painful truths of our own lives. And sharing those truths in the best ways we have. Shouting them out. Writing them down.

When – as staff, survivor, friend or carer – we speak openly and thoughtfully about our own encounters with self-harm, we challenge the silence and the stigma that surrounds the issue. We create meaning. We own our own experiences, our own lives. We shift the dominant account away from the medical and towards the personal. We meet each other as people. We draw attention to the real causes of distress. We highlight the enormous courage and resilience behind self-harm. We create connection. We construct firm foundations for mutual understanding and collaboration. We identify what works and what doesn't. We offer hope, comfort, reassurance. We are not alone. And so with every story, the world shifts a little, for the better.

Whoever you are, whatever your relationship with self-harm, wherever you are in your journey through this difficult, beautiful world, wherever you are reading this book – in your living room, on the night shift, in a cafe waiting for your friend, in a cell, in the five minutes before your next client, on a narrow bed in a lightless ward – I hope this book and the stories it contains (like the books I read all those years ago) offers you knowledge, insight, courage, consolation, hope.

And light.

Pass it on.

Introduction

Charley Baker

It seems fitting to begin this book by sharing my own narrative, my own encounters with self-harm. I initially thought about writing a relatively short, but academic, overview of self-harm for this introduction, providing facts and figures, citing reports and appraising research into the importance of listening to people's experiences. But this troubled me, for quite some time, as we began to receive submissions for the book. Because writing such a piece would have placed me in a position of knowledge, of 'knowing' about self-harm. And, as the submissions flowed in, I realised that I *didn't* 'know' about self-harm – not really. Everything that one *needs* to know about self-harm, and about how to respond effectively and compassionately towards people who are encountering and experiencing self-harm, is within these narratives. I do have 'knowledge' about self-harm – I have read a lot of theoretical material, guidelines, treatment approaches, autobiographical narratives; I have worked with and spoken to many, many people who experience self-harm. This is different, however, from *knowing*. The people who experience self-harm are the people who know about self-harm. Those who have so generously and bravely shared their stories here are the experts – not me, in my bubble of academia, research and teaching.

This book began its life with two significant events in 2011. First – and shallowly, perhaps – with an argument on Facebook. A good friend had been to a training event on self-harm and personality disorder, which she had found both powerful and positive. I commented that it was good to hear such education was occurring, as it was desperately needed to counteract some prevalent negative attitudes towards the two issues. Some friends of hers, professionals in different backgrounds, then repeated the very same negative attitudes I was referring to. That people who self-harmed were somehow less entitled to care and treatment than someone with an illness or accidental injury. That self-harm was 'difficult' to work with. That people who self-harmed were draining on resources and emotions. That their priority was always someone who sought help for something that occurred through 'no fault of their own' – though 'fault' seemed confined to people who had attempted suicide or self-harmed through overdose, and did not include people who needed treatment for, for example, a broken bone caused by playing sport, or someone who had diabetes and ignored their insulin requirements. When I countered these attitudes, I was told that it was up to 'me' to 'educate' people. Aside from the unfeasibility of 'me' educating professionals *en masse* about self-harm, the row did prompt me to think – about how people who self-harm had come to be seen as difficult, challenging and unworthy of care and support in some way, by people who are otherwise consummate professionals. In particular, I thought about how people are reduced to a physical injury and a concomitant psychiatric label, without the rich diversity of their individual lives being taken into account.

A conversation ensued between myself and Francis Biley following the publication of the acclaimed *Our Encounters with Madness* (edited by Alec Grant, Francis Biley and Hannah Walker) in 2011. Alec Grant, in the introduction to this book, talks at length of the importance of *listening* to people's stories, highlighting the multiple functions of narratives. Primarily, as Arthur Frank (1995) suggests, stories around illness, suffering or endurance can be healing, enacting an enduring testimony to the life lived both within and outside of the medical gaze. I strongly and passionately believe in the transformative and restorative powers of narrative – not least in humanising complex lived experiences of distress, pain and suffering, which are simplified and reduced by codification into a medicalised formulation. Lived experiences attest to personal strength, survival and recovery – commentary that can be missed when voices of power profess to speak *for* those who encounter self-harm in such medical language.

I put these two elements – my row on Facebook, and my belief in the power of personal narrative – to Fran. He agreed that, provided this wasn't another book *on* self-harm written 'by-professionals-for-professionals', and provided that there was no personal profit to be made for us as editors (there is not – all royalties from this book will be donated to Harmless, a charity working with self-harm in Nottingham), he would be happy to co-edit the book with me. We then approached

Clare Shaw, who has also generously shared her time, vast knowledge and personal experience in developing this book.

My own experience with self-harm spans the past 13 years, from the age of 18 when I first began work as a care assistant on a busy medical unit at a local general hospital. I was fortunate there, to encounter some fantastic psychiatric liaison nurses who countered the dominant perspective I heard – that people who had self-harmed were not 'really ill', that they were 'attention seeking', that their overdoses or lacerations were 'mainly superficial, therefore not a significant suicide attempt'. I did not initially realise that self-harm existed *outside* of an attempt to end a life; I did not realise it could be, conversely, a way of saving that same life. Of course, there were a large number of medical and nursing staff who were compassionate and supportive towards those who were admitted. But the attitudes remained, hidden beneath a veneer of professionalism which, at times, risked being somewhat coldly efficient rather than humanely compassionate.

Later, working in psychiatric services, I began to think more critically about such attitudes. I felt the hot fear of anxiety when someone I worked with self-harmed, the pull towards a paternalistic desire to keep someone safe and to 'fix things' for them. I felt confused when someone hurt themselves in spite of the 'best' I could do, fearing that my 'best' was not effective.

I met a huge number of clinical staff who were creative in their approaches to self-harm, caring and kind, and critically minded towards negative attitudes. These staff pointed me in the direction of thoughtful and thought-provoking books on self-harm, increasing my theoretical knowledge. I watched their kindness, humanity and understanding in action, absorbing the warmth and genuineness they displayed. I listened, and I learned, from people who hurt themselves, for a myriad of reasons and in a myriad of ways.

But I also heard, and continue to hear from people who experience services and from my students who are in clinical practice, cries of 'It's all for attention; it's just behavioural, don't feed in to it', and the like. I found some approaches to self-harm to be rejecting and punitive, such as withholding therapeutic contact if someone broke a 'contract' not to harm between sessions. I struggled to hear about people encountering medical and nursing staff who were dismissive and cold, or angry and unpleasant. I struggled, at times, to know what to 'do' for the best, not realising that 'being with' someone, staying with someone's distress instead of trying instantly to 'fix' it, validating their right to be upset or angry, or hollow or numb and – vitally – acknowledging their self-harm as a coping strategy rather than an automatic sign of psychopathology, could be the better approach.

Louise Pembroke's work was a huge inspiration for me, in particular around harm minimisation approaches to self-harm, and she has since generously allowed me to share her own work with my students. I no longer work in the NHS, but as a lecturer in mental health. Part of this role involves teaching both adult-field and mental-health-field nursing students, including sessions on self-harm, working with suicidality, and therapeutic working with risk. I use people's narratives in my teaching, and suggested reading usually includes autobiographies and collections of narratives – because I believe, passionately, that people should not only tell their stories, but that clinicians and those working with self-harm *need* to hear them. I do not believe that the negative responses that people have experienced when seeking help for their self-harm are caused because psychiatric and other clinical staff are inherently dismissive or callous. I think that self-harm can be difficult to understand, and that staff can be afraid of asking people about it (other than within a risk assessment or care planning framework) because they are worried about causing more harm, 'opening a can of worms', or fear not being able to respond effectively.

The most effective response in the first instance, I find, particularly for my students or for professionals who will have little contact with individuals because they are not in a long- term therapeutic relationship, is perhaps one of simple compassion. A compassionate response, to my mind, means a human response to the fact that someone has reached a point where life is so challenging that self-harm is the only option, or the best option available at that time. It involves connecting humanly and humanely with the person, not (as is told in many of these stories) treating only the physical wound or problem. It means listening *and* hearing. It means basic human kindness and empathy. This kindness and empathy, I think, can be initiated, nurtured, developed and strengthened by reading people's personal accounts of their own journeys through, with and beyond self-harm. Reading people's experiences, while distressing at times, can humanise the medicalised labels, acting as a reminder to the life alongside and outside of the visible and invisible wounds. They can provide for professionals a safe medium through which reflection and exploration, as well as knowledge, can develop. For people experiencing self-harm, personally or as a carer, these stories provide hope, useful strategies that have helped people, and routes towards a compassionate perspective. Because empathy and human kindness – the key elements I identified above – need to be self-reflexive. If you are encountering self-harm personally, you *do* deserve compassionate care and support. If you are encountering self-harm professionally, a compassionate approach to your own clinical supervision, peer support and professional development is important.

Should you currently be experiencing self-harm and not receiving support for this, we hope that this book will encourage you to seek help should you want or need to do so. There are some excellent support systems in place to help, not all run or managed by the NHS. If you have a supportive GP, or know of one at the practice you attend, this may be a good starting point. You may be lucky enough to live near one of the excellent sources of support highlighted in this book, like Dial House in Leeds (www.lslcs.org.uk/how-can-we-help/dial-house). National organisations like the National Self Harm Network (www.nshn.co.uk), Bristol Crisis Service for Women (www.selfinjurysupport.org.uk), Harmless (www.harmless.org.uk) and the Self-Harm Sanctuary offer web-based information and support. Bristol Crisis Service for Women also offers information on local support groups throughout the country, and young women aged up to 25 can access text and email support via their TESS service (0780 047 2908 / www.selfinjurysupport.org.uk/tess-text-and-email-support-service). In addition, the Basement Project (www.basementproject.co.uk), Mind (www.mind.org.uk/mental_health_a-z/8006_self-harm) and others listed above all produce accessible, useful information aimed at people who self-harm and the staff, friends and family who care for them. The Samaritans offer a 24-hour telephone helpline, along with other forms of support for those in distress and despair (www.samaritans.org / 08457 90 90 90). Finally, there are mental health support systems that are accessible via Accident and Emergency if you are in crisis or struggling.

The road to getting this book to its final published stage has not been an easy one. Our co-editor, Francis Biley, died during the initial collating of people's experiences. Fran was inspirational to me, believing wholeheartedly (though this belief involved some teasing) in my belief that I can 'make a difference'. His death left me awash with uncertainty and somewhat adrift with the book, oscillating between passionate belief in its value and worth, and fear that it somehow wouldn't hold true to his philosophy. But I hope this book would have made him proud, following as it does his deeply held beliefs in the value of humanising psychiatry and creatively approaching manifestations of distress, trauma and altered states of mind.

The structure of this book is deliberately quite loose. We have included a range of voices, predominantly from people who have personally experienced self-harm, but also those who have worked with and who care for people too. There was no easy division, however, between 'service users', 'professionals' and 'carers' – something that I strongly believe lies in the arbitrary, but powerful, divisions between groups of people. Many people I have encountered in my 13 years of working, in diverse ways, with self-harm, have used different services, while also being professionals from different backgrounds, and carers for friends and family. I myself do not fit easily into boxes. At different points, we all fall into different categories.

Nonetheless, the book starts with the voices of those who are most often not heard – the narratives of those who have direct, lived experience of self-harm. We move on to a consideration of finding the words to speak, think and write about self-harm, and then some more overarching formulations of self-harm by people who have personal experience of it. We look at the narratives of people who care for and work with those who self-harm, and then explore the experiences of young people and child and adolescent mental health services. Finally, we provide a 'then and now' comparison of two pieces that both emerged from secure inpatient women's services.

The vast majority of pieces have a 'thoughts' section at the end. Some of these are composed of hints and tips for clinical staff and non-clinical family members, friends and carers. Some are elements that people have found helpful themselves when struggling, navigating and coming to terms with self-harm. I learned much from these sections, and much from people's experiences. I hope that these narratives can prompt thoughtfulness, reflection and consideration of the ways in which self-harm is approached from clinicians and staff members, and the ways in which people experiencing self-harm can best be supported, cared for, and nurtured towards a time when life is easier. I hope that this book will provide people with hope, and with – as Clare says – light.

References

Frank, A (1995) *The Wounded Storyteller*. Chicago: University of Chigaco Press.

Grant, A, Biley, F & Walker, H (2011) *Our Encounters with Madness*. Ross-on-Wye: PCCS Books.

OUR ENCOUNTERS WITH SELF-HARM

2

Fight for life

Claire Shortland

Nobody grows up thinking their life will be one of self-harm, or one that involves a fight for life due to their own hands and mind. With the innocence of youth and very little understanding of what suicide really meant, I began from the age of 12 onwards to feel like I wanted God to take me away. I then began to self-harm at the age of 14.

Difficult life experiences would lead me to the edge of destruction and mean I would have to bring myself back from the hardest four years of my life. By the time I reached 14, I had been witness to domestic violence. There was one incident when I was six years old and had to flee with my mum to a women's refuge. That day I left behind several animals; it was only later that I found out my stepfather had taken their lives away, leaving only one dog to survive. At the age of six, I felt guilty: guilty for not staying with them, not stopping him and saving them from their fate. Other incidents included seeing my mum attacked in front of me, powerless to help, powerless to stop him. All of this had happened before I reached the age of nine, which brought its own haunting images. This, bullying, and becoming a carer at the age of 10 for my autistic sister and my mum, meant I quickly became an adult in a child's body.

Due to physical and verbal abuse, I not only went to bed every night wishing I could die but I began to self-harm. Rather than hurting people I loved for hurting me, I used self-harm as a method of punishment. I could not allow myself to shout back at them, to tell them they should not hit or call me what they did. Instead self-harm silenced the anger I felt. In adult terms, wanting to die would be classed as suicidal ideation. In a child's eye, it was simply a way to escape an unbearable pain. Because of nonstop bullying for missing school and, at 14, losing someone who was like a dad to me to suicide – my next-door neighbour, who was the only person I could lean on – the self-harm became more frequent. Being the last person to see or speak to my neighbour before he did what he did, I would carry the guilt of not saving his life around with me for years to come. Fearful of ridicule and further trouble at home, I kept the suicidal and self-harming thoughts a secret until I reached 18. It was my secret, my own dark little hell, but I would later regret this.

To this day, I know what the final breaking point was, the reason why I became so ill. At 15, after several incidents, I was thrown out of my mum's house. I went to stay at my sister's for a few days where I was told news that would bring further guilt. My mum and dad separated when I was younger because of his violence. Growing up I was told of the graphic incidents that had happened to my mum, one of which meant that my baby brother was stillborn due to my dad's actions. As a child, I was always close to my great nan. However, as I got older my grandparents and mum would argue. As grandchildren we were used as a weapon – if my grandparents and mum fell out, we would not be able to see them, hence I would be unable to see my great nan. While I was at my sister's house I phoned my nan. I was told she had died a year before. I felt an unbearable, suffocating guilt for not being there, not being able to say goodbye when she went. If I had known at the time she had died, I would have had to deal with two deaths within five months, and I know this would have destroyed me. I guess life has its own mysterious protective ways.

I went to live with my dad but, at the age of 16, he would be the second person to throw me out. There are no words to describe how scary it was to be standing on a street, waiting for a bus, not knowing where I would live or who would help. The abandonment was soon rectified by way of my sister taking me in. However, this would be the final straw. At the age of 18, my sister wanted to go and live with her boyfriend, leaving me potentially homeless. With the fear of being homeless and the thought of suicide already implanted, my head had come to the decision that I could not cope and would rather die than be homeless again. There are no words to describe the fear at that point; there was nobody to support me and things were like fragile glass with my mum. I guess these are the reasons why I have felt the way I have and why I feel the way I do. The reasons why I have become the person I am and, most importantly, why I self-harm and have previously attempted suicide.

Age 18 became an unwanted turning point. Amazingly, after much prompting, the general practitioner coaxed out of me what was happening. It was then I was diagnosed with borderline personality disorder. Despite rapidly deteriorating mentally, I fought to continue with my A-levels, even after my first suicide attempt. My first admission to the acute ward was a scary and lonely experience. What was happening? The images of me committing suicide were rife. It felt like I had two people in my head: one would repeatedly tell me to die and do what I was seeing, the other tried tirelessly to save my life. Wherever I was, wherever I went, the sensations of harming, the voice of destruction and the image of suicide would follow, like a dog to its owner. In my head I was going crazy but to some of the National Health Service staff I encountered, I was merely attention seeking. The diagnosis of borderline personality disorder gave me reassurance that there was an answer to my problems but also brought its own stigma. With memories haunting me and a mixed-up head, I attempted suicide three to four times a week, and my self-harm became life-threatening. I did not want to die; I just wanted to escape from the hell I was in.

I discovered an illogical solution to my mental images of jumping from a bridge. Others would never understand, but I reasoned that if I physically disabled myself by hurting my leg, it would save my life; I would not be *able* to go to the bridge. This brought its own problems. In my head, I wanted to be with the person who supported me once again, the one who gave me comfort and reminded me of the innocence of childhood – my next-door neighbour. I attended hospital where I was told that if I kept doing damage to my leg, by leaving foreign bodies in it, I would either lose my leg or die. For a suicidal person, this was the answer I needed. Unknowingly, the doctor had given me fruitful knowledge. If I kept the foreign bodies in my leg, I would die and be with my neighbour again. If I let the medical staff treat me and take them away, then I would lose the chance of being with my friend again, and any chance of not hurting anymore.

With everything else that was going on, I had also been involved with two partners – one who did something which meant that I will never be able to be in a locked building without knowing where the keys are again, and one who took me through a court case because of his actions.

Attending hospital was a mixed set of experiences. Some staff were amazing: they supported me, tried to talk me around and to give me hope. However, some would talk about me in front of me, give me treatment without painkillers, and not want to hear any reasoning as to why I did not want my leg to be treated. I once attended hospital after cutting myself and a doctor came into the room and started treating me with no warning, no painkillers and no communication. Another time a doctor walked into the room and treated my leg without even telling me what he was going to do. I had put my trust into the hospital and it would quickly decay.

I was seriously in trouble, and I thought I would succeed in being gone by the age of 20. I begged for hospital admission; I begged for them to save my life. Eventually, they did. The part of me who wanted to survive had won. I was sent to the Acorn Programme in York. It's a residential unit specifically designed to treat borderline personality disorder. There was a range of therapies offered, such as art therapy, DBT (dialectical behaviour therapy), psychotherapy and individual support. The programme saved my life.

I am now four years into recovery. Through becoming a Rethink activist and hearing about other people's experiences when attending hospital after self-harm or suicide attempts, I created 'Different Minds, Same Hearts'. The campaign exists to help improve negative attitudes and the treatment people receive when attending hospital due to self-harm or suicide attempts. It does not stand to criticise the NHS and its staff, but to try to improve staff attitudes, people's experiences and to reduce the stigma attached to these issues.

The most important thing of all is that self-harm happens for a reason – and everybody's reasoning for self-harm is and will always be different. Those wounds that lie beneath the obvious cannot always be seen or known about. I cannot blame the hospital for the problems I encountered. If we don't step into somebody else's shoes, or self-harm ourselves, how can we know what it's like? We cannot always fix a problem if we do not know why it has occurred. Hopefully the campaign will help to raise awareness of self-harm, and, by talking about my own issues, I will help in some little way to reduce the stigma that lies around it.

Thoughts

• Self-harm happens for a reason.

• Some, including myself, have experienced a childhood and early adulthood that is too painful and traumatic to put into words. That may be the sole, if not the only, reason they self-harmed – to cope with trauma.

- For people who self-harm, it is their coping mechanism.

- Never judge a book by its cover – or rather, don't see self-harm as only in need of medical treatment, but look at what lies deep within.

About the author

I am now in my steps to full recovery and happy to say my biggest milestone is not attempting suicide for four years this June. I'm now an activist for Rethink Mental Illness and have started the campaign 'Different Minds, Same Hearts', which is growing stronger each day. The campaign aims to improve attitudes and treatment people receive when they go to hospital after self-harming or attempting suicide, through raising awareness of these subjects via radio, TV and newspapers. The campaign is also developing training into the NHS using personal experience and through speaking to university medical students. I also volunteer for DORA, a self-help support group and funding organisation. A recent achievement was holding a self-harm awareness day, which was attended by over 100 people from various backgrounds and professions. I am also pleased to announce that I have started running a new local self-harm self-help group.

3

Justification

Naomi Salisbury

Last Friday I cut myself, as planned, but I really don't know why.

And I should know why, you'd think, after all these years.

In essence, I'm a fraud.

I've had years of therapy. I actually help to run courses on understanding self-harm. People tell me I'm inspirational, which I hate, and I feel it puts me under pressure not to fail, to get it right for everyone. I should have so much knowledge and understanding and insight. I know what to do: to try and work out why I want to self-harm at that time, to try and find something to substitute that gives me something similar, to try and distract myself. To reach out for help. And I have such good intentions.

I do all the right things. I'm good. I am a good patient. I don't want to cause anyone any trouble. I know what I should do. I don't do anything dangerous. And I know I'm not special. I'm nothing unusual. I'm just another woman who cuts herself; it's almost to be expected. I'm statistically very neat and tidy. But, luckily some might say, I don't use lots of services. I don't go to Accident and Emergency or even my GP that often. I take my pills. I behave.

My use of self-harm both fascinates and repulses me.

It leaves me powerless and it gives me power over myself.

But why am I fighting with myself? What am I even fighting for?

Some part of me doesn't care. It's not that I don't want to stop. It's that I don't care if I do. I don't care what the consequences are. Still some part of me thinks this is all I am worth.

On Saturday I felt wild. Raging with confusion about who I am, what I want. I wanted to climb out of my own skin and be someone else. Anything would have been better than feeling the way I was. All I wanted to do was damage myself. It was visceral. It was fierce. I was no one and I was nothing. I didn't matter enough even to hurt myself. I wanted to disappear.

I feel like I should have grown out of it by now. In training I talk about it so easily, but when I try to talk about it for myself, I can't do it. I'm deeply ashamed. I don't believe anyone else should feel like that, but somehow it's different for me. I think about what I've put my family and friends through. I think about how I will have to hide this week's cuts from people, not because they'll judge me or be angry, but because it will hurt them and I can't bear that. And yet I still do it. I know what I might lose and there is so much now, but it's still not enough.

I used to know why. For a long time I didn't. It just happened and for a time my whole life revolved around it. Get up, go out, wait for my flatmates to go out, come home to cut in peace, get on with the day. And repeat. And repeat. Every day. And I would fight with myself – physically holding my hand away from me – not to do it. Some part of me hated me, but some part of me cared.

Over time I began to be able to link it to things, like feeling angry, being upset by someone, or feeling alone and not being able to cope with that.

And then I stopped. And I really thought that might be it forever. It was like I had become someone new. Shed my old skin and started again. But I was still in there somewhere. Biding my time.

And now I'm not sure why anymore.

I think in part I just need to know I still can. That I still have it as an option. That I can still do this to myself, and that I can still rein myself in and stay in control. And that maybe it's holding back something so uncontrollable and dark and dangerous that I can't risk losing that form of control. Maybe without it I couldn't be all the things that make my life worthwhile. Maybe it's justifiable to be who I am.

I know that the more trapped I feel the more it helps. It makes me feel free.

But then it traps me too.

When I can't stop thinking about it. When every pulse-beat is an impulse to damage myself. When it springs unbidden into my head when I'm at work, or with my friends, or anyone I care about. Happy. Having fun. Enjoying myself. And suddenly it's there. Tiny, but insidious. Persistent. I know deep down I want to. The longer I resist the harder it will be and the more upset I'll get. If I just do it now I won't have to think about it anymore. I'll be able to focus on something else.

And then the rage with myself for not being able to cope. For always coming back to this. For not being enough. For not doing enough. For not hurting myself enough for it to be enough. For it not being over. For being a coward and a cheat.

Sometimes it's because I deserve it. Sometimes it's just to feel. Sometimes it's because if I don't I fear I might literally explode and fly apart. I feel myself unravelling, just like someone pulling apart an old knitted jumper. I can't feel my face. I slide out of the world. I'm disappearing.

Emotions are scary in my experience. They take you over and leave you bruised and battered. They sweep you along before you have a chance to realise what's happening, before you can catch your breath. Suddenly the world has changed and my feet are no longer on the ground. It's a fully physical experience. Everything becomes very loud and very bright. Sensory input goes up a notch. My sense of where my body is and what it can do is dampened down. I can't access it. It's not really mine any more. I lose track of everything. I can't speak. I try to communicate through my eyes, but no one understands. Surely they can see how I feel? But they can't. And I can't tell them. No one can hear you scream inside your own head.

I'm afraid of what I'm capable of. Of what's within me if I don't control it and keep it under wraps. Who might I damage apart from myself? I can't let that happen. At any cost.

It helps but at the same time it distresses me hugely. Sometimes I think about it constantly, graphically. It scares me. I want to be able to talk about that. About just how hard it is not to, not to discuss it after the fact.

Am I wrong to do this? I can't believe that I am. A lot of the time I'm quite happy. Things go well. But sometimes something dark and sinister and essentially unknowable threatens to take over. A shadow creeps over me. It's cold and frightening. It's dangerous. It wants to suck me in. And I can't let that happen. I've fought too hard to get to this point only to let it all go.

It's a heady mixture – shame and guilt and power, and I don't really know what to do with it. The truth is, I want to know I have this option. This option that I control and that no one else can withhold from me, or decide when I can have it. I never thought I'd be here saying this. I never thought this would be something of value for me or something I wanted. But I'm not ready to let go yet either.

Thoughts

- There is no one reason for self-harm. The same person can have different reasons for self-harming at different times. It's important to recognise this and not assume you've found 'the answer'.

- The severity of someone's self-harm or the level of functioning they have in the rest of their life is not an indicator of the level of distress someone is experiencing.

- Taking the time to listen to someone's experience and to acknowledge and validate their distress is essential, not optional or pandering to them.

- Trying not to self-harm can be very distressing and difficult, and is the time when someone may need the most support, rather than after self-harming when they may feel a lot better or at least different.

- Self-harm can be very containing, so expecting or demanding that someone stop using self-harm to cope is a very risky and ill-thought-out approach.

- The best way to find out how someone feels and what they need is to ask them – you don't need specialist training to show compassion.

About the author

Naomi is an apparently normal-looking human being who sometimes gets to live her life and is sometimes just masquerading. In no particular order, she is 32, loves cats, has used mental health services and self-harm for over a decade, is from Scotland, has been given a diagnosis of 'BPD' amongst other things, hates fish, has size six feet and a degree in linguistics, and is passionate about mental health advocacy and activism. She has worked in mental health advocacy and information services and is involved in experience-led training on self-harm and being given a diagnosis of 'personality disorder'. She has a bee in her bonnet about using language that reflects your values, and is respectful of difference and will not stop telling people this until they start doing it! She also strongly believes that diagnostic categories stem from a need to order the world to make us feel 'safe', sometimes to the massive detriment of people on the receiving end of such labels, and wouldn't it be nice if we just focused on what people say they need?

4

Filigree not gouge

Nic Tate

I have self-harmed, albeit with a protracted period of abstinence, for a large part of my adult life. I began when I was 15, for reasons that I have neither the time nor the inclination to go into, but it was not 'just a phase'. To me, self-harm provided some kind of answer – albeit not necessarily a good one – to the questions I was asking myself and the emotions I was feeling. I went into treatment, but left after the first, deeply unsuccessful session and never returned. The anger that I remember was, in hindsight, merely a defensive reaction, but I was not self-aware enough at the time to realise this. I continued self-harming for a while, but then did something stupid – I self-harmed in a public place – got into some trouble, and so sat on the urge for a long time afterwards, feeling ashamed that I had spoiled my one 'get out' mechanism. Years later, when that shame had faded and when I felt that I needed to, I began to self-harm again, because otherwise something much more permanent was going to break: me.

It was due to other life issues, more than the self-harm, that I eventually entered outpatient treatment again, and was this time given a provisional diagnosis of borderline personality disorder. In so doing, my mind and body became medicalised, my self-harming entering an established, and not very positive, discourse in which I was being told why I did certain things and manifested particular behaviours, rather than being asked for my sense of my actions or the meanings that I ascribed to them. In essence – insofar as I believe in essences – I was being placed into categories so that I could be treated. I am, to locate myself in such categories, a self-injurer rather than self-poisoner, with my chosen method being cutting. Moreover, I am a 'delicate' cutter (see the work of Ping-Nie Pao, 1969) – albeit bucking the trend by being no longer an adolescent – in the sense that I prefer a larger number of superficial cuts, rather than a few deep gashes. Oh, and I am male, which may or may not make a difference.

As a result of being so cautious in my own method of self-harm, I find myself sometimes jealous of other people's scars, when I notice them; it is as if their pain is so much worse than mine because their scars are so much worse. But thinking like that takes me to places I don't want to go – or at least, where I don't think I should go. It is like they manage to 'let go' of it more, whereas I keep it all locked in. But I don't think I can afford to let it all out, because I am in all honesty afraid of where I could go, of what I might do, if I let it out. As a result, I have not self-harmed in anger or rage for a very long time, and self-harming in the manner I do helps to actually keep the anger and frustration in check.

This is because of the fact that control plays a big part in my version of self-harm, as far as I can tell, and manifests in terms of patterns. It takes more self-control (as I see it) to continually cut at a particular area of skin, cross-hatch it, keep the lines straight and even, rather than losing control and slashing at myself. It is my method of retaining and keeping control, as my skin is about the only thing I have control of sometimes. It is my method of locking down (repressing?) emotional turbulence behind scab-bars. So the cuts may be on my skin, but the issue behind it, of control, gets under the skin, and is my way of dealing with the world when all I want to do is tear it down, shred whatever weird veil feels like it is in the way of my understanding everything. Thus, although I have had my moments of considering amputation (*yubitsume* or 'finger shortening') and burning, I have never done these because of the danger of them becoming outside of my control, and probably bringing other people into the equation.

To me, then, self-harm is more about control than the loss of control; cutting isn't about pain, but about the 'pattern' of crossed lines I draw. I have never 'showed them off' and never volunteered the information (maybe until now) that it is something I have done and might still do. I was careful that the cuts would leave scars but also never require medical attention. I only told someone I did it when asked a direct question, otherwise deflection normally solved the problem of having to actually tell someone what I had done. Was this shame or guilt? I don't think so. Rather it was (and is) the fact that I don't want people to make a big deal out of it or worry about it. The cutting was about me, not about other people, and so I was not going to give them the right to determine what my cutting means (or does not mean), when what it signifies is deeply personal, a way of writing my own truth on my body.

One of the most difficult problems I faced when seeking treatment was that medical staff could not understand the notion of a 'controlled' self-harm, and that they could not see beyond the self-harm. 'Deliberate' self-harm was understandable, containable, but 'deliberated' self-harm, self-harm without malice or anger – but which couldn't necessarily be described as 'attention-seeking' – raised all kinds of issues that they could not reconcile with their views of what self-harm was. One of the key times when this became a factor was when deciding whether dialectical behaviour therapy (DBT) was appropriate and entering the pre-treatment phase. The practitioner had to check with colleagues whether the 'obsessive' nature of the behaviour, and the patterns I inscribed, were contra-indicative of the general nature of borderline personality disorder. This seems, to me, to be using one definition against another, without actually considering the patient. A series of boxes are set up that you have to fit into, and my behaviour didn't; my behaviour, like my self-harm, seemed to be about crossing lines, rather than reinforcing them. As a result of the contract I would have had to sign (basically swearing not to self-harm), I decided that I could not proceed with DBT. I am currently on a psychotherapy waiting list and have been for the last nine months. To date, I am not self-harming, but I have the urge too often, obviously more so when I feel things getting out of control around me, when I feel frustrated or lost, when I am not sure where 'I' am. And, to date, no member of medical staff has ever given me a good reason why I should not self-harm, considering the way in which I do it. I know, somewhere, that self-harm isn't necessarily a good thing, but it is keeping me sane (for want of a better expression). So I have not 'given up' self-harm, I am just not doing it at the moment … but it's there if I need it.

Thoughts

- Self-harm is not an integral component of personality but an aspect of behaviour, and a limited one at that. For example, you are not a 'cutter', although cutting might be something that you do. To view the individual through this behaviour, to make it their sole or even primary defining characteristic, ignores everything about them that makes them a person.

- Self-harm, for some, is not about taking out their anger on themselves, or at least not always. It can equally be a way of keeping control, and keeping the negative emotions locked down. It might not be the 'best' mechanism to do this, but when it's either that or losing control – and whatever actions that may entail – controlled self-harm is preferable because that only affects you.

Reference

Pao, P-N (1969) The syndrome of delicate self-cutting. *British Journal of Medical Psychology,* 42, 195–206.

Patterns

An old proficiency:

Find your quiet place / somewhere doesn't matter / where. You unwrap / it the ritual necessary. Never in danger / take time.

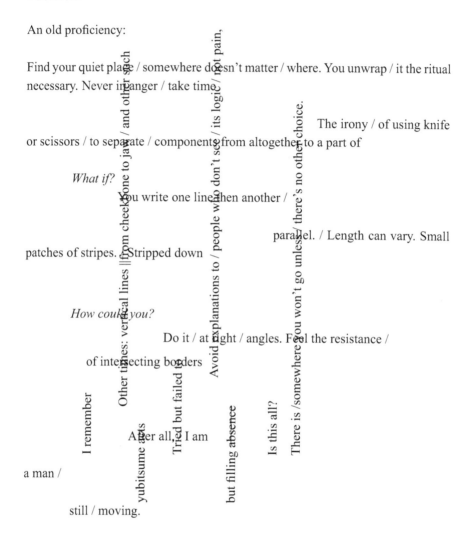

The irony / of using knife or scissors / to separate / components from altogether to a part of

What if?

You write one line then another /

parallel. / Length can vary. Small patches of stripes. / Stripped down

How could you?

Do it / at right / angles. Feel the resistance /

of intersecting borders

from cheek gone to jar / and other such

Other times: vertical lines ||

Avoid explanations to / people who don't see / its logic / not pain,

There is /somewhere you won't go unless/ there's no other choice.

I remember

yubitsume acts

Tried but failed to

After all, I am

but filling absence

Is this all?

a man /

still / moving.

For Mark Cresswell

A not-NICE self-harm algorithm

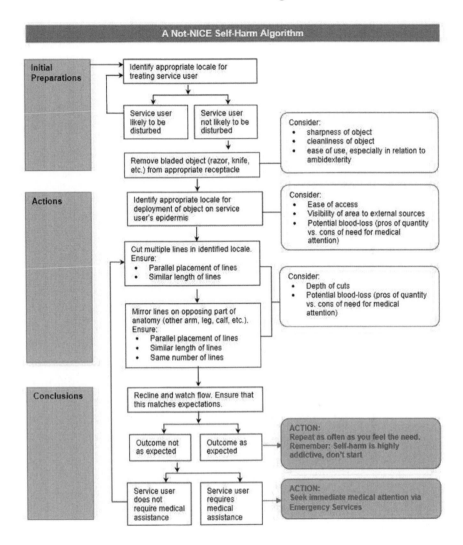

About the author

Nic Tate is an independent writer and researcher interested in the links between mental health and literature.

5

My journey through self-harm

J. A. G.

My journey with self-harm began in the depths of depression. It was something I had dabbled in as a teenager – a punched wall here or there – but only really as a call for attention, never with conviction or purpose. This time around I was a grown woman; the self-harm was private and served a very real purpose for me.

As my depression worsened over the course of time, the medications I had been prescribed only worked so far. I was in turmoil, unable to function properly, focus on a positive or even the possibility of a future. So much hurt and pain was building up inside, from both my current desperation and my past traumas that had contributed to me being there. As I searched every available avenue for some resolve, I found the need for some kind of release, some way to let go of just some of the pain I battled with daily.

It began with scratches up my forearm. I don't know where the notion came from, it wasn't an idea I had mulled over and decided to try, it wasn't a cry for help (I kept my arms covered), it was an impulsive urge I couldn't dissipate until satisfied. All I know is, from the moment the urge first took me and I acted on it, I knew it helped. I was searching for a degree of equanimity in my soul and the cutting served as a temporary measure.

As time went on cutting became my friend, and the release I turned to in times of upset and turmoil. If I couldn't cope, I cut. The more I did it, the deeper and larger the cut needed to be to offer the same satisfaction. I needed blood, I needed pain. As quoted in the lyrics of 'Iris' by the Goo Goo Dolls: 'You bleed just to know you're alive'. I could relate to that. The blood reassured me I was still alive as I felt so detached from reality and numb inside. I liked to feel the pain in my arm and the throbbing that lasted for some time afterwards. It transferred some of the pain in my heart elsewhere, albeit for a short while.

Those hours after a cut I felt at peace, calm and able to focus on my throbbing arm rather than the hurt inside and confusion in my mind.

For those who consider self-harm as attention seeking, a cry for help, you couldn't be further from the truth. I became very conscious of how I dressed, opting for long sleeves even on the hottest of days. I even wore long clothing in bed for fear of my husband – my confidant and best friend – discovering the mutilation I had performed on myself.

I cut in secret, either when alone, or in the privacy of a public toilet or my car. My 'cut kit' came everywhere with me. It was my safety net for when things got tough. As the cutting got worse, it was harder to hide, and when I ran out of excuses, and space, on my arm, I moved onto my stomach. After one nasty infection in my arm, and a visit to the out-of-hours doctor, I no longer cared much for the depth and risk of infection I was causing myself, so long as the release was found somehow.

I went on to have two further infections on my stomach and now carry numerous scars that will never fade. My CPN (community psychiatric nurse) and GP, who had become aware of the cutting, and who I no longer tried to hide the wounds from, kept a close eye and monitored as best they could – as best I would allow.

I was very ashamed of my habit, of the state of my arm and my complete disregard for my body. But at the time that was overpowered by the need to cut. I was given much advice from professionals on alternative measures to try when I felt the urge to cut, but realistically these were never going to touch the sides. Pinging an elastic band on your wrist, to recreate the pain felt without doing the deed, cannot have been suggested by someone who has ever had a relationship with self-harm. However, I feel blessed to have had a wonderful GP throughout my illness, who has always been there for support and reassurance, and provided a firm hand in treatment guidance when needed. Never did he treat me like a child or try to take my blades off me. For that I am truly grateful, as without my cutting to help me, however much an outsider sees it as unhelpful, I may not be here today. My CPN too has been, and continues to be, a source of much support and guidance. I feel lucky to have received the care, though not always agreed with, that I have had. No one can possibly begin to understand the need – and it is a need – for self-harm a person may feel, but not pretending to or belittling the actions' worth is a step in the right direction to helping someone through.

It has been months since I last cut, but only recently have I felt strong enough to remove my 'cut kit' from my handbag. I am ready to let go of that safety net. I am many medications and therapies down the line now and the depression is under control. There is a light at the end of the once very long and black tunnel I was in. I see my scars as war wounds – an outward sign of the inward battle I have fought and continue to fight. I can't guarantee that one day I won't return to cutting as a means of help when things are hard, but at this moment in time I don't feel it necessary.

The scars are a permanent reminder of what I have been through, and I will have to live with them. I realise cutting may not be a healthy way of dealing with emotion, but when desperation consumed me, I can honestly say that my relationship with self-harm helped me live.

Not everything faced can be changed. But nothing can be changed until it is faced.
James Baldwin

Thoughts

- Self-harm is rarely a conscious decision, more an urge that needs fulfilling.

- It is not an attention-seeking act, but a self-soothing method through turmoil.

- Self-harmers need support through it, not criticism against it.

- People need to look at the cause of self-harm, rather than the act itself.

About the author
I am a wife and mother of three active boys. I enjoy spending time with my family, reading, swimming and music.

6

To whom it may concern

Trish Staples

S uicidal? Not exactly, no. Why does everyone think my self-harming behaviour means I am trying to kill myself? That attitude reflects a complete lack of understanding and, what's more, it's insulting. As if you're telling me I didn't have the nerve to kill myself, almost taunting me. I agree that when I harm myself I feel desperate and I want to die … but wanting to die, to escape the world and whatever problems I am experiencing, is *not* the same as being suicidal. I have no particular plans, no chosen method or time and place. I have never planned to self-harm, it just happens. And when the urge to hurt myself comes over me, not once do I contemplate killing myself. So please, *please*, do not jump to conclusions or make assumptions about someone's self-harming actions – try talking to them instead, try to understand why they are doing it, and establish how it might actually be helping them.

E mpathy – one of those concepts that people think they understand but, more often than not, don't. Often confused with sympathy, empathy is not about feeling sorry for the person, is not about empty and meaningless clichés and offering a shoulder to cry on. Empathy is about experiencing the world, or a situation, the same way another person is. And that's no easy feat. Anyone can observe a situation, and base a response or reaction to it, from his or her own perspective. But how many are prepared to, as the Native Americans put it, 'walk a mile in another person's moccasins'? Empathy involves a great deal of discomfort – do we really want to feel for ourselves the hopeless desperation that has driven a person to self-harm? Are we actually comfortable with the idea that anyone can deliberately draw blood in order to cause pain to him or herself? Probably not. Yet that is the only way we can ever truly begin to understand why the person needs to, and does, self-harm.

L ife is short. Life is like a box of chocolates. Life is what happens when you are busy making other plans. Life is … life is. There are so many well known sayings about life that are intended to motivate us, to inspire us, to lift our spirits, to make us think. When I have self-harmed, the only 'sayings' I can usually come up with are that life is crap, not worth living, painful, unfair, unbearable, too hard … need I go on? Life is a subjective concept, and whilst many people may well be able to see and move beyond difficulties and negative experiences, others struggle to see a way through these obstacles, seeking ways to express their frustrations and dissatisfaction. And although there are those of you who find the idea of causing harm to yourself unthinkable, self-harm for many people is often the only way they can get beyond their current circumstances. And just as you would like to think that everyone else accepts your way of coping – whether it is through exercise, relaxation, talking, music, reading, prayer, etc. – please try to similarly appreciate another person's strategy for survival.

F ear is a major factor in public attitudes to self-harm, usually leading to stigmatisation and ostracism. Often, sitting comfortably alongside fear are ignorance, misconception, moral judgement and avoidance. If you don't let something affect you, it might go away. Wrong. Individuals have been damaged by personal events and circumstances for centuries, and even if self-harm was not as widely recognised, it too has always been around. Fear, and its accompanying negative, self-protective attitudes, serve only to promote the idea of self-harm as a selfish, attention-seeking and immature behaviour. A more radical, and admittedly scarier option, is to open your mind to the possibility that self-harm might actually be quite a normal response to intolerable situations and overwhelming feelings.

H elp is not automatically needed or accepted by someone who self-harms. Admittedly, some individuals will need assistance if wounds are too deep, or will appreciate someone's willingness to take care of them. But the majority of people who self-harm are predominantly 'independent' and act autonomously – self-harm occurs in private, others are not required to comply or accompany. After the self-harming actions, many people will feel they have achieved something – this could be the ability to feel, reconnecting with themselves and life, numbing themselves to events, punishing themselves, self-comforting, or any other perceived outcome. Mine was always a 'combo'– cutting allowed me to feel physical pain to overcome my emotional pain, provided me with an outlet for my guilt, was a punitive act I felt I deserved and left me with visible proof that I was hurting. I never once wanted help though. Self-harm was 'mine' and needed no well-intentioned yet meaningless words and reactions from others, nor did it warrant the sense of panic it sometimes appeared to create.

Acceptance of self-harm is crucial. I heard a saying once, something along the lines of, 'You do not have to agree with me [or my self-harming behaviour], but please accept and respect what I do.' Too many people think they know what is right for everyone else. This simply reflects an inability to empathise, and, more simply, to just accept that a person has choices. Of course others will choose to do things we may never in our wildest dreams consider doing, but does that make it wrong? Not at all. It's just wrong for some people, that's all. For the person who self-harms, it is the right way for him or her. The right way, the only way, the best way of coping. Because self-harm is not about inviting pity or sympathy, nor is it about taking the easy way out ... it is about coping, managing, surviving. I know that may seem strange, but unless you have ever been in a situation that has led you to choose self-harm, surely you cannot really understand it as a concept. Yet if you can find a way to accept a person's right to choose this way of coping, you may gain a deeper understanding, as well as the trust, of that person.

Respect, as mentioned in the previous paragraph, needs to go hand in hand with acceptance. It would be pointless to appear to accept a person's self-harming actions but then make remarks and comments reflecting that you actually don't accept it at all; that you think it is a foolish, selfish act; that you think the person harming themselves must be crazy; to pass judgement on the person's actions; to talk about the person in a derogatory manner. This shows not only a lack of acceptance but also gross disrespect. If you can truly listen to the person who is self-harming, if you can convey warmth, acceptance and empathy in your communications with the person, if you can keep what they have shared with you confidential, and if you can push aside any preconceptions or negative attitudes about self-harm, then you will be showing the person the respect they deserve. Someone who self-harms is a human being and deserves to be treated as one – not as an object of disdain and moral reprimand.

Methods of self-harm, and the motivation behind these acts, vary widely. Most people are familiar with cutting, but burning yourself, pulling out your hair, biting yourself, banging your head, inflicting bruises on yourself, drinking toxic substances, inserting objects beneath your skin, and several other methods are also used to achieve similar end results. I have already stressed the value of effective listening, acceptance and respect if you are talking to someone who has already hurt themself or is contemplating self-harm, but it is equally important to consider their motivation. What drives individuals to these actions? What are the intended outcomes? What do people hope to achieve? My self-harm was a way of expressing myself – it provided me with an opportunity to be in control of something when it seemed everything else in my life was beyond my control – it allowed me to substitute my emotional pain with physical pain – and it was my way of punishing myself for 'letting' traumatic events happen. None of these motives may sound rational to you, but at the time they made perfect sense to me. Other individuals I have met who have self-harmed have talked about needing to see the blood, feeling calmer after self-harming, or purging themselves using self-harming actions. Ultimately, the idea that everyone who self-harms simply wants to feel pain is a fallacy. If you want to work with or understand someone's self-harming behaviours, please take into consideration what has motivated the person and what benefits the person feels they will gain from the self-harm.

Thoughts

I do not profess to be an expert in the area of self-harm. But I *have* self-harmed, and *may* self-harm again in the future, which I believe provides me with an insight many others may not have. Writing this short piece about self-harm has allowed me to reflect on my experiences, and to remember what helped at the time and what did not. I would urge anyone dealing with people who self-harm to first challenge themselves to reflect on their attitudes to self-harm, and to identify any pre-existing opinions, assumptions and moral judgements that may ultimately stand in the way of communicating and working effectively with individuals who are already experiencing distress and do not need it exacerbated through stigma and ignorance.

About the author

Trish Staples (MA, MEd) is a qualified teacher, counsellor and trainer living in the UK. Following a diagnosis of MS in 1991, Trish experienced further significant losses that contributed to her experiences of depression and self-harm. Life events thus led to Trish becoming involved with a number of organisations in education, health and voluntary sectors, where she continues to use her personal experiences alongside learning, skills and knowledge to inform and support others experiencing similar situations.

7

Self-harm survivor

Rachel Claire Walton

Searching for my identity, who I am who is me,
Emotions so unpredictable like waves on the sea.
Leaning over the rails no longer able to satisfy my need for
    a release,
Feeling suicidal ready to jump as people look on in disbelief.

How did I end up so desperate, feeling so alone?
Am I ever going to escape from under this rockhard stone?
Reaching out for someone to help,
Mentioning the past and how I felt
Eager to succeed and prove people wrong,
Relearning coping skills to show that I am strong.

Self-esteem is still low but my self-image I can now bear,
Under control people now speak to me instead of just stare.
Remember something that I was taught: that 'you can't be
    sad forever'
Violence and me no longer connected together,
Important changes for my future I have had to make,
Various opportunities with both hands I now take,
On pressure all the time but I can now cope.
Realising that now I have hope.

About the author

My name is Rachel Walton. I am 24 years old and a single mum. I was born in Reading but now live in Derby. I am currently in a low secure unit but finally getting the help I have long needed that so many more people are waiting for and need.

8

PS. ... Help me

Caroline Roe

There's nothing remarkable about dying, nor about the day that I have chosen to die.

It is a very average Saturday evening. To the rest of the world it's just a day – a day where the sun shone and the wind blew. Where a girl went shopping with her mother-in-law and bought gifts for her friends.

But to me it isn't just as it seems, this very average Saturday. Instead, I am sat at my dining table, with a cold Budweiser and eating a fruit winder, thinking about ending my life. There is something very ordinary about my day to die.

I can hear the Lady Gaga song 'Speechless' singing to itself, upstairs, 'You left me speechless, so speechless ...', it sounds far away and the dishwasher's swishing is nearer and almost drowns it out, but I still hear it. Everything feels so odd. I feel odd. And alone. And speechless. I'm in such a terribly dark place, made ever darker by the serenity that seems to have descended upon my very empty house. It's 9pm and everything is in its place. The papers are filed, and every single item of clothing has been washed and sorted and put away. The kitchen sides are clear as if no meal has ever been had here before and my bed is made. I wonder what I should wear – to die in. Does that sound insane? Should it be my prettiest dress, or my jeans? Am I best known for my quirky ensembles, my accessories, or my boots? What would best cover the grimace that my face will wear ... a pretty hair slide? I doubt it. I am sitting at my dining table, at my big fake oak table that I love, looking out through patio doors into the gaping blackness that is my garden, only it's too dark to make out its shapes right now. I know out there is a lawn that is pleading with me to mow it, and big heavy tomatoes dragging their tired stems to the ground with their weight, their plumpness just starting to turn yellow as they think tentatively about ripening enough for us to devour. I love the garden. I love the way my hands will smell of those tomatoes for the rest of the day when I pick them! Only I won't get to pick these ones.

I am plagued by thoughts about ending my life; the rumination is perpetuated by distress. I feel overwhelmed by my existence. Thinking about death is a hard place to start to tell my story but thinking this way gives a sense of choice and control in a world where I have very little. This is as good a place to start as any, I suppose. This feels like my last chapter, and my first.

There isn't anything left to hold on to, except this writing. No company that I can keep that will take it all away. Just me and the tap tapping of my laptop keys, a sound all too familiar as I desperately attempt to record my life in some futile attempt to reach out to someone or to pass on my story to someone else. I'm not really sure. All I know is that I am *just* writing, writing for the sake of writing, writing to save my life? Perhaps I am also putting off the inevitability of the end. That very mortal full-stop that is suicide, it beckons, and everything feels so sad. Maybe if I keep writing I will chase away the decision that has already been made, perhaps I can bustle it onto the next page of my life somehow. Silly, huh? I also wonder what it is that I think I have to offer you, the reader of my woes. We shall find that out together.

For the first time in all of my life I have a home that feels like home, a wife whom I love dearly and friends that are as close as any family. It's not that my life is empty or soulless, quite the contrary. It is brimming full of stories to tell, and often laughter, and passion. The one thing that I hope people will know of me is that: passion. That everything I have ever done is done with passion – a real determination and care, to love completely and not ask for anything in return. Some would argue that that is half of the problem. No, my life is not empty; it is full, but not just of gladness. It is also full of pain, of regret, of torment and self-hatred. I masquerade by day as someone who has their shit together. But if you were one of the few that are given a glimpse into my *real* reality, you would know a different version of me to the girl who walks tall in her quirky clothes, the girl who tirelessly speaks out for people in need. And it is this girl that can't take anymore. I'm tired, really, really tired. It is this girl that I'm going to tell you about.

My name is Caroline, and I am 22 years old.

I dabble in writing and art, but by day I work with homeless young women, for the most part immersing myself in a world of troubled people who I try so very hard to help. I live both a very public and a very private life, the two being distinctly split between the *me* that I show to the world (this is the girl that I would like to be, that in another time and place, perhaps I could have truly been), and the *me* that stays quietly unknown. I wish I could converge the two, allowing them to meet and be known as one, but life has taught me to keep the aspects of *me* very separate.

Behind the closed doors of the projected version of myself, I am in a mess. I *am* a mess – a complete mess. This is a familiar mess. I know it and I understand it like I never have before, but I can't change it. My work depends upon my ability to help others build hope for themselves and affect change in their lives. But one thing I have learnt is that sometimes the only choices left for us to make are unfair ones, and sometimes there really are things that we cannot change. Life, as it is now for me, is one of those things, so I have anticipated this day for months. I have felt it coming closer and closer and I have pretended not to. I haven't sought help or spoken about how dark these thoughts have become. I haven't given anyone a chance to help me, because I haven't really wanted any help. I have approached today with a calm resignation.

There is a peace that descends when a decision to die is finally made, for me at least, although I have heard other people describe it. It's as if all the battling that has gone before just disintegrates, because however painful it still is, there is a knowing that it will soon be gone. All of the things that I wrestle with will fall away, and when I close my eyes (or not, as the case may be) it won't be to chase a fitful sleep that brings me no respite, it will be for a state of endless not-being. With that thought comes a wave of sorrow over letting go and letting down those that I love so, so much, but it's a sorrow that I too know will go when I go – a selfish but true fact.

I am questioning why my day today is stretching deep into the night; is it some futile attempt to find a different day again, a new light, a change in perspective? It's doubtful. I am certain that tomorrow will never be what I have longed for. I just don't seem to have the capacity to keep putting one foot in front of another but nor am I committing myself to the death I was so sure of when I began writing.

Maybe I will write until dawn, chasing away until tomorrow, what should have been today, or maybe I will etch into my skin more lines of sorrow to mark this day and fend off the decision that threatens to swallow me whole. My whole body wears the marks of this struggle; these scars are the private map that is the language of my silence. Just as the silence of this writing throbs with the emotion of this heavy aloneness, so does my skin. It lets out some of the scream that can't leave my lips. It says broadly and deeply that I am in pain and translates the language of my suffering into a tangible one. A wound of the soul born on the surface; it's still a private wound, one you won't see as I paint my face on each morning and go about my work. But it's there. They're there. And they tell my story.

Yes, that is what I will do. It's an easier trade-off right now: a small self-destruction whilst I wait for the finality of my life. I know some will think me mad – that the act of hurting myself right now is my only salvation. I know that it will stop these ruminations, halt the plague of thoughts that keep me driven to darkness and aloneness. It is a sad place to be. But tonight, in the darkness and suffocating sorrow, hurting myself might just save my life.

If you are reading this now it means I have had the courage to allow you to see into a place that I don't often share, probably for some reason greater than my own pain. Maybe in my struggle you [the reader] can come to know others. Maybe I can too. Maybe my insignificant drop in the ocean can touch your world and help you to understand a struggle. It also means, I survived.

Thoughts

- No person is destined to end their life and self-harm is an understandable phenomenon in the face of unbearable suffering, but it can be overcome.

- Self-harm can be a useful strategy in managing overwhelming thoughts and feelings – to help someone stay alive in the face of enormous struggle.

About the author
Caroline is now 33 and works as a director of a service that helps people who self-harm. She is a practising psychotherapist who also works to challenge and improve health and social care practice in the field of self-harm. Using both personal and professional experiences, she hopes to enlighten people as to the plight of those in distress. Caroline delivers training around interventions for improved working with people that self-harm and now has the privilege of working alongside those staff members who were unable to see her potential. Her recovery makes them hopeful for others.

9

Goodbye, I guess

Victoria Reynolds

This recent crisis has, like all my self-harming behaviour, been about more than one thing. It has never been simple for me and concerned professionals, who ask whether it's about control or release. It's much more complicated than that, and it's too difficult to explain to people who cannot allow their minds to go on that wild ride through history, guilt, conscience, dark, light, reality, belief, sanity, soul, sky, pain, size, death, life, dreams, movement and so on and on and on … They want one-word answers, answers that make sense in their minds, not what makes sense in mine. I have tried to give them something they can understand, something that is truly hurting me, because then they feel they can help and they are less afraid, for themselves as much as for me, some of the time.

I think I scare professionals – not because of what I do or think, but because I am not 'crazy' in a nice, easily diagnosable way, which would allow them to dismiss my way of thinking and behaving. Although the fact that I can be extremely strong-willed, articulate and will not quietly accept incompetence, patronising or bullying behaviour doesn't make things any easier for them, poor souls!

I feel so guilty about all the suffering, abuse, depravity, cruelty and neglect in the world. I feel responsible for the lives destroyed, the pain unacknowledged. For example, I watched a docu-drama about Myra Hindley and the guilt I felt tore me up. I should have been able to stop those lives being lost, and I did nothing. The fact that I wasn't even born when the killings took place doesn't really seem relevant. I did not prevent it happening but I have to acknowledge it. Little Keith Bennett's body was never found so he was my first priority: a litre of my blood in memory and acknowledgement of his.

I cannulated the artery in my left wrist and drained 850ml of blood. The rest I still have to make up, despite all the other cutting I am doing at the moment. Unfortunately I had to get the wound stitched up in hospital as my haemoglobin levels were so low and I could barely walk. I was pathetic enough to abandon my principles and had a blood transfusion. I now have Keith Bennett's blood on my hands; part of Myra Hindley is in me, and in order to change that I have to let the blood that was transfused, plus the remaining 150ml, out of my body. I am not yet sure whether I have to start all over again. My conscience has to think about that. I just can't bear it.

I have been so, so lucky in the friends I have. I have never deserved everything they have given me, particularly as it has always been so one-sided. I have never been able to equal the time, empathy, concern, care and support they have given me and they are all truly amazing individuals, most of whom fight their own demons and still find it within themselves to move heaven and earth for others.

How Could I?

Guilt.

Twisting, writhing, clawing

Through this battered body and mind.

I tear, I rip, I cut through all my senses
As sanity falls to the floor,
And panic's multiplied by pain,
Leaves me drowning in my own evil.
I fight to breathe,
And every breath becomes a further offence.
Appalling awareness:
The darkness and destruction I emit,
The agonising, horrifying knowledge
Of my monstrous mind.
All gives way to vile truth or lies.
Does it matter which?
Corrupting memories with depravity,
Desecrating the man who loved me,
If I could take it back, if I could atone,
I would.

Scared

Two litres yesterday.
Two litres tomorrow.
Two days later – two litres.
Can I survive?
Is it death I'm seeking?
My body is so weak
But I can't change this plan, trapped as I am within its quicksand,
And I'm sinking further …
I ask: what is it that I really want?
To escape my past?
To escape a darkness so vast that I crouch and cower from it,
Overwhelmed by its perverted power.
Will this loss of blood stem the flood of evil that flows from me?
And how do people fail to see such evil?
Don't they realise that I'm the cause of horrific holocausts?
Don't they realise how I corrupt even the moral, even the tough?
And so I continue to blood-let.
I will impede the evil
That I can't stop yet.

Reflection

So tired of the ugliness in the mirror,
Repeated day after day.
Examine every feature, every flaw,
But don't look into her eyes whatever you do,
She will turn you into stone.
She hates me, the face in the mirror,
Loathing what she sees, she longs to kill.
Blood-lust seeps through.
Glass is no barrier to her cruelty.
Her voice is a snarl,
She is disgusted with me.
One day she will burst out,
Clawing my face,
Stabbing, ripping, skinning,
Destroying the ugliness of me.

Victoria died in 2011

I met Victoria in October 2006 when she was referred to me in my role as Learning Advisor with the NHS Social Inclusion and Wellbeing Team. She was interested in pursuing her education, which had been interrupted by her life circumstances. She had achieved a Diploma in Higher Education in Criminology 10 years earlier, but had to abandon her studies before she achieved her degree due to ill health. I worked with her for five years and initially she attended art courses in the voluntary sector, became involved in volunteering, attended short courses in the community, and finally recommenced degree-level studies with the Open University, studying the nineteenth century novel. She was an outstanding student, achieving high marks despite the challenges and difficulties of her life and in the face of numerous hospital admissions. She also became a colleague, in that we worked together on a research project investigating the benefits of and barriers to learning for people using mental health services, and we published a paper on this subject. We discussed many times the possibility of publishing her poetry and she expressed her wishes that she should be published under her own name. Victoria was a caring, sensitive, perceptive, often very funny and warm, and extremely intelligent young woman who was very creative, whether using words, images, knitting or needlecraft. Her commitment to the activities she undertook despite the distress she experienced was nothing less than heroic. She is greatly missed.

Sue Atkinson

Victoria was an intelligent and articulate person, and yet as she grew into adulthood she became increasingly suicidal and felt a failure. Eventually, Victoria identified herself first and foremost as a 'self-harmer'. Victoria enjoyed the notoriety that she received as she developed new forms of hurting herself, while at the same time she was exhausted by it all and longed for happiness and normality. Victoria had demons and finally they engulfed her. Victoria's self-harm ultimately led to her accidental death. However, although I believe that it was accidental at that particular time, by looking at her journals it seems that she had often wished for it. I find Victoria's work disturbing and hard to view. I do not like the questions that the work raises, but perhaps these need to be asked.

Danielle Sleightholme

10

For girls like me

Mary T. Shannon

Six months after my son was born I began having flashbacks. I was checking on him one day during his nap when I looked up and saw myself as a little girl again, standing at the foot of my mother's bed with a splatter of freckles across my nose and cheeks and braids down to my waist. Mom was lying on her back with her legs spread wide, telling the girl to come closer – first in the kind of voice people use when they want you to do something, but when the girl didn't move, Mom told her again – this time not so sweet anymore. I could feel the queasiness in the pit of the girl's stomach, the tickling sensation of tears running down her face as they ran down mine. I stood frozen; rocking on unsteady feet as I watched my little girl self take a slow, small step toward the bed. She took another small step, and another, but then suddenly it all vanished. Just as quickly as the image had appeared, it was gone.

I stood blinking at the morning sun coming through the window, the blue and white striped wallpaper, the stuffed animals cuddled in the corner of my son's crib. My hands trembled as I wiped my tears. I did not want to remember. I did not! I walked out of my son's room and shrugged off that memory like you shrug off a chill that comes out of nowhere, determined to move on with my life. I was married to a good man – a respected physician, had a beautiful new baby to care for, and had just earned a master's degree in social work. I didn't have time to deal with memories I'd worked so hard to forget!

At first the flashbacks happened infrequently, but as time went on they nudged their way into my life like unwelcome visitors that refused to leave, poking and prodding and picking away at me until one day I realized ignoring them was no longer an option. Each flashback handed me a different memory, and each memory triggered another. It was like going home again, only I never knew when I was going or what I would find when I got there. I never told anyone about them, not even my husband. I was afraid if I told anyone they'd think I was crazy – or at the very least on my way to going crazy – so I kept them a secret. It wasn't until I began working with a therapist to find out why I couldn't hold down a job for more than a year or two that the truth began to leak out, little by little.

We were living in Berkeley, California, at the time and her office was in Marin, an expensive suburb that meant a long commute for me. Mary Beth was the quintessential California girl with long blonde hair, perfect skin and teeth, and a relaxed manner that made it easy to divulge things I normally kept buried. One day we were sitting in her light-filled office when she asked me to close my eyes and imagine myself as a little girl in the house I grew up in. Within seconds I saw a fuzzy picture of myself in the bedroom I shared with Mom, and suddenly burst into tears.

'What do you see?' Mary Beth asked.

I shook my head, unable to speak.

'It's okay, you're safe here,' she said softly. 'Take your time, and just start at the beginning.'

I tried to tell her, but the words wouldn't come. She handed me a Kleenex, then another, and another.

'It's okay, you don't have to say anything,' she told me. 'But what I would like you to do is write it all down. You mentioned how you used to write poetry, and how much you enjoyed writing. I think it'd be a good exercise for you. Start slow, and see what happens. Write about the house you grew up in, or you might even start with your earliest memory of your mother.'

I nodded, reaching for another Kleenex to blow my nose.

'I have a feeling that once you get your story outside of yourself and onto the page, the distance it creates will help you begin to heal. Just give it a try, okay? Promise me you'll give it a try. And remember, just start slow and see where it takes you.'

I left Mary Beth's office that day with swollen eyes, a promise to keep and a newfound determination. If I was going to be the best mother I could possibly be, I had to do this. I had to do it for my son, and I had to do it for my husband. But most importantly, I had to do it for myself.

The next morning I sat down at the computer with a cup of coffee and began to write. And I did not stop. For the next 13 years, I wrote. I wrote in fits and starts; wrote until I couldn't stand to put down another word, and then I'd sit back down and write some more. It was as if the words had finally found a way out and there was no stopping them. It all came pouring out of me. All the grief and rage, all the untold secrets, all the stories nobody wanted to hear – not even me. I began with my earliest and most vivid memory, and worked forward. I didn't know where the writing would lead but I hoped it would fill the empty space inside and give me roots – the space between loneliness and the business of life – a place to call home.

1959: Cincinnati, Ohio

It started when I was five, late at night in the room Mom and I shared. I'd hear her calling out for me, my name riding the space between asleep and awake like a song. I'd lie still as stone, pretending to be asleep. But then she'd call out for me again, and force me to touch her in ways I never wanted.

'You tell anyone and I'll beat ya to a pulp,' she'd warn, but even at five I knew better than to tell, and hid our secret so deep I sometimes wondered if God even knew.

On Sundays I'd go to church and silently ask God why Mom made me do those things in our room at night, but there was no answer. There never was. Sometimes I wondered if the church had a way of washing a soul clean, to scour it like you would a stain on a porcelain sink. I imagined the rinse water taking away the dirt on my soul and leaving nothing but a clean, shiny surface. I wanted to be cleansed like that, to be scrubbed so clean and shiny I wouldn't feel stained or dirty ever again. Who was I that my own mother would do such things to me? What was wrong with me?

On the nights Mom worked the swing shift as a keypunch operator I'd get to stay up late and watch television, sitting in my metal-framed chair with the green and white plastic strips across the seat. Waiting up for Mom always made me nervous. I was restless, twitchy; unable to sit still. One night I began tipping my chair back to see how far I could go without falling. Finally I did fall, hitting my tailbone so hard on the metal base that I let out a little scream. And then I did it again – only this time I did it on purpose. The pain was worse now – pain on top of pain. I got up and did it again and again, hitting the wooden floor as hard as I could. The more it hurt the more I had to do it.

I never cried. No matter how bad the pain got, I never cried. It was as if some part of me was testing me, seeing how much pain I could take and still not cry. When Mom came home from work it would be time to go up to our room, to the dark sounds and touches of the night.

I'd follow her up the stairs with a blank face and a throbbing back. I didn't know that I had fractured my own tailbone. All I knew was that something inside would not let me stop.

In school I remained invisible to the sea of girls who'd nudge up against each other and laugh without a care, girls whose mothers hugged them and kept them safe. Their laughter was a foreign language I could not speak, their world a culture I did not understand. One afternoon I came home from school to find Mom sprawled on her bed.

'Come over here and let me stick my fingers up inside you to see how big you're getting,' she told me.

I balled my hands into fists and dug my nails in, digging them in deeper and then deeper still. The next morning I lay in bed staring at my palms, the torn skin curled like petals on a rose, the crusted blood already blackened by time. I got out of bed and stared at myself in the mirror over Mom's dresser, hating the girl staring back at me, hating the life I had, hating everything in me and around me. I ground my teeth, closed my hands into fists and punched myself in the stomach, first with one fist and then the other, punching myself again and again until I broke into a steady rhythm. I had to do it. I had to numb myself with physical pain to get away from the pain inside me. It was the only escape I had.

When I grew as tall as Mom I began to fight back, and she threatened to get rid of me. I'd just turned 15 and didn't believe her. The next week a tall man with jet-black hair and brown-stained teeth showed up at the door claiming to be my father, whom I'd never met. It was raining the afternoon he came for me, and when I looked up at his milky brown eyes and wet, greased-back hair, I knew I'd been saved.

'Come on over here and sit on my lap so I can get to know you better,' he told me the following morning.

I did as he said, though the smell of beer and cigarettes was so strong I had to work to keep from gagging. When he wrapped his arm around my waist I felt his hand graze the side of my breast and pulled away.

'You sure are a pretty little thing now, aren't you?' he whispered.

I felt my cheeks burn and looked away, but suddenly his hand was pushing my head down and his tongue was in my mouth. He grabbed my breast and I pushed him off but he yanked me closer. I screamed for him to stop but he was strong and held me tight. I pushed harder, hard enough to get free, and ran out of that ramshackle trailer so fast I tripped, but kept on running just the same. After I reached the highway I hitchhiked back home, but Mom refused to let me in the house and called the county caseworker to come for me. When her maroon Buick pulled up to the curb I opened the door and climbed in without a word. I didn't tell her about Daddy, and I didn't tell her about Mom. I didn't tell her about anything. After she put the car in gear and started down the street I asked where she was taking me, but there was no answer. We drove the next 45 minutes in silence.

'This is an institution for unwanted children,' she said as we approached a large, run-down building.

Tucked away on the outskirts of the city and surrounded by a 20-foot chainlink fence, the Allen House looked more like a deserted warehouse than an institution for children, with its chipped brown paint and black metal bars lining the windows. When I got out of her car and looked up at the small, blank faces staring down between the bars it occurred to me that I could try and make a run for it. But just then the caseworker pulled me in and padlocked the door behind me. Once inside I was taken to the showers and told to strip and wash with disinfectant soap while a matron looked on. I soon learned that the matrons watched everything. Big-bellied and mean-faced, they patrolled the halls night and day looking for the slightest infractions to justify our beatings – straying a few inches out of the food line, not pulling the sheets tight enough on our cots, talking after lights out. What had we done that was bad enough to be locked up and treated like criminals? I was the oldest of the bunch, and couldn't help but wonder how long the others had been there. From the dark circles under their eyes and scraggly hair, I guessed it had been a very long time.

A week later I was placed in a foster home. Anxious to please, I did everything my borrowed family told me, for love didn't come easily for girls like me. And I knew it. One Saturday afternoon my foster mother found a half-smoked joint in my room and promised that come Monday morning, she was sending me back to the Allen House. I begged and pleaded with her not to send me back. I confessed that I rarely smoked and promised it would never happen again. I pointed to my good grades, my otherwise good behaviour, but it was no use; she'd already made up her mind. That's when I made up my mind too. That night I pulled a new razor blade out of its clear plastic case and started cutting myself. I dug that blade into my skin until bright, red blood ran from my wrist to my elbow. The more I cut myself the more I had to do it. I gritted my teeth and dug in. I was the one taking control now.

When I turned 18 I got a job and moved to the west coast, determined to put my past behind me. I changed my name, changed the color of my hair, even changed the way I dressed – everything I could think of to try and become someone else. I moved from one apartment to another, one neighborhood and one city to another, each time foolishly thinking I could outrun my past. But there wasn't a place on earth that would help me forget what I'd worked so hard to run away from.

It wasn't until I began the process of writing about my past, of locating my story outside of myself, that I was able to create order out of chaos and put the pieces of my life back together again. As I watched my words, phrases and paragraphs come together on the page I could sometimes feel the weight of silence begin to lift, the burden of isolation begin to disintegrate. Writing became the container for all my shifting emotions, the place where I found safety and solace, strength and understanding. It was where I began to live again. It was a place to call home.

Thoughts

I am 59 years old, and fortunate to be married to a man of great kindness and compassion. Our son will soon be entering medical school, but even now when I am sure that no one is looking, I sometimes gaze down at the thin, white scars on the inside of my wrists and feel a chill run up my spine. These are my battle scars, my battle against the ravages of pain and suffering that go a thousand layers deep. I have spent most of my life trying to run away from my past, trying to scrape myself clean and act as if it never existed, but I was running from a past that is impossible to run from. I hadn't learned yet that there is no such thing as a person without a past – that who we were is part of who we become. I hadn't learned yet to build on the ruins.

Negotiating and surviving self-harm means negotiating and surviving society's stigma against it – for until the stigma is banished the shame that accompanies it will not go away. The paradox about shame is that there is shame about shame. It is my hope that in sharing my experience here, the myths and realities of self-harm will be met with greater contextual recognition and understanding, and in so doing forge a new beginning toward restoring the kind of cultural compassion that we not only deserve but rightfully expect as members of a true and just society. Perhaps we can learn from these stories of pain, loss and vulnerability, and work toward an ethical responsibility for ourselves as well as others, for in the end it would prove to be no less than a triumph, and no more than an act of humility.

About the author

Mary Shannon, MSW, MS, is a psychotherapist, award-winning artist and published author. An expert in the field of narrative medicine, she is founder and CEO of Narrative Connections, a counselling and consultation firm dedicated to using story and art as adjunctive treatment tools for individuals, couples and healthcare providers. She is widely published in the areas of health and humanities, and has served as primary and co-faculty at conferences and seminars in the United States and abroad. Mary's memoir, *The Sunday Wishbone*, is currently used as a teaching tool in the Creative Arts in Therapy doctoral program at Drexel University in Philadelphia. She is represented by the Ann Rittenberg Literary Agency in New York. To view Mary's publications and art, visit www.marytshannon.com email: marytshannon@comcast.net

11

Not dying: Scattered episodes

Jackie Hopson

The nurses are afraid of me. They didn't bring me a cup of tea this morning, though I could hear the chatter and clatter of the trolley as the other patients were woken. This makes me angry. I am very thirsty. Hot tea would be a comfort. The curtains stay drawn around me. I think the nurses are pretending I don't exist. I would be glad not to exist. I pretend I don't exist. But I am still alive. Overdosing is no more reliable than bleeding. I woke up here and I am so angry. This has happened many times. I wake up in different rented rooms, on smelly carpets, or in different general hospitals, where I feel invisible. I have wires attached to me now, so it is difficult to move. I don't dare to call out for a drink. Now I have woken up I expect to be sent to whichever asylum is nearest to my present rented room. The punishment will start. I feel so exposed, in spite of the drawn curtains. The life of the ward is going on all around me, while I, a freakish monster, am hidden from everyone.

* * *

'See, Iris? See? She's a girl! She might have a boy's short hair but she's got boobs.' A nurse has wrenched me from sleep and made me sit up to reassure another worried patient. I am wearing a blue nylon nightdress that I've never seen before. I recognise this hospital ward, but don't remember getting here. I sink back under the covers, looking for the sleep to wipe away the present. I am not ready for consciousness and the hurt it brings.

* * *

In the ambulance, I feel too woozy to speak. My friend, Janet, is sitting near me, looking terrified. My head hurts and there is blood on my face when I put up my hand to feel the soreness. I had taken just one dose of the new pills my doctor prescribed yesterday. I remember feeling giddy, sick, and staggering back to my room. No one will believe this wasn't an overdose. I've had bad reactions before to stuff the doctor has tried out, hoping to help me. I can't speak now. I am not a criminal. I'll be locked away anyway.

* * *

A pool of blood spreads out around me. I am lying on the yellow rug and screaming. I can't cut deep enough to die. I am a failure at this, as well as everything else. I am taken away, shut up in a frightening place, where every door is locked and the windows barred. The nurses are all angry with me, pull me roughly, won't let me sleep in the day. Awake all night, I daringly ask for pills – but it's the wrong time now. I have to lie down and listen. But in the morning there will be ECT (electroconvulsive therapy) and the wonderful anaesthetic. I shall feel myself losing awareness – the best feeling in the world.

* * *

I vomit white sludge into a bowl by the sofa. I can't keep the poison in my body. My soon-to-leave-me first husband looks in at the door, then slams it shut. I stay here two days, maybe three. He brings me water wordlessly. Eventually I get up and go to bed. The next day I go to work.

* * *

Nobody knows where I am. I have moved to a new room in college and haven't told anyone. Two large glasses bubble scummily with soluble painkillers. I drink one and, nauseated, can't finish the second. I lie down and wait to go somewhere else. Later I get up and vomit a mess of blood. This happens several times. My bowels are loose and bloody too. My body is rejecting what my mind wants it to hold on to. A few days later, I get up and walk across town to my dear, kind doctor. I am alive but, curiously, deaf. I need his help. He wants me to get home to my distant family so he doesn't have to send me away again. But home is so much worse than the terrifying asylum. I shall have to be locked away once more. The punishment there is easier to take, since it comes from strangers. I am scared of my mother's disgust and anger.

* * *

My beloved second husband is dying. I cannot bear this. If I sleep for a few days, I may wake up stronger. Each time I come back to consciousness, I take another handful and slip away for a little longer. When the bottle is empty, I get up. My husband is frightened and lost. I should not have done this to him. Neither of us knows what to do.

* * *

My husband is dead. My small daughter and I walk through the rain on the Cornish beach. I am crying and hopeless. My daughter says she is hungry. We go to a cafe. The rain has soaked through her coat. I didn't know she was wet and cold. She eats beans on toast and I drink tea. I have to keep going until she is old enough to care for herself. Her life has got to be better than mine. I want her to have hope. Maybe I can share some of it.

Thoughts

Please try to hide your fear and disgust at those of us who self-harm. I am afraid of myself when I am ill. Good care has only reached me when my doctor was able to contain my fear and treat me as another person, not a disgusting monster.

About the author
I have spent most of my life as a service user and have been a frequent inpatient. Having been lucky enough to receive extensive psychotherapy, my depression no longer dominates my life. Although mostly unemployable (unless lying about my health record), I am now well and pursuing a PhD at the University of Sheffield.

My encounters with self-harm

12

Sue Denison

I began to self-harm in March 2005 when I was first admitted to a mental health unit. I was feeling very suicidal having lost my husband unexpectedly to a heart attack at the age of 40. I was 32 and had a two-year-old daughter. When admitted to the unit I was struggling to control my emotions. I felt frustrated, sad, tearful, hopeless and angry. I didn't know how to release these raw emotions effectively, so took to absconding from the ward to try and run away from my thoughts and feelings. Absconding obviously did not help, so each time I did it I was just returned to the unit, usually by the police.

After some time on the ward I started to look around me and wondered how other patients coped with their difficult feelings, emotions and stresses. It became apparent that 'cutting' was used by many patients to release tension, so therefore I decided to give it a try. I discovered that when I cut myself and drew blood I felt more in control and, sure enough, tension was released. I also felt that I needed to be punished for not coping with my husband's death and ending up in a psychiatric unit, so I felt able to justify my self-harm.

However, after some time the release of tension which I felt began to last for less and less time. This often led to me feeling even greater tension, and more angry for hurting myself. A vicious circle began as the less in control I felt, the more I wanted to self-harm to gain release.

Once again I began to look for new ideas to harm myself and gain release. These included cutting deeper, ligaturing, overdosing, jumping from bridges, stabbing myself, suffocating myself and burning myself with boiling water. The method of self-harm used depended on where I was and the situation I was in, for example, whether out in the community, at home or in hospital. As time progressed, my methods became more and more dangerous and impulsive in order to meet my needs with respect to relief of emotions. When feeling stable and in control, I was able to recognise that sometimes my acts of self-harm were a cry for help, a way of physically demonstrating to people that I was really struggling and needed help because words didn't seem strong enough, but at other times my self-harm was a suicide attempt.

Due to differing attitudes towards self-harm and people's judgements, I found it very hard to ask for help when struggling not to self-harm. Even when ringing the Crisis team, who are trained to deal with these situations, I was never quite sure what kind of response I would receive. For example, on one occasion I rang a dedicated mental health helpline, very tearful and distressed, needing to talk. The response I received was: 'Would you like to put the phone down and ring back in 15 minutes when you've calmed down?' Needless to say I never made a second call because I felt that the gentleman I spoke to didn't have time for me and I was just a huge inconvenience. Another time when I had plucked up the courage to call the local Crisis team for help, the response was: 'Oh are you having one of your little episodes again?' The call lasted for several minutes and was very unhelpful, leaving me still in a state of distress. Attitudes and lack of support like this often lead to people self-harming unnecessarily.

Unfortunately, my experience is that there is a great lack of education and understanding of self-harm both within the community and with professionals, and although I have had some positive experiences, unfortunately I have had more negative ones. If I am considered to be a danger to myself or others, the police are often called upon to assist. My experience is that on the whole they consider people who have self-harmed to be time wasters and/or attention seekers. I have often had inappropriate comments made to me, such as 'Pull yourself together' and 'We've got better things to do with our time than sit around with you waiting for doctors to come and assess you'. The police can also be very rough and intimidating which can heighten anxiety and feelings of being out of control. In my experience I feel that I am treated like a criminal – having my hands handcuffed, my legs tied and being bundled into the back of a police van cage – rather than as somebody who is unwell and needs help and understanding. When at police stations, because I have been taken there as a place of safety and because I am a danger to myself, it can be a very demoralising experience as I am often unceremoniously stripped to nothing, given an internal examination to look for drugs, then put in a suit which is strong and unrippable.

I believe that it would be very beneficial if police officers could be given some training on how to talk and behave around mentally unwell people so that they could develop a better understanding of what and why people find themselves in difficult situations and self-harm, then they could be more empathic, less judgemental and more reassuring, in what can be a very scary environment. It would also help the unwell person feel less scared about what is happening and going to happen to them.

My experience with mental health specialists overall is that they don't glamorise self-harm. On the whole they encourage patients to try and 'nip self-harm in the bud', but if this is unsuccessful and a patient does end up self-harming, they are ready and willing to talk about what led up to the self-harm when the patient is settled once again. They also often encourage patients to take responsibility for their own actions by cleaning up and dressing any minor wounds themselves if appropriate. This helps to put the patient back in control but also allows them time to reflect on their actions at the same time.

However, I find that a lot of mental health specialists will use information that they know about you to try and encourage people to think twice about self-harming. For example, they will ask me how my daughter would feel should I harm myself or permanently disfigure or disable myself, and what effect it would have on my family should I accidentally kill myself. This kind of conversation does not help, as when in a self-harming frame of mind it feels like emotional blackmail. It makes me feel even more angry and frustrated, which in turn can lead to heightened emotions and even more serious self-harm. Mental health specialists need to try and support patients during their initial crisis, de-escalating people verbally by talking calmly and in a reassuring manner, whilst at the same time being non-judgemental and non-threatening.

My experience of general nursing teams is very mixed, and it most certainly demonstrates that general nursing practitioners and doctors need to be educated as to why people self-harm. I have found that if I am taken to hospital by ambulance after self-harming I am often treated as a time waster. Staff talk in a patronising way and pass unsuitable comments and judgements without knowing any of my history. I usually end up staying at least one night on a ward, and again the nursing staff and doctors often treat me with contempt, knowing that my problem is self-induced. It feels as though they have no time for me and are judging me as a person and making all sorts of assumptions. It can be a very lonely place being on a general ward with nobody willing to talk to you about what has happened. I have even had nursing staff comment that I am there again and asking, 'How many times has it been this year?'

I have had very mixed attitudes from staff when attending Accident and Emergency (A&E) directly from a mental health unit. On one occasion the doctor treating me asked how I had obtained the injury. When I began to tell him he threw up his arms and said, 'Oh don't tell me, I don't want to know!' I felt this was very unprofessional and showed a great lack of care and understanding.

However, on a subsequent visit to A&E I was treated completely differently. I was full of apologies for being there, being a nuisance and wasting their time, because I was expecting to be treated badly, but the doctor very gently told me I had just as much right to be there and get help and treatment. She said how sorry she was that I felt so bad that I had resorted to harming myself, and if I wanted to talk she could make herself available. She then treated me very gently and with utmost respect, talking me through every step of the procedure she was carrying out, checking as she went that I was okay. This attitude was a complete revelation to me, which led me to write to her senior manager praising her compassion and understanding.

It is my belief that self-harm is generally perceived as a taboo subject, which people are scared to talk about because it is something they don't understand. A recent campaign aimed at educating the general public that one in four people suffer from a diagnosed mental illness had a disappointing outcome, as still only 24 per cent of the population know this information. However, I do think that it is very positive that so many celebrities have come forward to share their stories and experiences of mental health issues, and hopefully they can help to act as a voice to help combat the stigma of mental health.

Thoughts

- Self-harm is often used as a coping strategy when a person is struggling with difficult emotions.

- Self-harm is sometimes used by a person to physically and outwardly demonstrate their distress.

- Self-harm can escalate over time to obtain the required relief.

- Negative attitudes towards people often escalate episodes because the self-harmer doesn't feel they are being heard.

- There is a great lack of education regarding self-harm and why people do it, both within the community and amongst professionals.

- The police are often very rough, treating self-harm as time wasting/ attention seeking.

- More training for police officers in how to communicate with mentally unwell people would aid understanding, empathy and an awareness of people's needs when distressed.

- Using emotional blackmail often heightens negative emotions and can escalate self-harm.

- General nursing practitioners and doctors would benefit from more education in mental health and why people self-harm. This would assist understanding and help prevent unfounded judgements being made.

About the author

I was born in Manchester in 1972 where I lived with my mum, dad and older sister. At the age of 10 we moved to Stockport where I completed my primary school education, went to secondary school and then onto sixth-form college. Music played a huge part in my life and in 1990 I went to Lancaster University to train to be a primary school teacher, specialising in music. I qualified with a 2:1 in 1994. My teaching career began immediately after leaving university and continued until 2009 when I lost my job due to my illness.

13

Biting my lip when I'm screaming inside

Lynn Tolmon

Four months ago, I boiled a kettle and poured the water over my arm. Then I boiled it again, and did it four more times. It had been over six years since I had hurt myself deliberately, and if you'd asked me, I would have said I would never self-harm again. I had been your 'typical' teenage 'cutter', textbook really, but now I'm in my thirties and I thought I was a million miles away from all the influences that drove me to self-harm. But this was by far the worst injury I had ever inflicted, and I literally had no idea what had brought it on.

I don't remember the first time I hurt myself deliberately, but I do know that as a very small child I had often wished I could fall out of a tree and break my arm, because then my daddy would be proud of his brave little soldier. Children at school with plaster casts got treated like they were special, and I wanted to feel cared for. I always had scabs and scars; even mosquito bites always ended up with scabs the size of a ten pence piece – my mother must have spent most of her time saying 'Don't pick it!' – but I never broke a bone.

I had sucked my arm till I was perhaps eight. It was like sucking your thumb, but the difference was that your arm is fleshier, and I used to bite down as hard as I could, for as long as I could, till I could feel the comforting indentation in the flesh where my teeth had been. I would do that whenever I felt sad or lonely, or just bored. It was like sucking a dummy, but also like screaming into a pillow – a way to swallow my feelings when they were unwelcome.

When my mum said I was getting too grown-up to suck my arm, I had to give it up. I remember it as an upsetting time, a time of doing what the grown-ups told me, even though I desperately wanted to soothe myself, even though it had never been naughty before. This was also the time I started biting my lips.

Imagine you are having to bite your tongue in an argument – you are holding yourself back and controlling your irritation. Physically, you would probably find yourself squeezing your lips between your teeth. That's what I do. All the time. I spent my childhood and teenage years biting my lips together to control myself.

The more I am afraid I'll say or do something hurtful, the harder I bite my lips. As a child I remember hugging our family dog, and biting my lips, as if my love was unmanageable, and had to be controlled. Playing with other kids, I would feel the need to bite my lips, as if my excitement might be explosive, or toxic. Even hugging people, I would squeeze my lips together, so that the harder I hugged, the harder my teeth dug into my lips.

This is all perfectly understandable for a child whose father was suffering severe mental health problems – any display of emotion on my part could trigger rage or misery in my father, so I learned to swallow my feelings, to be 'seen and not heard'. My father had been raised in a family where sons inherit the precious family name, so he wanted me to be a boy, and I learned that boys get injured, boys are brave and strong, boys don't show their emotions. I knew I wasn't a boy, but I thought I could become one if I acted like one.

Then my father committed suicide and my stepfather came along. He was emotionally and sexually abusive, and my gender became a weapon against me, my body became a battleground. That's when I found my anger and powerlessness boiling inside me like infection in a boil.

I would be humiliated, punished, derided and sent to my room. I'd have spent the evening biting my lips, fighting the desperate seething chaos of my emotions, and in the privacy of my room, the only place I had autonomy, I would weep and feel my skin itch. My cat would be curled up on my desk, oblivious to the fact that in my head, unwanted thoughts would be invading my mind – snapping his legs, throttling him, smashing him against the wall. I needed to inflict hurt; I needed my agony to be displaced. My fingers ached to torture, to manifest the invisible horror that was going on in my head.

There was no way I could hurt another living thing. Especially the cat I loved. I fantasised about murdering my stepfather, watched him bent over the video recorder, wondering if I could stab him. But I knew that would hurt my mum, destroy her life. Nothing I could do or say would make me feel better without hurting someone else.

Though as I write this, I am looking at my first scar. I was sat at my bedroom desk, doing my homework, and trying to blot out the feelings thumping through my head – the powerless rage at my stepdad's horrible comments, the constant drive to destroy my sense of self. I had a paperclip, and idly fiddled with it, straightening out the bent wire and pushing it into the end of a finger. I scratched it unconsciously on the back of my hand, and an idea struck me: how hard would it be to create an actual wound? My childhood of scab-picking gave me a desire for a nice satisfying scratch. So I used the paperclip to scratch, over and over, till I had a perfectly straight injury on my hand. Then I did it again, leaving me with a lovely tidy line of damaged, bleeding skin, four inches long.

For that half hour, I hadn't thought of anything. I had been focused like a laser-beam on the process, the pain and the intended outcome. I hadn't been bothered by remembering my stepdad's cruelty; I hadn't been troubled by my own secret desire to be cruel myself. It was as if the physical pain had drowned out all that pain in my head.

From then on, when things got too much, I would find myself thinking about what I could do to myself. I learned to unscrew the blade from a pencil sharpener, then how to smash a disposable razor and extract the whisper-sharp metal. It was the preparation, the build-up, the hours and hours of waiting that made it worth the pain. Like opening your Christmas Advent calendar, feeling the pencil sharpener in my pocket while my stepdad called me a fat ugly waste of space, I could get through the day. He called me Child A.

I never thought beyond the injury. I just planned, prepared, waited, and cut. Then the fall-out would be a nightmare. Mum would sob, scream, make me promise never to do it again. She'd ask me if I was doing it to try and kill myself, or if it was to hurt her. If I tried to cover up the cuts, she'd demand to see what I was hiding. Just like when she made me stop sucking my arm, she made it so hard to cut. She made it about how much it hurt her. So I drank and ate. I binged on anything that would give me even a brief moment of oblivion, and managed to hide the evidence.

Once I wasn't living at home, with the freedom to do my own thing, I cut a few times, but mostly used drugs and food. I only had a few crises bad enough to warrant scars. It wasn't till my mid-twenties, when my sister and I were sharing a house and I was working in a high-stress job, that the cutting resurfaced. I had taken an uncharacteristic leap of faith and trusted a colleague enough to become friends. He let me down and left me devastated, sat at my desk, incapable of functioning under the weight of his abandonment. I could only keep myself going by planning, intricately, a huge bloody drama in the disabled toilet.

That, and my subsequent trip to A&E, a company psychiatrist, and the boardroom (where I was dismissed for gross misconduct), made me decide that this would be my last ever self-harm session.

What I didn't realise was that it wasn't my choice to stop 'being a cutter' that stopped the self-harm; being sacked removed the pressure enough to make life manageable. Subsequently, moving away from my family, I established a life that was, by dint of being dull, unlikely to drive me to self-harm. I worked damned hard to rebuild myself, and when I thought I was normal, I started building myself a life.

And that brings me back to the kettle. I'm not 'better' or 'fixed'. My life is different, but I am still susceptible to self-harm. I had taken on too much and stopped taking care of myself. With hindsight, as my best friend says, it was obvious what was happening, but at the time I would honestly have said I was fine, and that I don't know what triggered me to hurt myself. I had been let down by the NHS crisis team, I had taken on too much work at the community project I was helping to set up, and an unavoidable accident had seen me responsible for the death of a stray cat. I felt guilty, ashamed, worthless and undeserving. My head was a maelstrom of unbearable emotions.

I can't say I will never self-harm again, but I can say I know enough about myself to make it unlikely. If the worst comes to the worst and I find myself in A&E again, I won't beat myself up about it. Mental health isn't a binary state – it's not that I'm either normal or mental – it's a constantly shifting balance. Every moment of every day, the scales of my equilibrium have things added and removed, and sometimes those added weights are beyond my control. If I keep an eye on the scales, the adjustments can be manageable; if I ignore it, and let things get horribly out of whack, it takes drastic, and sometimes unhealthy, re-balancing.

So I try to be kind to myself and I try to make sure I express what I'm feeling. I have built a network of people who I can talk to, and learned how to channel my feelings outwards without it hurting others. I keep myself busy, but not to the extent that I'm blotting out my feelings. I take antidepressants when I need them, and I get out and about whenever I can. I try new things, like stand-up comedy and performance art, and am increasingly capable of handling things like rejection, disappointment or anxiety.

I think the most important change I've made is accepting help. There was a long time when I didn't dare admit that I needed help, even to myself. I thought I had to be self-sufficient in every way. When I am hurt by somebody cruel, I no longer say, 'Well, I probably deserved that' – I ask a friend and am comforted. There's a real sense of undeserving, a deep-down (misconceived) faith that nobody could ever willingly help a person like me, that my company and my needs are a burden or abhorrent. I know where this comes from and I am now learning to fight it. Changing this attitude means I can now seek and accept the love and support that most people take for granted, and which keeps most people from hurting themselves.

I will always be a self-harmer, in the same way that I will always have the occasional craving for a cigarette as an ex-smoker, or a drink after a hard day. My brain has just been wired that way. It doesn't mean there's anything wrong with me, it just means there's something wrong with how I'm feeling at that juncture in my life, and how I MIGHT cope with those feelings.

Thoughts

- Try new things. Finding out I'm terrible at netball was embarrassing, but I learned to cope with being terrible at things. And I found things I'm great at – and a few I'm getting better at.

- Be patient and generous with yourself. I wanted to be 'all better' and I wanted instant results, but it took me five years to go from heavily medicated and housebound to appearing on national TV and living my life.

- Do something scary. When I know how brave and strong I am, I don't need to cut myself to get that feeling of power.

- Write it down. A blog might feel too public, but a private diary or poem can vent those feelings you need to get out. The best place to write is your local cafe, because you're giving yourself some 'me' time somewhere nice, and if you're socially anxious, you can get used to being around people from behind your notebook.

- Take things a day at a time, even an hour at a time. I've had days when I didn't think I could withstand another minute of how I felt, but it always passes.

- Trust yourself. There is nothing wrong with you. We have survived the only way that's worked for us so far. You WILL find better ways, just like I did. You're the only person who can be an expert on you.

- Go to the library and take out every book you can from the self-help and psychology sections. The more I know, the more I know that works for me. When I feel anxious or twitchy, I can keep myself occupied by skimming through a book in front of the TV.

- Fight for what you believe in. I started out believing in the causes I support, but the more I've been able to do for them, the more I've come to believe in myself. Join a political organisation, an animal rights campaign, a union or a community project. Being proud of the cause taught me to be proud of myself.

- Get some sleep-in hair rollers. Last thing at night I have a shower and put my rollers in. It created a routine of self-care, and the positive response from people gives me a boost. Hearing 'Hi, Lynn, you look nice' makes me smile.

About the author

Lynn is a healthy, active, 34-year-old woman originally from a small fishing town on the south coast. She currently works with Liverpool Biennial, the leading contemporary arts festival in Britain, promoting their flagship work 2Up2Down by Jeanne van Heeswijk. Lynn is writer in residence at Homebaked Anfield. She lives alone with her three rescue dogs, and has a strong and supportive group of friends. Her hobbies include performing stand-up comedy and creating street art in her local area. She has overcome her father's mental illness and suicide when she was 11, and her stepfather's emotional and sexual abuse throughout her teens. Like many survivors of childhood trauma, Lynn spent her twenties struggling with debilitating low self-esteem, guilt and shame, and was told by doctors that she wouldn't live to see 30 if her self-destructive lifestyle continued.

Lynn attributes her survival and recovery to art and literature. She says that what sustained her in her darkest times went on to inspire her in her early recovery, and nurture her into her success.

14

Let the blood run

Pippa Hennessy

I felt like a freak.

I was 14 years old and I didn't have a bad life, all things considered. My parents were in the process of splitting up, but they were very civilised about it. I was close to my younger brother and ignored my (much) younger sister.

The main problems were that I was bored, and I was different, and I was lonely. I'd always been a weirdo – we didn't have a TV, which immediately placed me outside any peer group you cared to mention. And I read books, lots and lots of books. I didn't know anyone else who read more than a book or two a year, so I didn't have anyone to talk to about my passion. School was a nightmare place stuck in the middle of several council estates, not at all stimulating and full of bullies who were keen to make my life miserable. When I started there, aged 11, I spoke properly, used long words, and assumed the other kids would leave me to get on with my weird little life, as they had done at primary school. Not so. They identified me as someone different on the first day, and after that there was no let-up. I knew I was doomed when I realised even my friends thought I was just a bit too weird, and they (and a couple of the teachers!) were joining in with the bullies.

I tried to fit in, I really did. I worked hard, which made my parents and teachers happy, but didn't do me any favours with the other kids. Then I joined forces with the naughty kids and soon realised they didn't actually like me, they just let me sit with them so they'd have someone to tease. I tried being clever, I tried being stupid, I started smoking to appear cool, I played up in class to provoke admiration, I picked on kids who were even weirder than me so I didn't feel like I was at the bottom of the pecking order. None of it worked. I lost my friends, I lost my self-esteem, I lost any feelings of connection with my parents. So I became a 14-year-old, lonely, bored, miserable, confused freak.

My parents were too busy with their own problems to take much notice of me. I don't blame them – they'd both been brought up during and after the war, in families where the children were left to get on with it. Ideas of security and love and affection didn't figure much in their lives. My dad was an only child, my mum had a sister six years younger than her, so they didn't see the problem with having to be emotionally self-sufficient. At the time, it felt like they didn't love me very much, which was (of course) my fault. I had been very close to my brother, but he'd found a different way to deal with being different – he'd joined the marauding gangs of council estate kids, and was being sexually abused by an old man who lived up the road. He had his own problems and he was growing away from me. I didn't understand it at the time; I saw it as another loss.

There's a phrase that people used a lot about me back then: 'She's just looking for attention.' So I was not only a freak, I was a silly girl who was constantly demanding something I was not entitled to expect. My increasingly outrageous attempts to make my life more bearable provoked incomprehension, anger, or plain indifference. I ran away from home and when I was finally found (in Edinburgh, of all places), instead of being pleased to see me again, or even relieved that I hadn't been harmed, my parents simply seemed irritated that I'd disrupted their lives. Once I'd arrived home and been told off by a policeman, the episode was not mentioned again. I never told anyone that I'd narrowly avoided being raped during that escapade.

Yes, I was looking for attention. I knew that was part of what was going on. I also knew that made me a Bad Person. It never crossed my mind that I was looking for attention because I actually needed it, because I wasn't getting enough of the right kind. I needed proof that I mattered. In that respect, my parents' policy of 'not rewarding bad behaviour' failed miserably. Sure, they didn't reinforce my 'bad behaviour' by responding to it, but that doesn't work if you don't respond to any sort of behaviour.

So, I was a 14-year-old freak, desperate for attention. And if I didn't get the positive kind, any kind would do. Yes, I was self-absorbed (to the extent that I didn't notice what was going on with my brother, and I didn't notice that one of my friends was anorexic) but I was also deeply miserable.

One Sunday, I was sitting in my bedroom thinking about my English homework. Our teacher was a bit of a rebel – he played guitar in a band called the Geisha Girls, who were notorious for stripping naked while on stage at The Hexagon – so he tended to set homework that was mildly interesting. He'd asked us to start writing a diary, and had suggested covering the exercise books he'd given us for the purpose with wallpaper, or maybe pictures of our favourite bands or football teams. That was far too dull for me. I decided to colour mine in red, so it looked like I'd bled all over it … then I thought, 'Why not actually bleed all over it?'

It took much of a day to coax enough blood out of my fingertips, using a pencil-sharpener blade. The result was disappointing. Once the blood had dried on the blue cardboard cover it looked more brown than red, and not at all shiny. So I ripped a picture of Billy Idol out of *Smash Hits* and taped it over the top, then filled the first few pages with random ramblings designed to shock the teacher.

Although nothing much came of it, I couldn't stop thinking about that experiment. The pain was fascinating. I didn't like it much at first, but after I'd gotten used to it, it kind of felt nice. More to the point, it kind of felt *something*. I'd grown used to suppressing my emotional pain, because it (or rather, its outward expression) was 'self-centred' and 'attention seeking'. It had been invalidated and I had internalised that judgement. This pain, on the other hand, was perfectly valid. My skin had been cut, there was blood and there would be scars. It was real.

Cutting my fingertips wasn't the way to go though. Having sore fingers was inconvenient and I kept catching the flaps of skin on my coat pockets or getting strands of my hair caught in the cuts when I brushed it. And the pencil sharpener blade was rubbish. I discovered you could buy razor blades from Boots, and cutting my forearms was much better. After cutting several times, I would stop and watch the beads of blood spring from the thin red lines, glistening and perfect. Using the razor blade was less painful, and it made the cuts less ragged. I didn't cut deeper, but I did cut more.

I didn't keep it secret at first. I'd walk round with my sleeves rolled up. I told other kids how I got the cuts. When teachers asked, I said I'd fallen into a thorn bush. I could tell they didn't believe me, but they didn't do anything about it. The other kids just looked at me as if I was mad. My parents more or less ignored the cuts – Mum once said I should think about the scars, they'd look ugly on my arms for the whole of my life (which didn't affect me at all – I couldn't see beyond tomorrow, let alone into adulthood). Apart from that, and the time she lost her temper with me (which at least showed she cared, but had the adverse effect of reinforcing the behaviour!), she never said anything to me about them. I don't know if Dad even saw them. I guess he must have.

Eventually, I found my way to a youth counsellor. It was just what I thought I wanted – someone who would listen to what I had to say and who would (I hoped) help me feel happier. I'm not sure what I got from those weekly visits. Talking about my problems didn't make my parents take more notice of me, or make school life any easier. We discussed the self-harm often – she saw it as a concrete problem we could tackle together. I didn't really know why I cut myself, but she kept asking, so I tried to understand what was going on and explain it to her. The nearest I could get was that it proved that I could handle any emotional pain that anyone else inflicted on me, if I could cut myself and deal with the physical pain. It showed I could heal.

The counsellor was concerned that I was one step away from slashing my wrists, which I outwardly encouraged because it ensured I continued to get her attention. It wasn't true though. I never seriously considered suicide (I did take a couple of overdoses, but not enough to put me in much danger of actually dying).

After a while, I gradually stopped cutting. I discovered that getting drunk on cheap cider was a more effective way of blunting the raw edges of my life, although I did occasionally reach for the blade when things got too difficult. Then I went to university and (so I thought) everything sorted itself out after a miserable first year.

It wasn't until over a decade later, in 1995, that I first learned I wasn't the only person to self-harm. I found a short article about Princess Diana's self-harm in *The Guardian*. I can still vividly remember the shock and then the relief I felt. Being *The Guardian*, the article gave some context, mentioning that self-harm was much more common than was once thought and that it was far more than simply attention-seeking behaviour. For the first 40-odd years of my life, that article was the only source of information about my self-harm that didn't cast my behaviour in an entirely negative and freakish light.

So. I got through university and came out six years later with two degrees and a husband. Over the next few years I developed a career in computing and had two sons. I had moderately severe postnatal depression after both births, but that was treated quickly and effectively by a brilliant specialist team at Queen's Medical Centre in Nottingham. Life was pretty good.

Then things slowly fell apart, between the ages of 32 and 42. My marriage broke down when I realised I'd been denying my sexuality. I fell in love with a woman who soon dumped me, had to take increasing responsibility for my children due to problems with my ex-husband, worked my way into a demanding, high-stress job, and gradually slipped into deep depression. As a result, I was off work for over five months, much of which I spent sitting on my sofa watching TV. As soon as I was back at work I was made redundant.

I spent several months trying to get back into computing and eventually realised that would be the worst thing I could do. So I started studying for a BA in Creative and Professional Writing. I'd always wanted to return to study and I thoroughly enjoyed the work. However, I also had to make a living and look after my children, who by that time were in their mid-teens. So I took every opportunity to make contacts and get experience relevant to the writing industries. I got a part-time job with a local publisher, got a teaching qualification and started leading workshops, became an active member of several local writing organisations and societies, took extra classes to improve my own writing … in short, I turned into a workaholic. I didn't (and still don't) see this as a bad thing – although I hated working in computing and resented every minute of my 40-hour week, I love the writing-related work I do now. It's even more varied these days, but still basically the same, and I don't mind that I spend every waking moment writing or working.

The problem was that I wasn't yet emotionally robust enough to take the stress at that time. I don't think I had managed to fully escape the depression that had lost me my job, and I was busily taking on a workload that a healthy person would baulk at. I could feel myself slipping back downwards into despair – that state of hopelessness where you *know* you are never going to be happy again and that life is never going to be any better.

So, I started cutting myself again. This time I had a greater understanding of what was going on in my head and I was almost clinical in my use of self-harm. I accepted that the act of cutting (and the pain of the unhealed wounds) helped relieve the stress I was putting myself under. I had to build a new career from scratch and support myself and the kids in the meantime. Therefore, I had to work hard; I didn't have time to sink into lethargy the way I had a couple of years before. Cutting was simply a way of coping with the unavoidable pressure.

The old 'silly attention seeker' label was still attached, and I was deeply ashamed that I'd reverted to what I saw as childish behaviour. I didn't tell anyone for a long while. Eventually, I let something slip to my GP (deliberately? – maybe) and he referred me to a wonderful community psychiatric nurse, who kept me stable and pointed me in the direction of the equally wonderful Harmless.

Harmless is a charity set up to help people who self-harm. They provide support in many ways. I talked to a counsellor and read an anthology of writing by past and current self-harmers. I couldn't believe there were so many people who felt like me, who'd responded to such a wide variety of problems in a similar way. I was shocked in fact. How could this self-destructive behaviour be so prevalent and so poorly understood, even by many of those who harmed themselves? I realised I'd been lucky, in that the negative reactions I'd come up against had been relatively mild. Yet even so, I had a deep-rooted 'knowledge' that self-harming made me a Bad Person, and it would take more than empathy with and sympathy for other people's experiences to persuade me otherwise.

I don't want to give the impression that my life has been bad. It hasn't. I've had a lot of luck, and a lot of happiness, not least thanks to my sons. But I believe the best stroke of luck I've had was being accepted for a clinical trial for people with recurrent severe depression, which gave me a year's access to tailored psychiatric support and a year's course of cognitive behavioural therapy (CBT). It was hard work, but it was a life-saver for me. Not in the literal sense – I don't think I'd have killed myself, because I couldn't bear the thought of what that would do to the kids. But the life I was living four years ago was relentlessly miserable, not a life I'd wish on anyone, not a life at all.

There's no point going over the work my therapist and I put in over those 12 months – you'd probably be thoroughly bored by the time I finished. The interesting aspect of it is that the therapist and the psychiatrist both virtually ignored my cutting. They'd ask, every now and then, whether I was still cutting and how severe it was. But apart from that, we didn't talk about the self-harm, or the reasons behind it. I didn't notice this avoidance at the time – I believe it was deliberate, although I never asked them. And bizarrely, I didn't notice when I stopped cutting. Somehow, over the space of a week, I went from cutting several times a day to not cutting at all. I couldn't say when the last time I cut was – I didn't notice not cutting!

That was the point at which the therapist helped me understand more clearly why I had been cutting and the lessons to be learned from my behaviour patterns (there are always lessons to be learned in CBT – it's inescapable). I think it's worth listing them here.

- The emotional pain I'd been feeling was valid. I didn't need to have physical pain as well to deserve sympathy, or to prove to myself or others that I was miserable.

- The cutting gave me a level of control over my emotional state. I could regulate the physical pain, deciding how much and when. It was something I had a choice about.

- The release of endorphins due to the pain helped relieve stress – it was actually a form of self-medication (not one to be encouraged as a default, admittedly).

- The physical pain and the sight of the blood felt real, and it reminded me that the physical external world exists and matters.

Now it's a year since I finished the CBT, and I haven't cut myself in that time. I did cut a couple of times in the month or two after I stopped cutting daily, but my therapist helped me not to panic or see it as slipping backwards, it was just what happened on the odd day that was worse than the rest. Yes, I still think about it every now and then. It's a bit like quitting smoking. The temptation will always be there, and I accept that. But I'm lucky – I've got my life back. And I'm going to hang on to it with all the strength I've got.

To My Body

I need your mouth to speak
my silent body

I roll my words down your tongue

my ink lies
in charms
under your skin

protect me from this world
to which I am not immune

if I draw a knife

along	and	across	you
along	and	across	
	and	across	
		across	

your pain heals mine
for a time

but

whose blood falls
around who?

can you
be
without me?

can you let me
be?

Thoughts

The reactions to my behaviour as a teenager – that I was silly, attention seeking, and didn't deserve any sympathy – were completely counter-productive. They focused on the behaviour rather than the cause, and they made me feel like a bad person, driving me deeper into depression and isolation and setting the pattern for my self-harm in later life.

In contrast, the reactions to my adult self-harm – acceptance and acknowledgement of my distress, and an overwhelming validation of my need for help – enabled me to accept my own feelings and behaviour, and overcome the negative connotations I'd automatically attached to them.

Self-harm … is it harm? I'm not so sure that label was useful to me. Certainly when I was cutting in my adult life the aim wasn't to harm myself. It was to enable me to deal with an unbearable situation. And in that respect it was helpful to me. I'm not sure this matters so much, but it is one reason I like the charity's name: Harmless.

Most importantly, self-harm should *never* be seen or described as something to be ashamed of. This leads to those who harm themselves hiding their behaviour and piling even more pressure on themselves to Stop Being A Bad Person. Which, in itself, is going to increase the pressure to self-harm and will not lead to the underlying issues being resolved.

About the author
Pippa Hennessy is a writer, teacher, publisher, editor, proofreader and typesetter. She is a single mother who spends her days rushing around trying to get on top of her to-do list with boundless enthusiasm and varying degrees of success. After leaving university in 1990 with a BSc in Psychology and a PhD in Computer Science she worked as a programmer for several years before being promoted into middle management. In 2008 she was made redundant, and has since managed

to defeat depression at the same time as completely changing her career and studying for a BA in Creative and Professional Writing. She has published poems and short stories in various magazines and anthologies and is working on two novels and a collection of poetry.

15

Self-harm

Richard L. Peacocke

'Like a thief in the night' (1 Thessalonians 5:1–5), that's what they say when something happens unnoticed. In the case of Paul's letter, it is the Second Coming of Jesus Christ at the end of days, but it can be used for more personal things. In my case, it was the departure of my phlegmatic demeanour, which has stood me in good stead over years of bomb disposal, prison nursing duties, court appearances, and dealing with my ex-wife. A numbness has been inserted in its place.

The dulled, numbed emotions developed over several years and have maintained their dominance ever since, taking any raised emotion and damping it down to the same porridge stodge pool as the rest.

Occasionally, when my guard is dropped because of tiredness or emotional overload or feeling safe for some reason, such as being in the bosom of my family and friends, hidden away from the dangers of the world, a musical interlude or a memory or a piece of art will spring out at me and start my eyes to tears. These moments are ruthlessly suppressed by the porridge pool, and normality returns. I cannot afford the luxury of these feelings, allowing them free rein (or reign) over my alertness. That way there be dragons. Thus, people have to work hard at being my friend; not so many want to do that and so they drift away. I am sure that some see it as a challenge and do make the effort, but they have their own problems. However, when I find one such person, I value them greatly and am utterly aware of how fragile the relationship is.

So, when someone or something looks to be threatening it, the pain often becomes unbearable and I have to do something about it for my own sake. I have to bring myself back from the self-destruct panel. I have to protect myself. In such circumstances, the emotions well up fiercely and the porridge pool is not strong enough to pull them back down to it. The logical mind says: 'Wake up, old man! You've got to do summat here or you'll be stuffed, and no mistake!' (or words to that effect). In fact, it doesn't come as words in a cod northern accent like that, but as a realisation that things are getting out of control. I need to do something fast and drastically. I cut myself. I take an overdose. I switch off entirely and become, for a time, someone else – who knows who, just someone else – for longer or shorter periods. I respond to the situation at hand, wandering off, putting myself in harm's way as a means of ending the pain, dissociating.

I suppose that the rarest thing I do is to cut myself. It is much more common for me to take an overdose of my tablets. I do not know why this is but it seems to be the way I have of avoiding the pain. Some time ago, the way I dealt with things was to pull out my beard hairs one at a time with a pair of eye tweezers, or sit myself in a scaldingly hot bath and watch my lower body go scarlet. In the beard case, my reasoning was that I was saving myself having to shave, but in reality it took a long time to achieve a hairless chin and the pain, for what it was, was acting as a distraction for me. I don't know what I was thinking of in the bath; I was too young and it was too long ago, or maybe I do not want to remember – such is dissociation.

Another time I was tempted to self-harm was when I was of the opinion that my fiancée and carer, Stephanie, was talking about me behind my back to my care coordinator, David. On this occasion, I felt the need to cut the back of my hand with a rusty modelling knife blade. I made four superficial cuts to the back of my left hand in straight lines and almost immediately regretted having done so. It was so patently obvious that I had cut my hand on purpose that other people joked about it. My care co-ordinator was not phased at all. He took it all in his stride and noted it down in his file. But then, he was trained in self-harm matters.

By far the most common method I use to self-harm is to take a non-fatal overdose of my tablets, my medication. I have no idea why I do this, but perhaps the very act of doing it gives me back some control over my life. Obviously, having taken the tablets, I feel quite shame-faced. However, as far as I know these overdoses have caused me no harm. The worst that has happened was when I took too many Haloperidol capsules and slept solidly all through the night, waking in the morning with a headache. Of late, these self-destructive urges have been waning and I have felt more stable on my medications and in my living conditions.

Often people talk about crying for help, but I do not think that is it in my case as I never ask for help after self-harming. There are times when the prospect of dying is almost welcome. I think, rather than being actively suicidal, I am being devious. For example, if I die it might be seen as an accidental overdose and not suicide. I do not know why this is important to me, but obviously it is. After all, should I die, who will be able to chastise me? I will be well beyond anyone's reach, but it will be a black mark against my name, even though I would not know about it. However, 'Sod's law' says that there is an afterlife and I would be left staring down at all the upset I have caused. Of course the thought of causing all that upset is a strong reason not to take things too far. The reason for self-harm remains, however, in having control over areas of my life when I feel that control is slipping and that I am losing control. My ability to inflict damage on myself under controlled circumstances is a very important part of my life.

Castle Mud

The world becomes too much to bear
With eyes or ears or taste or touch,
And so I close myself away
From eyes or ears or taste or touch.

It's easier in the warm confines
Of this old castle made of mud,
With my enemies there with me,
Away from the cold sight of God.

What need I for security
When I'm locked in from the outside?
Walk through the gate while it's ajar?
It's always been locked from outside.

Richard L Peacocke, 2000, Dorset

Thus is my vulnerability laid bare. The Freudian death drive is strong within, but only under certain circumstances and at a time of my own choosing, which allows a little free will – does this make me a metaphysical libertarian working within the concept of a free will that requires the individual to be able to take more than one possible course of action under a given set of circumstances? It also gives me comfort for my old age, as there is no way I would allow myself to become totally dependent on someone else and live just for the lack of dying. The seeming lack of long-term hope is merely realism to my mind – and am I now a determinist, a compatibilist? I do not think so.

The phenomenon of hope, which also lies at the root of any meaningful recovery, can best be understood in the context of my experiences of being in the world. If all understanding is self-understanding based on pre-understanding then Weinsheimer's dictum can be better appreciated (Weinsheimer, 1985, p. 166): 'Understanding is projection and what it projects is expectations that precede the text.' In the case of the disruption and fear engendered by suffering dissociative states, including depersonalisation, and the self-harming practices that creep up on me, only hope for a better and more settled future keeps me going along my personal recovery path. In this sense, the self-harming is fulfilling a self-protective role, albeit suppressed.

A shift towards a fuller understanding takes place not from a neutral observer's position, one who is detached or removed from the immediacy of the experience, but via the intimacy of understanding that comes as a part and parcel of the hermeneutic circle. This is my aim in this writing: to help you, the reader, to experience from first hand, or as close as you can get, my emotions and the reasons for my actions, and in experiencing this, to more fully understand me. Within this context, understanding is emergent when we circle from the whole to the parts and back to the whole again, constantly forming and continually revising our understandings about the whole as more parts of it come into view. As I do this, I help you to form and reform prejudices. It is important to remember that prejudices are not false judgements, they are conditions of understanding. Thus, instead of getting rid of our prejudices, we should choose from amongst them. We must be constantly questioning our beliefs and our understandings as we become prepared for the text we are exploring to say something new to us.

There can be no doubt but that the experience of self-harming focuses one on the living that is to be done. I think the lessons learned are sparse from this story. I was in a sorry place and one way of dealing with it was to self-harm. That self-harm fell well short of suicidal intention and was used more as a method to pull myself up short and focus myself on my shortcomings is evident from the text above. It is also evident from the text that most of my self-harming was done privately, without the knowledge of others, except for when I scratched my hand with a rusty modelling knife and regretted it almost immediately because it had the effect of advertising to the world that I had self-harmed. This was not something that I required the world to know. I felt ashamed that I failed to keep private that which should have been kept private, that others knew of my weakness. There is prejudice and stigma attached to mental ill health, and evidence of self-harming is often seen as a badge of that same mental ill health, thus attracting the stigma. I did not want this stigma to reflect on my fiancée to her detriment. Therefore, I kept my self-harming invisible to the world. For example, it was mortifying for me to admit to the doctor that I had taken all my Haloperidol capsules and required a renewal of the prescription. This mostly strictly controlled privacy worked against my receiving any help, which meant that I was left out in the cold.

Thoughts

- Self-harming makes me feel ashamed.
- Self-harming is often a private and hidden activity.
- Self-harming is often a pain- and emotion-controlling activity.
- Self-harming should not imply suicidal ideation.
- Self-harming attracts stigma and discrimination.
- Hope is a protective, allowing movement towards recovery.

About the author

I have been a mental health services user for the past 12 years. In that time I have been diagnosed with several mental illnesses, the latest being post-traumatic stress disorder. In most of those 12 years I have intermittently self-harmed. I am an ex-soldier, ex-prison officer and I trained as a mental health nurse. I have also completed courses in psychology and anthropology at master's level. I am currently completing my doctorate with Bournemouth University. I am now married and relish the stability that family life offers me. I have not self-harmed for over a year.

Reference

Weinsheimer, J (1985) *Gadamer's Hermeneutics: A reading of truth and method.* New Haven, CT: Yale University Press, p. 166.

'X78' and 'Welt'

Nic Tate

X78

Is this me – cross for a name,

a year that went & multiplied,

new life tarnished by genetics?

I, no, we love and hate what is

metal; a cold tang for you and I

to mark this cross-hatched sign,

clot ourselves together with intent

kisses sharp enough to harm.

Welt

This world is made up
of ridges, lacerated &

lashed. Touch raised
scars to trace its top-

ology. Imagine the up-
heaval beneath leather

as your body sketches
a world's lived-in skin.

Fading scars

Anon

I finally feel that I have reached a point now where I am able to look back on my periods of self-harm and talk openly about the impact this has had on my life. I have suffered with depression since I was about 14 years old and have had many different hospital admissions and experiences. I didn't actually start self-harming until I was 17 years old, after I had spoken to a fellow patient, Jo, who self-harmed and spoke of the relief that this gave her.

I must admit, when I first saw her scars from cutting I felt very uncomfortable and was shocked that someone would actually do that to themselves. Never in a million years did I think that I would do it, or even be capable of doing it to myself. I was relatively new to mental health services and bar my own experience I had no knowledge to draw on to even begin to understand the process of self-harm.

When life next became unbearable I remembered the discussion I had had with Jo and was willing to try anything that might help me. As people who suffer from mental health issues will be very aware of, there is a feeling of desperation that runs alongside it. I started by scratching patterns on my hand and arms with a pin. I almost felt in a trance-like state when doing this and although very superficial I did feel the pain and start to feel a slight release, which I in turn associated with success. Oddly, I didn't have an issue with the physical side of self-harm and had strong notions that as long as it was helping me and I was alive, then how bad could it be? I did, however, have massive issues with the effect that this could have on my family and friends, and also what people would think of me if they saw the scratches and started to ask questions that I was in no way ready to answer or deal with.

I soon became very embarrassed by the patterns and scratches on my hand and arms. I believed them to appear childlike and silly, and because of where the markings were I struggled to keep them covered up. I thought my sense of self-worth was as low as it could be, but by adding self-harm to the list of what people referred to as 'my issues' I dropped quite a bit lower, as I now had physical proof as to how much of an embarrassment I had become.

The next step in my self-harming journey was to use the blades from inside disposable razors to cut my wrists. Again, this started in a very superficial way but the fine lines that I traced produced a lot more blood and could easily be covered up with a thick bangle, therefore encouraging me that I had found a way to continue with my new addiction without it being as noticeable. This was a win-win situation in my eyes.

This carried on for many months; my life revolved around sleeping for as long as possible and then when awake cutting on a regular basis, three to four times a day. I can only imagine now what my parents must have been going through and I am quite selfishly glad that I do not have full and accurate memories of this period of my life. I am sure that the amount of medication that I was prescribed was responsible for this. On the odd occasion that I have spoken to my mum about this time I am quite astonished at the difference in our stories and recognise how self-absorbed I was. I was living in my own bubble with no thought as to how my mum was coping, trying to work and be there for me all at the same time. The stress I put on both of my parents must have been phenomenal.

Although the cutting was a regular occurrence I also cut in the same place, opening partially healed wounds over and over again, cutting deeper and deeper down in my wrist. Many times we dressed the cuts with steri-strips when really I should have been getting stitches. My final phase of cutting involved a Stanley knife but I knew I had gone one step too far with this, as I applied the same pressure that I had been doing with the blades and quickly ended up surrounded by a pool of blood. It looked like I had tried to commit suicide but at this point that was never my intention. Don't get me wrong – I have made several attempts at suicide, but always through overdosing rather than cutting.

By this point in my life I had been admitted to an adolescent unit in Manchester where self-harming was forbidden. The majority of residents continued with self-harming but in secret. I did a lot of work with Mary (my key worker) and although we never had any major breakthrough or dawning of realisation, things did seem to click into place for me.

I was allowed to leave hospital on the condition that I had a job lined up and a suitable routine to return to. I was on a mission by this point and had made a definite decision to try and get my life back on track.

Things were very up and down for me for several years and when things were down the self-harm did return, though not as severe or for any great length of time.

I finally got a job I loved as a travel agent and although I might not describe myself as stable I was at least managing to hold down a full-time job.

In time I outgrew the job and decided again for a change of career. I saw a job advertised for a mental health support worker with Community Links Northern Ltd in Leeds and applied. I found the whole set-up of Community Links brilliant – it was such an eye opener to me to be accepted on my life experience rather than my qualifications, as it was due to my mental health that I never achieved the academic success that was expected of me.

I am still working for Community Links nearly nine years later and have been fully supported through my relapses and other emotional traumas by a fantastic management team, whom I will be forever grateful to.

I am now in a position that I never thought I would achieve. I have been married for three years, with a baby on the way. Although I didn't know my husband at the times when I was self-harming, he is supportive when issues arise for me and tries his best to understand. I realise how difficult it is for people to understand depression and self-harm when they haven't lived through it.

The scars I am left with now are jagged and are very delicate to the touch, sending tingling pains through my wrist when accidentally knocked. Although faded they are still noticeable and as much as I forget they are there, other people notice them and ask questions. There are now several children that I see regularly and I have been asked very innocently by them what happened to my wrists. I still haven't been able to come up with a suitable reply so I tend to make something up on the spot – this seems to be working for now. Colleagues have also asked me about my past and luckily I have been able to give them an outline of the truth without feeling too judged. So again, I am grateful for this. As I stated at the beginning of this piece, it has taken me this long to be able to talk about my self-harm – nearly 20 years – and writing this in itself has been therapeutic to me.

I continue to appreciate all that people have done for me and the support I have been lucky enough to receive throughout my life.

Thoughts

- Try to differentiate between teenage behaviour and signs of depression.

- Seek medical help as soon as possible to try and prevent sinking deeper down.

- Look into counselling and don't dismiss alternative therapies, as hypnotherapy worked wonders for me.

- Don't hesitate to seek a second opinion if you do not feel like you are getting the advice/support you need.

- The final and main point for me is to keep calm and always try to think you will come out the other side, however difficult it may be and impossible it might seem at the time.

About the author

Born in the summer of 1979 I arrived to be greeted by a caring family including my parents and 18-month-old brother. Growing up in Lancashire I had a close-knit group of friends and was very happy. I was 14 when I first suffered from depression and was diagnosed with clinical depression, which played a large part in shaping the rest of my teens. My school and college years were a difficult time with my illness. My family and friends helped me through it. At 19 I became a travel agent. I enjoyed finding holidays for people almost as much as going on them myself. I did not, however, enjoy the increasing focus on selling and decided on a complete change of career. In 2004 I applied for a mental-health support worker position over the hills in Yorkshire with Community Links. Having struggled significantly with agoraphobia this was a massive life decision for me, which luckily paid off. Within months I had met my future husband and eight years later we are expecting our first child together. I still love what I do and I have made some wonderful friends along the way.

18

Working through self-harm

Nicki Evans

I first started to self-harm 10 years ago, although I had a few previous incidences during school. At first I cut myself very superficially and kept it well hidden. I felt so ashamed that I was so driven to damage myself. I considered myself to be warped and sick in the head for a long number of years. The extent I went to to keep my self-harm a secret became a time-consuming task, and one at which I considered myself an expert, as I kept my distressing feelings and emotions deeply hidden. What began as self-harm that I considered relatively minor and superficial, escalated and tipped quickly into something far more serious and dangerous, as distressing events in my life and depression seemed to completely consume me.

I hated life and was full of self-loathing. I felt angry and frustrated that I could not function in a world I felt that I did not belong in. I often felt like I had no right to exist. Self-harm seemed a perfectly logical response; indeed, it seemed the only clear thought in my chaotic mind. I had no regard to the damage I was doing and started a cycle of going to A&E regularly to have my cuts seen to. However, the attitudes I often encountered and the shame I felt in going to A&E eventually resulted in attempts to deal with wounds myself when they needed stitching. This has left me with some very bad scars.

My life existed then with the sole purpose for me to slowly destroy myself in ever more damaging and creative ways. Anything that was harmful I repeated, anything positive I rejected.

I often hear that self-harm is a coping strategy, but I feel there are also other reasons for this behaviour, and referring to self-harm as a coping strategy alone does not fit entirely accurately for me. I do not doubt, however, that if I had not harmed myself then I would have taken my own life. I have felt, at times, very disassociated and numb to the world around me. I felt trapped inside myself, with ever-growing frustration and despair at not feeling that I could communicate and express myself. Self-harm was a means of expressing how distressed I felt with myself in the most extreme manner – an external action, expressing a very internal feeling of profound, deeply rooted unhappiness.

I withdrew and isolated myself from the world I feared. I had a fear that if I truly expressed how I felt I would lose all control, and turn into a very aggressive, volatile person; so a lot of the time I did not talk to anyone. All my feelings and emotions were kept buried inside and the only way to cope under the buckling pressure I felt was to self-harm. Eventually such emotions have to surface, and I quickly found myself under the care of mental health services, and in and out of psychiatric hospital, with 10 lengthy admissions over the next eight years.

At times, I was on regular courses of antibiotics due to infection and spent vast quantities of money on first-aid products, as well as being prescribed very strong painkillers. This paved the way to addiction, and a descent into illicit drug use that took me years to completely break free of. It was then that I felt self-harm was becoming a necessity. I even knew the brand of razor blade that was easiest to take apart. I would ritualistically prepare steri-strips and bandages, making sure there was going to be no mess. I cut myself daily without fail, to a routine. Some people make a cup of coffee a few times a day. I self-harmed with a similar attitude.

I felt a sense of curiosity in self-harming yet equally felt appalled with myself for these thoughts. I was torn by constantly feeling I was not human. I often felt no pain when I hurt myself, which made me do something far worse, almost to try and confirm in some way that I was human. But it proved nothing to me. What is it to be human? Would we know if we were not human? I continuously asked myself and tried to answer questions revolving around: 'Why are we here?', 'Who am I?', 'What is reality?' This kind of thinking can drive someone nuts, but it made me who I am. I have learnt not to consume myself with too much existential thinking; though I still query everything around me I do not let it stop me living as it once did. A querying mind is a happier one, I feel, than a passive mind, yet I know you cannot query everything every minute of the day. Surrounding much of my self-harm was the need to control, to impose order on something, even if that something was holding me back and keeping the cycles of negative thinking firmly fixed.

The world felt unhinged and frightening, hurtling at a catastrophic pace while I felt helpless looking on. I believe that this feeling of being out of control can never be described adequately. It invaded all of my senses, and I felt like all my being was hurtling both mentally and physically to a dark demise within something infinitely vast.

Self-harm was a fight against the human condition that I dwelled on and panicked about (albeit very internally). The world seemed far from my grasp and pointless.

The feeling of being out of control internally and externally was something that slowly increased and worsened the deeper into my distress I went, reaching a point where my self-harm was so out of control and there was nowhere worse my mind could go. I felt I had systematically gone over so many unanswerable questions and resulting crises that I had to move away from this cycle of thoughts and actions, and not cling to their familiarity. So gradually, and often unnoticed by me, the dark, infinite, out-of-control feeling was replaced with more 'normal' uncertainty and worry about what the future would hold.

Diagnoses and treatments

For a long time I did not think that I would get out of the debilitating depression I felt. I hardly went out, I felt so medicated that I did not have the energy to do much and I was mindlessly bored. I often felt like an observer of the world around me – which I doubted existed – and that I was observing myself with very little control over my life. I felt unable to do anything about it for a long time and I self-harmed to the extent I did, as I did not think it mattered – I would not live long and it was all too unbearable.

Much of what I describe in my own experiences reveal 'criteria' for what I feel is a devastatingly damaging diagnosis – borderline personality disorder (a.k.a. emotionally unstable personality disorder). Whilst this labelled a lot of the behaviour patterns I had found myself repeating destructively, and the extremes in emotions I felt, I feel I would have been better off never learning of such a diagnosis. The diagnosis made me feel defined, and equally confined, by how I was characterised by others, rather than learning to think for myself and know myself. There was a danger that in my search to understand the diagnosis through reading and research, I never recognised how entwined with the illness I had become; everything I read was taken as more fuel for my negativity, even if I read hopeful and optimistic accounts of recovery. Positives were turned to negatives, as I so often compared myself to others and their achievements, often being harshly and ruthlessly critical of myself. I felt I could never achieve anything and anything I did had to be 'perfect.'

I found that the relief of knowing the distress I felt was recognised and that I was not alone was short-lived. In many ways we are alone. I felt many doctors had heard my words of distress and had seen my destructive ways many, many times before. I felt like a parrot reciting negativity and anger. The recommended treatments were just trial and error, of going through every medication, over and over, until I made the decision that medication was not for me. Medications and their harmful effects became, in my mind, another form of self-harm, one that psychiatry was participating in wholeheartedly. Once I started to challenge its use and question its effectiveness to help me in any way, I made steps towards making decisions and practical life choices for myself that were beneficial to my wellbeing.

Talking therapies only started to make an impact when I became less medicated. Emotions became blunted for me, and I feel the true problem cannot be seen clearly when a huge quantity of medication is involved. I found it paradoxical to be treated, on the one hand, with medication that prevented me from expressing myself, and on the other, to sit in therapy, which is all about expressing and communicating feelings. It's difficult to speak from the heart when you're numb.

Today I no longer take antidepressants, antipsychotics, anti-anxiety medication and mood stabilisers as I did years ago.

At that time, I was greatly influenced and triggered by others' self-harming, even things on the TV. (I can name a few movies that I practically re-enacted in various ways.)

Often, I got a lot worse when admitted into psychiatric hospital. I was very focused and hell-bent on cutting myself. I can only begin to imagine how difficult and frustrating it is for the NHS staff and mental health professionals, seeing someone continuously hurt themselves who is unwilling to consider any help or see past what they are doing to themselves, on a day-by-day basis. Any challenging of what I was doing long-term, was met with the repetitive answer that I did not have a future to live, so it didn't matter how I hurt myself.

Things change

What I did not learn for a long time, is to take responsibility for my actions. I was not always sensible in how I self-harmed; I tended to do things to extremes. Aside from cutting, I would burn myself with cigarettes, eat next to nothing, take illicit drugs and take regular overdoses that would at times lead me to be admitted to general hospital. At the end of the day, I and only I am responsible for my actions. Even when my state of mind was very erratic and my thoughts disordered, I still had a sense of what was a healthy lifestyle choice and what was not. I just spent a few years ignoring my own common sense.

In hospital on various occasions, different approaches were applied to me at different times. Sometimes I was told I would be discharged if I self-harmed. This made me self-harm dangerously and seek no medical help, withdrawing further into myself and staying out of the way of staff. There was no way I could be stopped from hurting myself; I was impulsive and opportunistic in finding things that would harm me.

A different approach was that I was allowed to take some responsibility for my actions: I agreed that if I cut myself I would get it looked at by a nurse and that I would talk about it more. This worked far better; not only did I go to nurses more if I self-harmed, but more importantly, the severity of the cuts became superficial and eventually far less frequent.

My initial acceptance of this kind of approach was, in hindsight, the start of wanting to change, and to realise that my repeated un-cooperation and defiance, was ultimately hurting only myself. I was growing weary of my own repetition.

Gradually over time my circumstances and outlook changed for the better. I felt like I was starting to outgrow my self-destructiveness. I saw things I was missing out on and wanted to be a part of. I felt self-harm was knocking my confidence, and every time I went a week without doing it was an achievement. A month went by with no self-harm. Six months later the habit was replaced by healthier, more people-orientated activities, which encouraged socialisation, not isolation.

Given time, I feel better able to recognise what can make me feel so out of control, depressed and anxious. Whilst some things in life are unavoidable, there are many things that can be avoided. So these feelings can be reduced, whether that is by being more active and eating better, or more obviously avoiding drugs and the lifestyle that comes with drug taking.

In the past I considered 'people' as part of the problem, not the solution. The very notion of wanting to be around people, who enriched my knowledge and life, would have filled me with nauseating fear a few years ago. I would have rejected such sentiment, but attitudes change. I believe no one could have stopped my self-harming. Only I could do that, and I had to do this in my own time, when I was ready. I started to want to look after myself, and began to see a future that was not constant torment. It is one of the most liberating feelings to no longer consider suicide as a way out if things get unbearable.

One consequence of my self-harm is that it has affected my general confidence and how I view my body. I don't wear short sleeves in summer, unless I'm feeling brave, or in company where I feel comfortable enough to do so. I feel unable to go swimming or enjoy holidays in the sun, when I would love to do so (sun cream is a must on scarred skin). I cannot wear shorts without showing some very severe scars. I love fashion and it's difficult avoiding clothes I would love to wear just because they are short sleeved. It's worse during summer in the heat.

The scars can affect many things, and in time I may get braver and not concern myself so much with people staring at my arms or asking me, 'What happened to your arms?' At the moment I would find it difficult to answer people who do not understand, although I did tell someone that I had an argument with a very angry cat once – that may amuse others less than me!

In time I'm sure I'll be more accepting of these scars on my body. They are part of me and represent to me how far I have come, that I survived the destructiveness that could have cost me my life.

I have not deliberately harmed myself for three years.

Self-harm was a huge part of my life for such a long time and I never considered I would stop. It has taught me much about myself in a very extreme way, and I feel that I had to go to the dark depths of despair in order to start the journey out of it. I am in a much more fulfilled point in my life now. The things I have gone through have been as much about growing up and gaining maturity as the labels given to me by the psychiatric profession. Rejection of such labels in a rational, calm way, and taking control, fights against the apathy and despair that can inadvertently come from involvement in mental health services. More open, honest discussion about self-harm is needed; many professionals avoid talking about it as if even this can cause people to go and do it. But ultimately, I believe that being more open and honest will lead the way for people to take responsibility for their self-harming. Telling people to stop doing it, which I have encountered on many occasions, is not helpful.

Thoughts

- Even when distress seems overwhelming and out of control, when it's easy to think nothing can ever change, things do, slowly. Change is not always easy to recognise and putting thoughts into actions can take time, years even.

- Thought and consideration should be given to how people who self-injure are treated in hospital environments, such as psychiatric units, A&E and walk-in treatment centres.

- Wider understanding and more open discussion of the complexities of self-harm should be encouraged, as better understanding is gained from those supporting someone who self-injures.

About the author

Having been given a diagnosis and medication, I feel that challenging ideas and practices in mental health has proven crucial for me. I am now aware that there are many unimplemented routes, which do not include hospital environments or being heavily medicated, that lead to a better sense of wellbeing. I am currently a service user consultant, with a fondness for animals, especially my dog, the outdoors, travelling, photography, website design and writing poetry as a means of expressing myself. I also have an interest in group work, which I have been involved with, including a 'Thinking about medication' group, writing groups and a 'Walk and talk' group, which are run in my local town of Shrewsbury in Shropshire.

19

A letter home

Caroline Roe

22, Hopelessness,
Endless,
Struggle.

March 2002

Dear all who have met and treated me,

As I begin to write this I know you won't remember my face.
I am anonymous to you. I remain an enigma.

When I come to you for help, why do you hate me so? I
do not put myself here, in this place full of echoes, at the dead
of night for the sole purpose of burdening you. I am sorry and
I wish you could know that.

I am not forthcoming with my answers to your questions
because I am not sure of the answers. You ask me if I intend
to hurt myself again, or if I have thought about killing myself,
or if, when I took these pills, I intended to die. But my head
is so full of struggle that I can't find the answers for you.
'Why did you do it?' I don't know, it doesn't make sense
to me either, that hurting my body eases my suffering, but I
can't say that to you – that's not the answer you want to hear.
You are just asking these questions because you have to. You
need to know whether a security guard should be placed at
my bed, whether I am going to try and leave, and try to kill
myself … I contemplate for a moment what you want me to
say, but I can't judge that right now. Your face is unfaltering

in your determination to get me through your department as quickly as you can. There is no warmth towards me and I know why. I have stared at these ceilings week after week and you are tired of fixing me. I understand why you would be, but your approach fuels a self-hatred in me that is only worsened by being here. I cannot be scared out of my pain because you are tired of my presence, or just simply tired. I feel guilty for existing, so you don't need to tell me that I am a drain upon your resources and time, I already know it.

Sometimes I wish that my thoughts would form more clearly and that courage would equip me to find the voice to tell you who I am and the world that I have come from. But the shame that I carry keeps my head hung low so that you cannot look into my eyes. You only see this as 'being difficult', but I am trapped and I wish you could see that and help me to get free. Maybe if I were articulate you would respect me more. Every day I struggle to find the right words to use to say how I feel, but words are a translation of feelings that go so deep sometimes that the right ones are hard to find. Would you understand? Would you want to listen? I am not so sure anymore.

If I could find words right now, I would tell you that I didn't do this for you to notice me or to get attention. All I really want is to be left alone and not to be as visible as I am right now, laid vulnerably out on a bed, in a room full of other people, with bright lights and loud voices. I want to be anywhere but here. I did this because I don't know what else to do. That sometimes my head swims with emotion that rises up from struggle, from experiences that I will never tell, and I don't have the strength to save myself. When I hurt myself, things get clearer for a little while. My head stays above water for a little while longer – it's like letting the plug out for a bit so that I'm not going to drown, not just yet. I am not proud of what I do or that I cannot cope like other people.

I'd like to think that when you have pumped me full of drugs to protect my liver and you send me home, that I won't see that look in anyone's eyes again, but we both know that I will. You look at me that way because you have no hope for me. Neither do I, and as long as those two things remain true, I don't know how I am supposed to climb out of this living nightmare. Hope drives change, and without hope, neither you, nor I, have anything.

So please don't look at me like that, not anymore. Your hopelessness is crippling me further. And please don't call me 'the overdose in bay three'. My name is Caroline and I am scared. If you asked the right questions, I might be able to let you know the answers. That I have no help or support. That I really, really need some, but there's nowhere to go with this. That you don't need to say the right things to me to let me know that you care, but that if you did care, it might be the only warmth and human contact that I have access to. It is not your job to fix me, it is mine – so don't burden yourself with that frustration.

I am just a girl like you, or your sister, your friend, your daughter – not a threat, nor a nuisance. And your care could be the difference between me leaving here with hope or despair. That is not your burden to carry, but if you wanted to reach me, you probably could.

With regards,

Caroline
(The girl in bay three who took an overdose tonight because she ran out of options.)

FINDING WORDS: WRITING SELF-HARM

20

'I do not believe in silence': Self-harm and childhood sexual abuse

Clare Shaw

I am no technical expert in language or the legacy of sexual abuse. I'm not well versed in theories of language, linguistics or development. What I am though, is a self-harm trainer, consultant and activist, and I've spent many years trying to make sense of self-harm – my own and others' – in a way that makes sense to other people. I'm also a poet, and as a writer and a teacher I have a massive personal and social commitment to the value of expression and communication. And I'm someone who survived sexual violence and general mess and 'fucked-aroundness' in childhood. As you can see, I'm still searching for the right language.

At the moment I wrote those lines, I realised that this is exactly the piece that I wanted to write. Because searching for the right language is at the very heart of my life, my struggles, my drive, what it is to be alive, what it is to love each other, to be with each other, what it is to survive sexual abuse, what it is to self-harm. So that's what I'm bringing to you – my own search for the right language for my own experiences, and how that played out through self-harm, and how it's played out through language, and through life and its calm days and hurricanes.

I do not believe in silence

Because, tonight –
however I try – I cannot get downstairs
without waking my daughter
I do not believe in silence.

Because of the Warboys enquiry,
because of the one hundred-plus women he raped –
because of the policeman defending the findings
unable to utter the word –
'this (herrrrm) crime, this (ahem)
assault, this category (cough)
of offence' –
I do not believe in silence

because of the stairs and the banister's crack;
the sound of the lock
and my hand on the door – the fifty-tone creak –
the magnificent echo of light-switch and click –
I do not believe in silence.

Because of Neda – and everyone's sister –
and the man who said 'Don't be afraid';
for the sake of my daughter, because of the burka,
because of the patter of rain;
because of two hundred-thousand years of human history,
thirty-seven of them my own –
I do not believe in silence

for the sake of my arms, the wrists especially.
With respect to my legs
and my belly and chest
and the comfort long due to my throat

because of nightclubs at one am
and shouts in the street and feet in pursuit
and shops that don't shut;
because of sirens and the dealers downstairs;
because of Levi and Akhmatova;
because of the blue-lipped prisoner;
the itch and the scratch of my pen;

I believe in the word.
I believe in the scrabble of claws
on uncarpeted floors.
I believe in my daughter's complaints.
I believe in the violin, the E-string,

the see-sawing bow; the cello
straining its throat.

I believe in the heart and its beat
and its beep and the dance of the trace
on the screen, I believe in the volume
of colour turned up, and my blood
which was always too loud

Because of the nights, and the sweats,
and the same rowdy thoughts;
because that one afternoon
when I nailed my own voice to the air
and because there was nobody listening
and through it all
birdsong
and the sound of cars passing -

I do not believe in silence

(*Head On*, 2012, Bloodaxe UK)

I wrote this poem in response to *A Book of Silence* by Sara Maitland (2008). In it, Sara engages with silence as an undervalued experience, pursuing the goal of total silence from the Yorkshire Moors to the Outer Hebrides to the Sahara. But what this beautiful, thoughtful book prompted in me was the realisation that whilst there are times in my life when I relish peacefulness, I could not accept silence. First, because I rejected the idea that in this noisy, colourful world of ours there could ever be anything that could rightly be described as true silence, but even more importantly, because I realised that even if there was true silence, I would never want it in my life.

Why? Because alongside the inner silence of spiritual practice, is the experience of being silenced. Alongside the religious call to 'the discipline of silence', is the obligation to break the silence around sexual abuse, domestic violence, the impact of psychiatry. Alongside silence as a calming, enriching experience, is silence as a tool of oppression and a strategy for maintaining brutality and inequality. Joseph Jordania (2009) suggests that silence in social animals is a sign of danger – the cessation of contact calls. The silence that falls over the forest in the presence of a predator is the silence of fear.

So it began to seem to me that the pursuit of silence as a positive experience is rooted in privilege: by which I mean the absence of coercion, the presence of choice, of resources. Or at the very least, that before we can in good faith value the positive qualities of silence, we must speak out – about ourselves, and about what continues to go on in this world.

The bottom line is, silence does my head in. It does my head in because the world is beautiful precisely because it is noisy and messy and never still. But also because this beautiful world is full of cruelty and injustice and we should never be silent about that. Beyond the big political statements, it does my head in because silence hurt me badly and it continues to hurt me. I'm going to visit that story and I'm going to bring that story around to self-harm – to the 'blood which was always too loud'. I'm going look at self-harm as one of the powerful ways we attempt to break silence in the absence of words. And in doing all of this, I'm going to tell you my own story.

To do this, we're going to start from the assumption that self-harm is functional and meaningful. People do it for a reason. Actually, this is way more than an assumption. It's a reality. I self-harmed because it worked. It made me feel better. I wouldn't have done it otherwise. Survivor accounts tell us that self-harm is a way of surviving, preserving and affirming life in the presence of what is often experienced as intolerable distress (e.g. Arnold, 1995; Hawton et al, 2003; Camelot Foundation and Mental Health Foundation, 2006; Newham Asian Women's Project, 2007; SANE, 2008).

We cannot assume that we know why someone self-harms. The functions of self-harm not only vary from person to person but can vary for the same person from hour to hour; seemingly contradictory functions can sit side by side, as they can for any human action. For me, I self-harmed because in the context of a chaotic, sexualised family background, it gave me one thing I was in control of: my space, my action, total ownership. But there were times when it also gave me a way of rescinding control and abdicating responsibility – of saying, 'This is too much for me. I need someone to take some of this away.' And sometimes, in the presence of terrifying levels of pain – loss, grief, fear, despair, anger – self-harm feels like the only way I can survive. I self-harm to feel better, to distract myself, to release some of the bad feeling. I simply need to get through the next hour or so; these personal needs are far more important than the desire to communicate my distress to anyone else.

We cannot assume that the function of self-harm is always communication. But we should be alert to self-harm as an expression of a feeling, an experience, a need. A way of making distress, which is so infuriatingly intangible, real and concrete in the form of physical harm. Something that can be seen, witnessed, understood and contained. Something that can be held, which can respond to treatment and which can heal.

I recall an occasion when, having just told the story of my childhood and adolescence to a group of mental health workers, I was asked, 'So for all of those years, did you not try to tell anyone what was going on for you?' Well, the fact is that I spent all of those years doing my utmost to tell. It was made perfectly clear to me from an early age that it was unacceptable for me to communicate my experiences, needs and feelings directly. So instead of using words, I began to use the other means I had at my disposal. I starved myself, I stole, I vomited, I cut myself, I banged my head, I wore black, I overdosed, I beat myself up. I'd say I was speaking very loudly, very articulately. I'd say I did a pretty excellent job of expressing the fact that I wasn't happy.

But a message is only as good as the listener allows it to be. In a referral letter I was given access to, I found out that I was considered to have: 'borderline personality disorder' (BPD) and an 'inability' to express myself, 'leading to a tendency to self-injure'. So, at the point that my first poetry collection was being published to critical acclaim, Phillip, my cognitive behavioural therapist, informed me that my problem was that I was unable to express myself.

From Jimmy Saville to the Catholic Church, we are now more aware than ever of the powerful and widespread strategies used to silence people who are sexually abused, and those who believe and support them. Grooming for compliance; belittling, normalising and minimising abuse; deliberately undermining victims; outright threats – there are many individuals and organisations (e.g. NAPAC, n.d.; Warner, 2000) who can tell you with depth and clarity about these and other processes, and the part they play in perpetuating abuse. But I want to focus specifically on how, at the level of communication, and within the act of communication, I was silenced again, as many of us are:

- when we are denied the right language for our experiences;
- when the languages we use are not understood.

I ran to a large stone house, set up the track away from the main road. I avoided the flats. Knocked on the door. A boy my brother's age answered. 'A boy took me in the bushes and made me take down my pants' I said, knowing even as I spoke the words, that they were a million miles from what I'd just been through. So in that moment I learnt to translate what I'd experienced into a language suitable for others to hear and all the words and the sounds that could have come near describing the horror, the terror swam to the back of my brain and remained there, and is still there.

It's one thing to have language; it's quite another to have the right language. A language that speaks to the self, for the self, about the self, from the self. A language that is owned and felt, that feels right, that makes sense, that fits the self and its experiences. After I was raped, my family referred to it as 'the incident in the churchyard'. It was 10 years later that I began to refer to it as rape. And it was about the same time that I began to reframe my experiences of growing up in a neglectful, chaotic, sexualised home environment as damaging. Abusive. It's still a word that I struggle with. I'm still searching for the right language.

What happens when we don't have the right language? At 22, having spent my adolescence believing there was something weird, odd, broken within me, I was predictably and inevitably diagnosed with BPD, that most controversial diagnosis, which is so hard for those of us who self-harm to avoid. When I object to a term that pathologises, stigmatises and blames me more effectively than the old categories that have historically been used to damn those of us who stepped out of our gendered line – hysteric, moral imbecile or witch – I'm often told, 'It's just words'. Only words! There are few phrases more incendiary for a writer. It's not only words to tell me that the core of my being is disordered. It's not only words to ignore all the skills and qualities and values that make up me. It's not only words to fix something as fluid and changeable as my personality in an immutable, one-dimensional category. It's not only words when I'm told that the distress I experience is the result of my own pathology and that the strategies that brought me through are merely symptoms of a disorder.

Language itself is not JUST words. It's the passing on of information; a way of evoking emotions and responses in others; a way of enquiring about and knowing the world; a way of forming and expressing our impressions, opinions and identity. It's a primary way of having our needs met; it's performance and action, interaction, instruction, regulation, direction. Without the right language, we struggle to make our own sense of our own lives, to communicate our needs or our feelings, to be understood. We are alone and we don't really know who we are or why we are. Our life, our world, is not our own.

But the truth will out. As the Welsh poet Gwyneth Lewis (2003) says: 'I speak six different tongues/so keeping mum isn't an option.' People find a way of speaking out, even if that speech is their silence. The challenge then is in the listening.

Self-harm may be the strategy that someone uses to deal with the multiple pains of being abused, including the despair of being unheard. It may also be the most powerful language someone has. Are there some experiences that are beyond words? It's a question that, as a writer, I always see as a kind of provocation, because the task that I set myself in poetry is to give expression to that which cannot be expressed in commonplace language. Poetry offers us lots of ways of doing that; one of the greatest is the metaphor: the use of one thing to represent another. Metaphor allows us to create our own language; to state more powerfully than direct language allows; to meet reality from a different direction, and in doing so, to make it more real and more knowable. But metaphor demands effort not only of the writer, but also of the reader. We have to engage, we have to be willing to go with it, to see beyond the surface. That's the challenge of listening to self-harm.

Having had my own abuse silenced by normalisation; having learnt to belittle and euphemise my own rape; having the consequences of this violence both damned and hidden by psychiatric diagnosis; and facing the denial of my truth and integrity by those closest to me, I found my own powerful metaphors in injury. The wound that was my violation. The scar that is my language. In a recent writing workshop, I was invited to look – really look – at my arms. And what I saw was: geology, archaeology, pattern and history. I saw pattern and signal, graffiti, calligraphy. I saw art and nature. I saw literature. My arms are code and map, and you can read them if you ask me and they will tell you about suffering and horror, but they will also tell you about strength and hope.

Let's think of the impact of any injury. What does it state to the witness? 'I am hurt. Notice me. I have been through bad things. Be concerned. I am brave. I am vulnerable. I need care. Look away. I need to be a priority. I am tough. I may die. I am invincible. Help me.' And self-harm, I think, speaks even louder than this. It speaks not only to the witness, but also to the person who self-harms. My self-harm said to me: 'You are alive. Your life is difficult. You are hurt. Your pain is valid. You are courageous. You are strong. You are deserving of care.' These were things I desperately needed to hear.

But just as listening to an account of abuse can be profoundly challenging, so can listening to the language of injury. Self-harm has a profound emotional effect, and in the absence of reflection, support or information, this impact is often translated into negative assumptions and responses.

We are all aware of the tendency, enshrined at the personal and institutional level, to 'blame' victims of rape or abuse and those who support them. They were asking for it; they provoked it; they have false memory syndrome; their accounts are fabricated, elaborated, fantastical; they are somehow to blame. And so for self-harm. When an act provokes feelings of extreme sadness, frustration or horror, how much easier it is to blame the person who self-harms for those feelings, to refuse to engage with them or address them, and to dismiss the self-harm as 'attention seeking' or 'learnt behaviour' or 'superficial'?

How much easier is it to respond with disbelief, blame, vilification? And how profoundly devastating? Instead, I invite you to listen. Have respect for the communicatory power of self-harm. We respect poems or films, pieces of art or music that leave us moved. Let us respect the powerful expressive function of self-harm, and do our very best to engage with what it may be telling us – not just about trauma and pain, but also about the incredible, unending desire to survive.

These days I prefer words. I am a writer. And I work across the UK, and beyond, as a freelance self-harm trainer and consultant, working alongside individuals – Sam Warner, Jude Sellen, Fiona Venner, Helen Spandler – whose work I have admired for years. Words serve me better than wounds. They are more lasting, versatile, and impactful. They make more sense to more people. They bring about change. More people are able and willing to listen. It's easier on them – and me. I have stopped inscribing my own self and started inscribing paper. Started to write my own words and my own story, not just on the page but on life. I am still searching for the right kind of language. I think I always will be. And sometimes, that language is spoken in injury. But mostly, it's in the word.

I believe in the word.

I do not believe in silence.

Thoughts

- Self-harm may be usefully understood as a powerful language for communicating distress.

- The distress that is articulated through self-harm may be related to past or current experiences of sexual violence, abuse and trauma.

- There is an ethical imperative on all of us to speak out against sexual abuse and violence.

- There is also an ethical and professional imperative to listen – whether someone communicates in words or through less direct means such as self-harm.

- Listening to distressing experiences can be a distressing experience, and can give rise to defensive attitudes and responses.

- There are parallels and shared territories between the unhelpful responses experienced by victims of sexual abuse and violence, and the responses experienced by those who self-harm.

- Support, self-care and critical reflection are vital when working helpfully and thoughtfully with self-harm.

About the author

I live in a beautiful part of West Yorkshire with my daughter, my cats and a network of wonderful friends. Like most people, I've had some horrible experiences in my life and some amazing ones too. For example, I have the best career in the world: I'm a poet, with two Bloodaxe collections to my name; and I love performing my own work and enabling other people to discover what a transformative experience it is to find your creative voice. I'm also a self-harm trainer and consultant, working independently and in partnership to enable services to respond helpfully to people who self-harm. I have a particular interest in the links between self-harm and language, or more widely, mental health and creativity, and I've been given the opportunity to explore this through recent projects involving academia and mental health services. Other good things in my life include rock climbing, cider and my vast collection of Chumbawamba CDs.

References

Arnold, L (1995) *Women and Self-injury.* Bristol: Bristol Crisis Service.

Camelot Foundation & Mental Health Foundation (2006) *Truth Hurts: Report of the National Enquiry into Self-Harm amongst Young People.* London: Camelot Foundation and Mental Health Foundation.

Hawton, K, Rodham, K, Evans, E, Samaritans & University of Oxford, Centre for Suicide Research (2003) *Youth and Self Harm: Perspectives. A report.* Oxford: Samaritans.

Jordania, J (2009) Times to fight and times to relax: singing and humming at the beginnings of human evolutionary history. *Kadmos* 1, 272–277.

Lewis, G (2003) *Keeping Mum.* Tarset: Bloodaxe.

Maitland, S (2008) *A Book of Silence.* London: Granta.

National Association for People Abused in Childhood (n.d.) *NAPAC Homepage.* www.napac.org.uk/ [accessed 30 June 2013].

Newham Asian Women's Project (2007) *Painful Secrets.* Newham: Newham Asian Women's Project.

SANE (2008) *Understanding Self-harm.* London: SANE.

Shaw, C (2012) *Head On.* Tarset: Bloodaxe.

Warner, S (2000) *Understanding Child Sexual Abuse: Making the tactics visible.* Gloucester: Handsell Publishing.

21

Research and recovery

Sarah Chaney

When I tell people that I'm writing a PhD thesis on the history of self-mutilation they are generally intrigued but, more often than not, somewhat perturbed. There are two particular questions I have been asked over and over again. The first is: 'You mean self-cutting?' This brings one of the main arguments of my thesis into sharp relief. My research focuses on the late 19th century, a period in which one can find many descriptions (within and outside a psychiatric context) of self-castration, enucleation, amputation, hair-plucking (the term 'trichotillomania' was coined in 1889), knocking, burning and skin-picking, which were generally not considered suicidal. It is rare, however, to find record of injuries made using a sharp implement, other than cut throats, which were always regarded to be suicidal. This is not to say that such acts of self-inflicted injury did not occur. Rather, they were not singled out as the main paradigm of self-mutilation and, indeed, psychiatric definitions of the term in this period often did not include self-cutting at all. This reminds us that definitions of self-mutilation, self-injury, self-harm – call it what you will – *cannot* exist separately from those doing the defining. Self-mutilation is not a natural entity, but a collection of disparate acts carried out by equally diverse individuals. In various periods, patterns have been created by excluding certain individuals or acts in order to support particular generalisations. But what, one might wonder, ever made it seem desirable to combine so many different things under one general category in the first place?

This isn't really the place to delve more deeply into the answer to this question; it simply seemed an important issue to raise before moving on to the second query with which

I am often met. Sometimes it is asked hesitantly, on other occasions more directly. Twice, I have been bluntly asked outright, in half-joking tones: 'Why are you writing about that? Are *you* a self-mutilator?' It's a question I feel uncomfortable with on many levels, but also an issue I consider important, and one which I have spent much of the last three years trying to work out how to answer successfully. But let's start by addressing some of the problematic assumptions in such a question. First, there's the idea that one's research must necessarily be associated with personal experience – a strange conjecture, given that one of the people who asked me had just given a paper on the role of the non-human in the laboratory environment! Presumably he didn't consider himself a non-human, so why must I be a self-mutilator? Is there something about the particular topic that encourages the assumption that one must practise it to be interested? What's more, what *is* a self-mutilator? The descriptive noun suggests that self-inflicted injury defines the very essence of someone who practises it. But even those who feel that self-harm has taken over their lives have many daily experiences that do *not* involve, or even relate indirectly to, self-inflicted injury. This is certainly something I reflect on in my own research, given that most of the sources I examine describe encounters with the medical profession, whether in asylums, hospitals or general practice. By probing the topic of self-mutilation through such records, I run the risk of doing just what the medical practitioners I study do: classifying people by virtue of just one act or experience among many.

It's difficult to recount my own history, for similar reasons. Writing an account of self-harm suggests that this is necessarily the most important element of the story, but that is often not the case. It also makes it easy to retrospectively create a tidy narrative, in which each element progresses in a seemingly straightforward fashion from the previous one. But life isn't generally like that. When I stop to reflect, I am aware that I have adopted most of my explanations for injuring myself subsequent to the events. I don't even know what I would define as my first act of self-harm. I know I had a fascination with endurance, even as a small child. I always wanted to be the one who could keep her bare legs in a freezing stream, or hold onto a hot pan for the longest. Fascinated by religion, at age 12 I became obsessed with John the Savage in *Brave New World*, and spent long periods pretending to be crucified because I wanted to know how it felt. But can we possibly say that one 'naturally' progresses from this to repeated private acts of self-inflicted injury? I doubt it. It's only later that a chain of causal links appears to emerge, and we should be on our guard for the way this can mislead us.

Then there are the psychological explanations. I was a shy and quiet child. I was deeply affected by the death of a close friend when I was seven, and I remember crying with loneliness in the school playground in subsequent months, perhaps for years. I was bullied by my teachers for the ease with which I cried, and frequently held up for ridicule in front of my peers. I hated them for their cruelty, but slowly I learned to hold the tears in. In later years, I would explain that cutting myself was a way to let all this emotion out. But did I really feel or believe that the first time I did it? Or did I discover this explanation subsequently? I was certainly a teenager before I began to relate all my problems back to the death of my friend, although, in all probability, I was withdrawn before this even occurred. I was certainly introspective. I remember very clearly, as a small child – perhaps four or five – freezing in the middle of doing things because I was suddenly struck by an uncertain horror as to who I *was*. Did an 'I' really exist? How could one *prove* that it was real? Sometimes the world appeared so overwhelming that it seemed it would swallow me up, and I would never know where I ended and it began.

I was 14 when I first decided to cut myself. I say 'decided', as if it happened clearly and distinctly. It didn't. I hid razor blades at the bottom of my underwear drawer for months without even really having an explanation; they just somehow made me feel safe. Sometimes I would take off the paper wrapper and look at them. I liked their inconsistent nature. They looked so small, so shiny and beautiful, but faintly menacing, as if they somehow held within their molecules the essence of the violence that could be inflicted with them. I felt the same way about blood. When I cut myself I felt guilt and exhilaration all at once. It struck me as a peculiarly religious experience. I also burned, scratched and bit myself, but these acts seemed less pure to me. It was the blood that reminded me that I was alive.

My cutting worsened when I went to university, as did my shyness, my misery and my sense of isolation. I visited a GP once, when I was about 19, when I suffered insomnia so badly it was affecting my work. I also rarely menstruated, something which had worried me for years. He dismissively told me that this was probably because I was 'sporty' (brushing off my answer that I did no sport whatsoever as irrelevant) and the lack of sleep was because I was 'an anxious person'. He prescribed me an over-the-counter herbal remedy for the latter. I didn't discover that was what it was until I got to the chemist, and I was furious; did he not consider I would have tried *every* over-the-counter remedy (and every strange folk cure I could track down on the internet) before visiting him? This has since struck me as the typical attitude of many GPs (although I think the situation has been improving in recent years): the assumption that their patient has little or no insight into a condition or knowledge of possible remedies and that the GP is their first port of call. I'm not sure how often this *is* the case for any patient but I imagine there are very many occasions when it is not.

I was 20 when friends persuaded me to openly admit to a doctor that I couldn't cope. My self-harm was escalating and I was breaking down in public with increasing frequency. One particularly awful incident involved me running screaming around the East End of London throughout the early hours of the morning, chased by friends as I veered in front of cars and threw myself at walls. Back home, my flatmate and boyfriend fought physically over who was to blame for my condition and our neighbours called the police, who simply laughed when my flatmate asked if they would drive us to hospital to get stitches in the gaping wound in my arm. The nurse in A&E was very kind and chatted to me amiably, which calmed me down as she bandaged the wound. I don't even remember the faces of the doctors who stitched me up. They seemed very remote even at the time, as if I was simply a machine to be fixed, but could not be engaged with on any level. They did ask me if I needed crisis intervention and I felt a huge relief as I agreed that I did. They told me someone would call, but they never did. I decided this was because the doctors knew there was nothing really 'wrong' with me, and that I'd better just hurry up and die instead. I collected proof of this as best I could for a long time. I intentionally phrased questions to others to ensure that their answers would support the idea that the world was a painful and unpleasant place, which brought nothing but misery to anyone, and that the only solution was to die. Death itself seemed very remote, however. The idea was pleasant – like a deep, unbroken sleep – but since I rarely slept more than a couple of hours a night, it seemed equally unattainable.

I still remember the GP I finally spoke to about my problems. He was lovely – a middle-aged Asian gentleman who jointly ran the surgery with his wife. He drew some circles on a piece of paper and spent a long time trying to explain how I had to move from one circle to the other. I didn't really see how visualising the world in two-dimensional circles would help me, but he was so animated about it that it felt like someone genuinely cared. He put me on Prozac (fluoxetine) and referred me to a counsellor who told me I wasn't very helpful for thinking I was a bad person – something of which I was well aware. The fluoxetine had similarly little effect, other than making me unusually chatty for about an hour after I took it. I would time taking it just before social occasions, which I suppose had some benefit. I took it religiously for years, mainly, I think, because it suited me to have a biochemical explanation for my problems. Later, I tried a variety of other antidepressants, all of which seemed to have a multitude of very different effects (making it seem rather odd that they were marketed as one and the same thing), and I fervently encouraged myself to believe in their efficacy, in the hope that I would get the maximum 'placebo effect', even if that was all they did.

With other doctors I have had very varied experiences, ranging from accusation to lack of interest. Many GPs, in my experience, have an extremely negative reaction to the very idea of self-harm. Once, I read in a magazine about a make-up service offered by the Samaritans. They would teach you how to cover up scars, but you needed to be referred by your doctor. I moved around a lot, so I was with a new GP. He had never met me before but bluntly said, 'What's the point in referring you? You'll only go and do it again.' I wasn't actually hurting myself at the time, and his refusal to write the letter angered and frustrated me. I wondered how one was ever supposed to move on from the stereotypes surrounding self-harm. On another occasion, a different GP showed absolutely no interest in my medication review, but then I received a letter from the local psychiatric unit saying she had referred me. I was confused and disappointed. I'd trusted her, and didn't understand why she hadn't told me in advance. I never went back to see her again, although I did go to the psychiatric unit, where they were even more disinterested than the GP. They were obsessed with self-harm, and repeatedly tried to refer me to specialist services for 'managing' it. Unusually forthright, I told them I didn't feel it was an isolated problem, and that I would refuse to go to anything that suggested it was a condition rather than a symptom. There was a long back-and-forth exchange, in which the psychiatrist said he would refer me anyway and I said there was no point because I wouldn't go. He did refer me. I didn't go.

I consider two factors much more important for my eventual recovery than medical intervention. One was my return to higher education; the other was personal support. The internet made a big difference for me. When you're shy, it's much easier to type to people than talk to them face to face. Then when you meet them, as I discovered, you already feel like you know them, making conversation much easier. I gained a very close group of friends in this way. I remembered what it was like to have interest in life and to want to do anything other than hide, and I felt able to stop injuring myself for the first time (although I did return to it in my mid to late twenties). It was also the first time I didn't have to hide my scars. Although the group was nothing to do with self-harm, people were very accepting. My friends and I had long philosophical and psychological discussions on this topic, and many others. None of us felt 'normal', for a variety of different reasons, but as a group we were protected from that.

My conversations with friends aided my return to historical research some years later, as did my own experiences. I wanted to question the way in which these experiences can often be interpreted so glibly by others. It frustrates me that evidence of self-harm can cause others to make so many assumptions about a person. This can be a problem even where the concerns appear to be motivated by kindness: several times I have had my abilities questioned in a work situation simply because someone saw my scars. Even when I had already proved my worth, the suggestion that I had injured myself in the past suddenly made others concerned that I would not be able to cope. There is often a fine line between kindness and discrimination. Yes, self-harm may be a mechanism some people use for dealing with stressful situations, but it doesn't follow from this that they are unable to cope with *anything*.

I am very aware that my research – in particular my concerns about categorisation, classification and reflecting diversity – stems from this. I do not believe that all mental health practitioners – or even all GPs! – are hostile to or disinterested in self-harm – many are not. Nonetheless, the nature of their work makes it even more important for them to regularly question their assumptions than might be the case in other fields, remembering that they are dealing with people and not conditions. While my research is historical in nature, it thus has strong contemporary resonance. It would be misleading, perhaps, to complete my thesis without acknowledging this. It would also undermine certain of my aims: how can one seek to reduce the stigma around a topic if one can't even admit one's own association with it? Finally, it would prevent me sharing what is, in many ways, a positive story of recovery. I have a strong belief in the value of education as confidence-building and empowering, something that, in my experience, psychiatric medicine is not. This thesis has been my therapy. I have had no contact with mental health services (as a user) for four years. A year ago, I stopped taking the antidepressants that had been my security blanket for more than a decade. I discovered I was now happier without them. My research has given me belief in my own capabilities, the strength to question the assumptions of others and, most importantly, the view that 'normal' is a statistical term, not a goal we should hope – or perhaps even want – to achieve. Ironically, the very acceptance of this idea has probably brought me closer to the norm, on some levels, than I have ever been before.

Thoughts

I hope this short extract from my experiences highlights several of the problems I have encountered in medical attitudes to self-harm. Personally, I don't believe that self-harm is necessarily problematic, although I admit that it can be a considerable problem. The irritated manner in which many mental health professionals insist on focusing on self-harm as 'the' problem (whether or not it *is* the immediate or only concern) can be both patronising and dismissive. If a person has used mental health services for a number of years, staff should be aware that their patient may well have plenty of insight (and may have had before they even arrived at the service in the first place). In addition, a lack of transparency and honesty, and a failure to follow through, can be immediately distressing, as well as ultimately rejecting, leading to the assumption that there is no care available and increasing the isolation of a potentially vulnerable person. It's trite but true that a little kindness often goes a long way (even if it's just drawing a few circles on a piece of paper!).

About the author
I am currently completing a PhD thesis on the history of self-mutilation, following an MA in the history of medicine. Many of the questions I explore in my research have been shaped by my own experiences – something that I consider contributes to, rather than diminishes, their impact. I struggled with shyness and depression from my teens into my late twenties, and frequently injured myself. I am now in my early thirties and living in London with my cat. I do not consider myself to have self-harmed for at least five years, although those who find my incessant nail-biting annoying may disagree! I strongly believe in the value of questioning categories, stereotypes and preconceptions on every level, and hope I succeed in my intention not to be judgemental in my attitudes to others. You'll know if I trust you, because I won't be wearing too many layers of clothing in hot weather.

22

A research encounter with self-harm: Using pictures and words

Amanda Edmondson, Cathy Brennan and Allan House

In this chapter we describe our experience of using visual images to change the way we explored the reasons for self-harm, in a research project in which one of us (AE) talked with participants about their experiences of self-harm.

People with personal experiences of self-harm are sometimes approached by researchers like us whose aims, amongst many, are to increase our understanding of why people are motivated to harm themselves. However, the way researchers have typically approached this question has been shown to be limited in its approach and not always considerate of those being researched. Subsequently our understanding of what motivates some individuals to initiate and maintain self-harm remains incomplete (Himber, 1994; Klonsky, 2007, 2009; NICE, 2004; Rodham et al, 2004; Suyemoto, 1998; Nock, 2012).

Rather suitably then, researchers are urged to consider 'what works' (Creswell & Plano Clark, 2011), and when faced with research problems that traditional approaches have failed to address adequately, Latham (2003) suggests pushing at the boundaries of convention to create innovative 'methodological hybrids' (p.1993). This is not a rejection of traditional methods; instead it is recognition of their limitations in certain circumstances and a challenge to think what, if anything, can be added to current knowledge by using more creative methods.

With this in mind, we found choosing a method that would allow us to access people's personal experiences of self-harm particularly thought-provoking and resonant with some of the research tensions put forward by Spandler (2001). After exploring young people's experiences of self-harm, she too wrote about the limitations associated with conventional approaches. The foreword to her book, written by Bernard

Davies (2001), criticised those researchers who withdraw into their professional institutions and develop proposals that employ methods they believe to be most effective in drawing out knowledge they believe to be of relevance. Instead, she encouraged researchers to adopt a more participatory approach, an approach which enables those upon whom the research is focused to contribute to and advise on 'what works with them', whilst highlighting what does not work and why.

In light of these discussions it was fundamental for us to consider, from the perspective of those who have personal experience of self-harm: 1) what is important to them about their experience of self-harm, and 2) what is the most helpful way to access this knowledge, whilst highlighting any potential barriers. By doing this we hoped to gain a better understanding of self-harm.

A different approach

The value of adopting a visual approach with people who find it difficult to express themselves verbally has been well documented (Pink, 2004; Sweetman, 2009; Bagnoli, 2009; White et al, 2010; Whitehurst, 2007; Erdner & Magnusson, 2011), as have the reported benefits of adopting a visual approach in other sensitive subject areas such as cancer (Frith & Harcourt, 2007; Radley & Taylor, 2003a, 2003b) and mental health (Erdner & Magnusson, 2011).

Adopting a visual approach then was something we considered potentially valuable and something that might 'work'. One of the methods used in visual research is photo elicitation: 'a method in which photographs (taken by the researcher or by research participants) are used as a stimulus or guide to elicit rich accounts of psychosocial phenomena in subsequent interviews' (Frith, 2007, p.1340). This method was first put to use by John Collier and the Cornell team to look at psychological stress in the 1950s (Harper, 2002) and is said to promote self-understanding, expression, communication and focus during interviews (Drew et al, 2010), as well as being useful in accessing unpredictable information and establishing rapport (Hurworth et al, 2005).

Using participants' own images in particular, enables them to think about why a particular image is important and prompts them to provide explanations for the images (Hurworth et al, 2005). This reflection encourages a better expression of experiences; the images unlock the stories (Liebenberg, 2009) and may provide a far richer narrative than any questionnaire or focus group response could offer (Hurworth et al, 2005; Cooper & Yarbrough, 2010).

When using photographs within a research context the technique 'auto driving' can also be employed. This technique places emphasis on enabling the participant to 'drive' the interview, in theory, changing the typical research relationship and 'changing the voice' (Frith et al., 2005, p. 190). Having control over the research interview can be useful in enabling participants to prioritise issues that others might see as irrelevant and encourages participants to communicate issues in their own terms (White et al, 2010).

Auto driving may therefore be a very useful technique to combine with the photo elicitation method; combined they may provide a way for people who self-harm to express themselves differently.

Searching for ways to access people's complex and highly sensitive experiences of self-harm, without considering an approach which might work with people who have personal experience of self-harm, could simply serve to replicate what we already know. Being creative with research methods to generate new ways of understanding, on the other hand, may generate thinking away from the usual responses that people report when questioned, allowing a different form of expression for people who self-harm whilst offering us a more effective approach to explore and (re)consider self-harm from a new angle.

Using pictures and words

The different ways participants experienced using pictures and words to describe their experience of self-harm will now be presented, followed by our own observations and experience of using this approach.

A positive experience

Most of the participants involved in the study reported having enjoyed using photographs and words to describe their experience of self-harm. They felt able to capture images they felt were representative of their experience of self-harm. Using photos specifically was described as 'helpful', 'a good thing' and 'interesting'. One participant compared the use of images to translation:

Yeah it's helped. Your experiences you could translate into something that somebody else could understand like, like the volcano how you would explain that, whereas you show them the volcano its more obvious than words I suppose people will understand volcanoes. – Annie

It's quite a good thing because if like if you were just to say come in and talk about it, I wouldn't know where to start or anything and it's a good like, it's a talking point like the picture you can say "I've taken this picture because ... " and then it leads, like, like I did with the picture of my dog like it's a picture of my dog, but it causes this and that you know what I mean? – Tori

Participants seemed prepared in that they had chosen in advance of our meeting what they wanted to disclose, both visually and verbally. They seemed able to take control of the interview through initiating discussion of particular topics and taking the lead on further discussion, for example, when they wished to move onto another topic area. There was also a sense of ease within the meetings, perhaps because the use of pre-prepared images served to minimise any anxiety which might arise through unpredictable questioning.

Using pictures and words combined to describe personal experiences of self-harm seemed easier for some than for others. Some participants seemed to have a very clear idea of the images they wished to take and the places they needed to visit to capture those sorts of images, whilst others had a combination of pictures they had taken in the 'spur of the moment' which they felt reflected their experience, and more select pictures. For most of the participants, taking the pictures was described as something that gathered momentum over time.

A challenging experience

The biggest challenge for our participants seemed to be the initial question of what to take a picture of, followed by finding the images they wanted. For some this was a practical difficulty in that they were unable to capture specific images, such as an image of the sea, a heron or a pressure valve. Others spoke of difficulties associated with capturing the intangible features of their experience, such as different emotional states or memories:

Finding images for stuff like emotions and things like being angry, it's like I just, I don't, I don't understand how I can take a picture of anger, like I guess I could take a picture of something that causes the anger which I did, erm, but it's not always from there that causes the anger if you know what I mean like it could be like three or four things in a day have gone wrong. – Tori

I wanted, like I can't remember like pictures in my head of memories but I couldn't like that would like instantly fit the situation like and when we first

met and how instantly we clicked and stuff, it's like I can't take a picture of that and stuff it's like a memory. – Sarah

Other challenges seemed to relate to embarrassment and uncertainty about the task and it was apparent in some participants' accounts that certain images were considered but not taken or brought along. For example, Tori spoke of wanting to take a photo of something that would relate to her premenstrual tension but didn't feel able to capture this visually; this seemed more due to embarrassment than practicality. She also described thinking about taking a picture of her laptop because anything electric was 'packing up on her' and causing her frustration, however, she didn't take the picture as she felt she was 'over-thinking' the task.

Similarly Emma, one of the younger participants, was the only participant who failed to present with images and it was possible that she struggled to understand the nature of the task. When asked what sort of images she would like to have taken to best help her to describe her experience of self-harm, her examples (a place associated with her friend's murder and her favourite shop) didn't seem obviously related to her experience of self-harm.

For some, producing images might have been perceived as a test. On several occasions participants apologised for their images or a lack thereof and seemed to lack confidence when showing their images as though they felt under pressure to produce several images of great interest. On those occasions the power imbalance between the researcher and the researched was notable, which then led to questioning whether or not participants felt in control of the interview, how conscious they were of their personal images being looked at, and what impact, if any, self-consciousness might have had on the data collection process – that is, the types of images taken or not taken. In turn, this led to a consideration of whether using images left participants feeling exposed and vulnerable, and consequently not in control of the research process.

Some of the challenges related to what participants did not want to capture. Taking Emma's example of the place where her friend was murdered, she spoke of how she would have liked to have taken a picture of this place but felt unable to as she found it too distressing. She described not wanting a constant image of that particular place with her (on the camera and accessible to her):

It would have upset me even more because I'd looked at the picture and kept looking at it and saying, 'Listen, delete it', because I'd need that I don't want that picture in my head anymore. – Emma

It seemed painful images were also missing from other participants' collections. For example, Theresa spoke about wanting a picture of a rose, which although it wouldn't seem to be too difficult to capture, she hadn't. The rose was representative of her grandfather's death, which marked the time 'when her world started to disintegrate'. It's possible of course that there were practical difficulties in capturing the exact rose.

Nicola was also reluctant to capture images that represented her daughter. She reported how she did not want to associate her daughter with the topic or the task, yet at the same time she described how her images failed to represent the guilt she felt in relation to her parenting:

> *I'm not gonna have my baby involved in this, I'm not gonna have her* (sigh) *but that, that is a big thing because I'm not being a proper mum, you know erm* (cries) *I can't, I can't, I can't, I can't* (cries) *I'm not a proper mum. It's not her fault, but I am not a proper mum and I don't know what the picture is that you could say that.* – Nicola

Finally, it is worth noting that none of the participants wanted to keep their images after the meeting, therefore none of the photos had a life beyond the study. We didn't explore the reason for this choice but wonder, given the topic area, whether, like the participants in Frith and Harcourt's (Frith & Harcourt, 2007) study who had taken pictures of their experience of chemotherapy, the participants preferred to render their images of their self-harm experience as 'unavailable for future remembering' (Frith, 2011, p.64).

The narrative structure
Participants often spoke of and used images that were representative of both past and present experiences. Some described their experience as an order of events spanning from their childhood/youth to present day, and some described their experience as an order of events since the onset of their self-harm. A temporal structure however, wasn't present in all of the participants' narratives; the experience of two of the participants in particular (Nicola and Emma) seemed to lack any particular structure and their stories moved back and forth between different times. Notably, Emma's account didn't use any images, so it's possible that she didn't approach the interview prepared with a story to tell and instead focused on detailed specifics of recent incidents of self-harm, which triggered discussion of both past and present events. Nicola captured the most images and so for her perhaps having too many images made it difficult for her to structure her story.

Having an abundance of images proved difficult to manage within the interview and the analysis, and in hindsight it might have proved valuable to pose a restriction. Too many images resulted in participants saying less about each image in order to work through them, whereas having fewer images drew out a more detailed narrative. Also, having more images often led to increased interview times, which were very challenging for the participant and the researcher. Narratives became more difficult to discuss and follow, but equally, stopping the interview might have interrupted the narrative structure. A large number of images also posed problems when moving onto the analysis phase and listening to the audio recordings; it wasn't always obvious which images were being discussed when there was swift movement from one image to another. On occasion, the images were used as a substitute for language and subsequently the audio wasn't very indicative of which images were being looked at and commented upon.

Content

In reporting their experiences, both individual experiences and experiences involving others were described, and several different, difficult topics were raised, such as: sexual abuse; death; relationship difficulties, both familial and relational; violence; religion; homosexuality; alcoholism; and other mental health problems or diagnoses.

Self-harm was described by some participants as something that was deeply interwoven into many aspects of their life, whereas for others it was more focused and attached to specific issues such as relationships.

Discussions captured history in relation to self-harm, specific triggers, methods of harm and perceived functions, which included significance of places and people. For example, participants expressed, both visually and verbally, the significance of certain spaces in relation to their experience of self-harm. Two participants specifically took images of their living space to describe different affective states and contextual features of their experience of self-harm. Outdoor spaces were also captured to symbolise different memories and events that were related to self-harm. In terms of people, familial relationships were mainly discussed, followed by social relationships, namely intimate relationships and close friendships. Participants were asked to avoid taking pictures of others, though they were informed that they could take pictures of items/objects to represent others. Images used to directly depict family members or significant others, however, were few. Only one participant clearly captured an image that was representative of a family member (see Figure 1: Richard):

Figure 1: Richard

It wasn't really a heron, it was my way of replacing the figure of my mother with something else and it was a particularly nasty sort of moment between me and my sort of infant self and my mother and so yeah, so I mean as things start I've been, I'd felt the urge to self-harm or been self-harmed on by myself erm for years because of this replacement bird for erm for, for someone that done me harm basically for an incident that was harmful, painful and I'd used, I'd used an image of a bird to er, you know. – Richard

Use of images

Participants' images varied immensely and participants used their images differently. Some used very few images and spoke of them quite literally, some participants took several images and seemed quite reliant on their images to tell their story, and some used their images more metaphorically. For example, one of the participants used an image of a bird to discuss her sense of freedom (see Figure 2: Theresa).

Images were used to capture cognitions, such as memories, thoughts and reasoning, and feelings, such as fear, pain (physical and emotional), sadness and frustration. They were also used as a way of drawing comparisons to describe loss and desires. For example, one participant showed a collection of images that represented agility and fluid movement, something he described as both a loss and a desire (see Figure 3: Oliver).

Figure 2: Theresa

Figure 3: Oliver

Figure 4: Tori

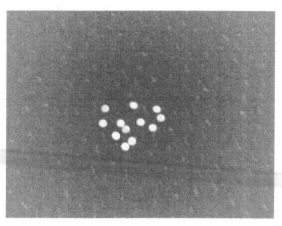

Figure 5: Nicola

Interestingly, none of the participants chose to capture images of their injuries and only two of the participants captured single images of their method of self-harm (see Figure 4: Tori and Figure 5: Nicola).

Images themselves also featured as a pertinent point in some people's experience of self-harm. For example, Nicola, Oliver and Richard expressed the significance of visual images, though in different ways. Nicola spoke of images being a source of upset for her due to the absence of pictures displayed of her in her mother's home; so for her images themselves, or the absence of them, represented feelings of sadness. Oliver, on the other hand, gave the impression of someone who was very involved with using images to express himself and his experience of self-harm. He brought along several images of artwork that he had either produced himself or that he had bought, and seemed familiar with using images to express his thoughts and feelings. Lastly, Richard gave the impression that his experience of self-harm was very visual, in that he used images to literally depict the visual content of the flashbacks he suffered, which acted as triggers to his self-harm. For these participants then, the visual was shown to be somehow relevant and aligned with their experience of self-harm.

Finally, at the very end of each discussion each participant was asked if they felt able to choose, out of all their images, one image that best represented their experience of self-harm. Half of the participants felt able to do this and selected only one image; however, Nicola and Theresa selected more than one image – interestingly, both of them had a larger collection of images to choose from – and Richard felt unable to select only one of his images as he felt most of his images were equally important. The images shown overleaf are a collection of those deemed most representative of self-harm for the group of participants involved in this study.

The images captured a range of features, most notably the private and internal experiences associated with self-harm. The theme of communication also featured in the images: Annie and Sarah's photos both captured indirect forms of communication and interaction, and a possible shift from private to public.

A researcher's experience of using pictures and words

Quite often self-harm is described as private and so to be 'shown' the internal and external aspects of a person's experience of self-harm was a very dear experience. We felt privileged to be given access into people's

Tori

Nicola

Theresa

Nicola

Nicola

Theresa

Sarah

Annie

Oliver

lives and spaces, including their homes and bedrooms, in this visually enriched and (what sometimes felt to be) quite an exposing way.

A novel approach, but is it for everyone?

Using images in research with people who self-harm was a novel experience for all of us and we reflected on how we might have engaged with such a method. We wondered whether particular people might be more likely to engage in this sort of task than others – perhaps those people who consider themselves to be more visual or creative. In turn we were prompted to consider what impact this might have had on the sorts of data gathered. Related to this was how different researchers have different stances in relation to pictures. Whilst most of the researchers felt themselves to be more 'visual', one of the researchers described themselves as 'not very visual', and it took a while for them to get into the stride of working with and analysing visual data. So, it is not an approach that comes naturally to everybody, which may seem a little surprising given what a visual world we live in.

Using images as data

Images can have multiple meanings, sometimes referred to as polysemy. The polysemic properties of images are said to be greater than those of words (Penn, 2000, cited in Frith et al, 2005). Images can be used to represent all manner of subjects and can be interpreted in so many different ways. There were many occasions where seemingly mundane images unveiled complex narratives relating to self-harm and it proved difficult at times to know quite what was being communicated. For example, when we see a bedroom, do we see a refuge or a place of abuse? Pictures can usually only be understood when accompanied by a commentary if the understanding we are after is of the individual who took them. One of the challenges was therefore to present an analysis of an image which was considerate of a number of different, though not exhaustive, reference points, for example, the participant's interpretation of the image and its communicative intention from their perspective, as well as other cultural and social references, including our own. The complex analysis of data with multiple meanings provoked us to bring order and organisation to the data and present it in a linear and structured way, though this did not necessarily mirror the way in which it was presented to us. Similarly, we noted a tendency to translate or code pictures verbally and then look for themes in a traditional way. This might have led us to miss something of the power of using images, but we aren't confident of a way out of this.

To summarise, using photos and words to discuss experiences of self-harm was both a helpful and challenging experience for the researchers and the researched. Images were reported to aid expression and communication, and were sometimes seen as a substitute for language. Using images enabled participants to prepare and present what they felt was important in describing their experience of self-harm, which hopefully in turn enabled them to feel in control of the research process. Using this unstructured approach with images allowed for the unveiling of complex, unpredictable and detailed narratives which may not have been accessed through interview alone.

Nonetheless, not everything can be captured through images, and perhaps not everyone feels able to visually represent their experiences through images, which might result in access to only those people and topics that are. Asking people to provide this sort of data might also result in feelings of embarrassment, which in turn could inhibit communication.

The challenges associated with analysis of this type of data are ever present and potentially vulnerable to sceptical scrutiny.

Thoughts

- As well as considering research design in terms of methods and research questions, research design also needs to be considerate of the population being studied. In turn, this might help address potential barriers to recruitment.

- It's important to consider how different research methods might be perceived by participants; tasks which might seem simple and accessible may not always be perceived in the same way.

- Though this is the first study to adopt visual methods and apply them to the topic of self-harm, there are a growing number of research studies employing visual methods in other health-related and sensitive topic areas. Nevertheless, whilst encouraging others to consider visual methods we would also offer caution, in particular we would suggest consideration of the following:

- Limit the number of images participants are asked to take – this might help focus the photo generation phase and subsequent interviews.

- Consider how the visual data will be managed and analysed.

- Consider some of the ethical challenges when working with visual data. We would strongly recommend reading Kate Gleeson's chapter within *Visual Methods in Psychology* (Reavey, 2011) and Andrew Clark et al's article on ethical issues in image-based research (Clark et al, 2010) at the very outset.

About the authors

Amanda Edmondson's background is in applied psychology and she has worked in a number of roles with people who self-harm in both a research and clinical capacity. Amanda is currently funded by the Economic and Social Research Council (ESRC) and is completing a PhD focusing on the functions of self-harm, supervised by Dr Cathy Brennan and Professor Allan House.

Cathy Brennan is a lecturer in Public Health at the Institute of Health Sciences, University of Leeds. She has an interest in the use of visual and participatory methods in research to explore experiences and understandings of health and illness.

Allan House is a Professor of Liaison Psychiatry in the academic unit of psychiatry and behavioural sciences in Leeds. Since 2005 he has been Director of the Leeds Institute of Health Sciences. Allan is also a member of a multidisciplinary research group, which undertakes research into psychosocial aspects of physical illness. Allan has worked with adults who self-harm, both as a researcher and as a psychiatrist in general hospital practice. He is interested in developing research partnerships between academics and service users and carers.

Authors' note

We would like to express our thanks and appreciation to all of the participants who took part in this piece of research, and those who consulted on the design. Without their time, effort and what was sometimes a challenging contribution, the completion of such a rich and detailed piece of research, including this chapter, would not have been possible.

References

Bagnoli, A (2009) Beyond the standard interview: The use of graphic elicitation and arts-based methods. *Qualitative Research*, 9(5), 547–70.

Clark, A, Prosser, J & Wiles, R (2010) Ethical issues in image-based research. *Arts and Health*, 2(1), 81–93.

Cooper, C & Yarbrough, S (2010) Tell me – show me: Using combined focus group and photovoice methods to gain understanding of health issues in Guatemala. *Qualitative Health Research*, 20(5), 644–53.

Cresswell, J & Plano Clark, V (2011) *Designing and Conducting Mixed Methods Research* (second edition). Thousand Oaks, CA: SAGE Publications.

Davies, B (2001) Foreword. In H Spandler (Ed), *Who's Hurting Who? Young people, self-harm and suicide* (pp. 5–9). Gloucester: Handsell Publications.

Drew, S, Duncan, R & Sawyer, S (2010) Visual storytelling: A beneficial but challenging method for health research with young people. *Qualitative Health Research*, 20(12), 1677–88.

Erdner, A & Magnusson, A (2011) Photography as a method of data collection: Helping people with long-term mental illness convey their life world. *Perspectives in Psychiatric Care*, 47(3), 145–50.

Frith, H (2011) Narrating biographical disruption and repair. In P Reavey (Ed) *Visual Methods in Psychology: Using and interpreting images in qualitative research* (pp. 55–68). Hove: Routledge, Psychology Press.

Frith, H & Harcourt, D (2007) Using photographs to capture women's experiences of chemotherapy: Reflecting on the method. *Qualitative Health Research*, 17(10), 1340–50.

Frith, H, Riley, S, Archer, L & Gleeson K (2005) Editorial: Imag(in)ing visual methodologies. *Qualitative Research in Psychology*, 2(3), 187–198.

Harper, D (2002) Talking about pictures: A case for photo elicitation. *Visual Studies*, 17(1), 13–26.

Himber, J (1994) Blood rituals: Self-cutting in female psychiatric inpatients. *Psychotherapy*, 31(4), 620–31.

Hurworth, R, Clark, E, Martin, J & Thomsen, S (2005) The use of photo interviewing: Three examples from health evaluation and research. *Evaluation Journal of Australia*, 4(1/2), 52–62.

Klonsky, ED (2007) The functions of deliberate self-injury: A review of the evidence. *Clinical Psychology Review*, 27(2), 226–39.

Klonsky, ED (2009) The functions of self-injury in young adults who cut themselves: Clarifying the evidence for affect regulation. *Psychiatry Research*, 166(2–3), 260–8.

Latham, A (2003) Research, performance, and doing human geography: Some reflections on diary-photograph, diary-interview method. *Environment and Planning A*, 35(11), 1993–2017.

Liebenberg, L (2009) The visual image as a discussion point: Increasing validity in boundary crossing research. *Qualitative Research*, 9(4), 441–67.

NICE (2004) *CG16: Self-harm: The short-term physical and psychological management and secondary prevention of intentional self-harm in primary and secondary care*. London: National Institute for Health and Clinical Excellence.

Nock, N (2012) Future directions for the study of suicide and self-injury. *Journal of Child and Adolescent Psychology*, 41(2), 255–9.

Pink, S (2004) Visual methods. In C Seale, G Gobo, J Gubrium and D Silverman (Eds) *Qualitative Research Practice* (pp. 361–76). Thousand Oaks, CA: SAGE Publications.

Radley A & Taylor D (2003a) Images of recovery: A photo-elicitation study on the hospital ward. *Qualitative Health Research*, 13(1), 77–99.

Radley, A & Taylor, D (2003b) Remembering one's stay in hospital: A study in photography, recovery and forgetting. *Health*, 7(2), 129–59.

Reavey, P (Ed) (2011) *Visual Methods in Psychology*. Hove: Routledge, Psychology Press.

Rodham, K, Hawton, K & Evans, E (2004) Reasons for deliberate self-harm: Comparison of self-poisoners and self-cutters in a community sample of adolescents. *Journal of the American Academy of Child and Adolescent Psychiatry*, 43(1), 80–7.

Spandler, H (2001) *Who's Hurting Who? Young people, self-harm and suicide*. Gloucester: Handsell Publications.

Suyemoto, K (1998) The functions of self-mutilation. *Clinical Psychology Review*, 18(5), 531–54.

Sweetman, P (2009) Revealing habitus, illuminating practice: Bourdieu, photography and visual methods. *The Sociological Review*, 57(3), 491–511.

White, A, Bushin, N, Carpena-Méndez, F & Ní Laoire, C (2010) Using visual methodologies to explore contemporary Irish childhoods. *Qualitative Research*, 10(2), 143–58.

Whitehurst, T (2007) Liberating silent voices: Perspectives of children with profound and complex learning needs on inclusion. *British Journal of Learning Disabilities*, 35(1), 55–61.

REFORMULATING SELF-HARM

23

The self-harm spectrum: A personal journey

Sandra Walker

'It's your artistic personality!' the nun said as she dragged me back from the first-floor window I was halfway through, having screamed my intention at the top of my lungs before throwing myself dramatically outwards. I was 15 or 16, in full adolescent flow, approaching exams in a boarding school where I was known for being sensible and musical with literary tendencies. That this behaviour was extremely out of character for me was not acknowledged. No one was told – my parents only found out 20 years later and were horrified that they hadn't been informed at the time. Was this response the right one? I don't know, but it was a nice excuse for them to be able to brush it under the carpet and pretend it didn't happen. A cry for help? Maybe, but it felt more like a rage of frustration and anger over the lack of control I felt I had at the time. It didn't work as a cry for help anyway because no one offered me any, but the crisis diminished and nothing catastrophic happened.

Some years later I began training to be a mental health nurse and one of the tutors was a psychosexual counsellor. To say this man saved my life is not too much of an exaggeration. At the time I was using drugs of all sorts, in a seriously dysfunctional relationship and experiencing flashbacks from childhood abuse. By the time I realised I was pregnant I was beginning to reach a place where I could begin to build some self-esteem, and this combined with the counselling helped me straighten out. Then the postnatal depression hit after the birth of my second son and with this came the cutting. It didn't help to make me feel better in the way some report, but it was a release of the emotional turmoil and I didn't know what else to do when my distress became unmanageable. I was a community patient at this time and was generously offered the diagnosis of 'personality disorder'. I was a junior nurse by then and although the diagnosis had not reached the height of its popularity, I was well aware of the damage a diagnosis like that could do to me in future years. So, I chose to stop attending my appointments and was discharged by default. However, this was not before losing my nursing job because of my mental health problems and there was no attempt at follow-up by the service I was attending. I remember looking ahead of me shortly after my first daughter was born and thinking that I had two paths to choose: I either carry on like this and end up as a serial patient, or I get out of the situation and start again. I chose the latter. I was lucky that I could see the choices – some are not so lucky.

Once I managed to get back to work years later, I did well. I developed a fascination with self-harm, unsurprisingly, and got a job working in an emergency department (ED) managing a team of mental health practitioners providing assessments for people in the acute hospital with mental health issues. The majority of the people we saw had self-harmed. I was aware at the time of the attitude of many of the staff in the department and, along with the team, provided training about self-harm in order to try and improve the reception that people who had self-harmed received when attending the ED. The longer I worked there – it was about six years in total – the more varied the people, types and functions of self-harm.

I did my degree part-time; my dissertation topic was around self-harm and I was discovering that the majority of the literature I was reading did not appear to understand self-harm as a concept in itself, but saw it as a suicidal behaviour. Things have begun to change now, but we are still in a position where much of the research that has been done into self-harm has come about by accident as a result of it turning out to be one of the most common factors present in completed suicide (Duffy & Ryan, 2004; Coyle, 2001; Barr et al, 2005).

When I began my journey towards a doctorate in 2009, still focusing on self-harm, I became aware of the vast differences in the literature regarding a sensible and suitable definition for self-harm. Some definitions – for example, the National Institute for Health and Care Excellence (NICE) (2004, 2011) (which provides clinical guidance for services delivering care for people who self-harm), Favazza (1996) and McAllister et al (2002) – appear to be attempting to move away from linking self-harm to suicide. However, this then leaves out those people who have variable intent or who are motivated by a wish to die. Richardson (2004) provides a short definition: 'Deliberately inflicting injury on oneself.' This allows for any intent and avoids any judgement being made about intention beyond the word 'deliberate', but does not prompt one to ask why the self-harm happened. I needed a good definition for my research and was unhappy with the way that intent was not explicitly mentioned in many, so I devised this one: 'Any act intended to cause physical harm to the self.'

This definition encompasses all forms of self-harm and draws attention to the need to discover the intent, which will be different and variable for each individual. It also allows for the fact that although physical harm may result from the actions, there can also be a psychological benefit from these same actions.

Policy documents have serious trouble separating suicide and self-harm, and the literature is littered with articles that bounce from self-harm as a coping mechanism to self-harm as a suicidal act. The research indicates that the two are interlinked whether we like it or not – the fact remains that whilst some people will self-harm with no intention of ending or even risking their lives, others will self-harm with the intention of ending it all. There is a huge range of other possibilities, so it is impossible to pigeonhole everyone into one category. Is there a danger of us becoming embroiled in the issue of separating the two (self-harm and suicide) and is this distracting us from the real issues? In order to make more sense of this and for use in the training I regularly delivered, I created a self-harm spectrum (Figure 1, overleaf) in order to crystallise my thinking. The spectrum incorporates both self-harm and suicide, accepting that they are interlinked, and the tool that helps us to decide whether they apply or not is the person's intent. Favazza (1996) was an eye-opener for me, as his book helped me confirm something I had become aware of in my role in the ED: that there is a whole spectrum of behaviours that could be regarded as being self-harm, many of which are culturally sanctioned.

The negativity shown regarding self-harm is indicative of the ignorance that surrounds it. Considering the spectrum, it becomes easier to explore how ordinary, everyday behaviours, such as nail biting because you are nervous, have a correlation with cutting to release emotion. Where is the line that tells us when a behaviour is self-harm and when it can be considered acceptable? My assertion is that the intent that lies behind the act is the most important factor. If someone drives at 100 miles per hour, crashes into the central barrier on the motorway and dies, this is a tragedy. If the driver enjoyed driving at high speeds and was fully aware of the dangers, this clearly differentiates him from the driver who has had enough and deliberately hit the barrier in order to

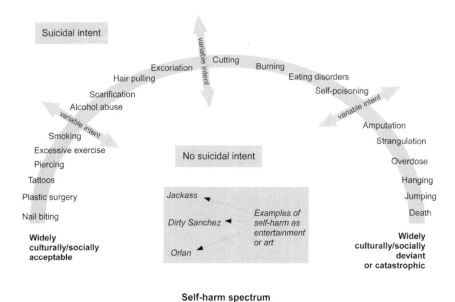

Self-harm spectrum

NB. This list is for illustrative purposes and is not exhaustive

kill himself. The intent is key here, but the outcome is the same. In this instance we would only be able to guess at the intent, but in many cases we have the opportunity to look beyond the act to the person behind it, to connect with them and enter their world.

There is much room to manoeuvre within the spectrum. By this I mean there may be differing levels of intent that make the same aspects of the spectrum more or less acceptable. To illustrate, consider a person base-jumping for pleasure who has no intention of dying, and another who wishes to die and attempts to jump from a high building. It is the intent of these two people that decides if their behaviour is one that should cause society concern. If they are a consenting adult with full capacity, the activities they engage in for fun should be no concern of ours. If they are suicidal, it would be acceptable to intervene and assist if possible in helping the person find ways of making life worth living again. Consider also a person with chronic obstructive pulmonary disorder (CoPD), who can barely walk 100 yards without becoming very breathless, who has a zest for life and a happy personality but smokes like a chimney, fully aware that they are killing themselves. This scenario is slightly clouded by the issue of addiction, but why is this person more acceptable socially than the one who cuts their arms in order to cope with the stress of their job?

At what point does plastic surgery become destructive? When the silicone from the implants leaks? When the rat poison injected into the face prevents an expression? When the fat injections make the lips look like a fish pout? This also highlights the issue of personal values. For example, I would consider injecting poison into myself completely unacceptable, but I have had plastic surgery to correct the damage done to my stomach following childbirth. What is or is not 'acceptable' varies from person to person, culture to culture, and depends completely on time, context and intent. We can only comprehend these things if we are able to talk about them and take an interest in the person, rather than judging their actions or behaviours.

Practices we may consider culturally unacceptable now were commonplace at other points in history, for example, self-flagellation for atonement of one's sins. Understanding that self-harm has been present in our society for centuries, if not longer (Favazza, 1992), puts things into a wider perspective where the hysteria surrounding it begins to seem a little unnecessary. The idea that self-harm can be a creative behaviour may be difficult to swallow, but those who have successfully used cutting or burning to help themselves stay alive may disagree.

I have always liked tattoos. Using the skin as a blank canvas for expression makes perfect sense to me. Having been through a traumatic relationship breakdown, in 2010 I felt it was time to get the tattoo I had been promising myself for five years. I knew what I wanted, so made the appointment and gave the studio my design. On the day I was nervous; I knew I wasn't good with pain and wondered how it would all go. There was a feeling of rebellion as I sat in the chair – my ex was against women having tattoos, so there was a feeling that I was giving him the finger just by being there. The transfer was on, it looked great, I knew it was going to be good and I steeled myself for the first needle prick. The outline was not as bad as I had expected, but the shading of the colours, with needles going back and forward over already damaged skin, was agony. I was resisting the urge to pull away all the time, I was allowing myself to be harmed. There was a conflict there. I talked to the artist about his experiences and about my research and he said he had tattooed many people who he felt used tattooing and piercing as a legitimate way to harm themselves. The pain was intense for nearly an hour, but the experience of resisting the urge to pull away and coping despite the pain was a very powerful one. Once it was done I felt elated. The tattoo looked (and still looks) beautiful and I knew I had made the right decision. I felt I had turned over a new leaf in this chapter of my life and the tattoo expressed this. Whenever I see it I feel good about myself; it is a representation of the struggles I have overcome over the years and a celebration of the person I am now, despite the pain. I was struck by the commonalities here with the way some people who self-harm talk about it as a physical representation of their emotional pain – a coping strategy, a way of staying alive – and the way scars can remind them of the pain they have survived and the journey they have made (Tantum & Huband, 2009). The tattoo provided a powerful release of emotional pain and a rite of passage for me. It is a fine line between harm and healing.

When I set out to write this chapter I wasn't entirely sure what my aims were. Having written it, one aim is clearly to broaden the thinking around self-harm, from being a dysfunctional behaviour, to being something that has actually been part of our culture for as long as we have. This link to culture may hold the key to reducing stigma and increasing understanding. Primarily though, I want to encourage all to look beyond the act to the person behind it and discover more about them. It is my contention that self-harm is becoming and will continue to become more socially acceptable and recognised as a legitimate coping mechanism. If this is the case, then harm minimisation strategies, such as those suggested by Pembroke (2007), will become essential in order to avoid unnecessary disability. Pathologising every behaviour our society finds disturbing is an expensive and unnecessary route to go down. Only by finding out about the person do we discover what they need, what the self-harm means for them and if intervention is required or not. The emotional distance of diagnosis and stigmatisation of self-harm only keep the uneducated in a state of ignorant bliss. The challenge to us all is to connect with each other and accept that we are as gloriously different in our modes of expression as we are in our dress sense!

Thoughts

- Self-harm has been part of most cultures for centuries.

- Understanding this link may hold the key to reducing societal stigma.

- Self-harm is a legitimate coping mechanism for some and can be considered a life-affirming act in some cases.

- Self-harm is inextricably linked to suicide on a spectrum and the only way of defining where people who self-harm are on this spectrum is to discover the intent of the individual.

- It is essential to look beyond the act of self-harm to the person behind it.

- Intent is the key!

About the author

Sandy is a Senior Teaching Fellow in Mental Health at Southampton University. She is a qualified mental health nurse with a wide range of clinical experience spanning more than 20 years. She has a long history of mental health problems but has had no formal contact with services for 17 years. In addition to her university work, she is a professional musician and does voluntary work for various mental health organisations, including being the coordinator for the Hampshire Human Library – an international initiative aimed at reducing stigma through interaction and education of the public. She is the Creative Director of the Sanity Company, which publishes books aimed at helping children and young people develop good mental health and problem-solving skills.

References

Barr, W, Leitner, M & Thomas, J (2005) Psychosocial assessment of patients who attend an accident and emergency department with self-harm. *Journal of Psychiatric and Mental Health Nursing*, 12(2), 130–8.

Coyle, B (2001) Suicide and the young. *Community Practitioner*, 74(1), 8–9.

Duffy, D & Ryan, T (2004) *New Approaches to Preventing Suicide*. London: Jessica Kingsley Publishers.

Favazza, AR (1996) *Bodies Under Seige: Self-mutilation and body modification in culture and psychiatry* (2nd edition). Baltimore, MD: Johns Hopkins University Press.

McAllister, M, Creedy, D, Moyle, W & Farrugia, C (2002) Nurses' attitudes towards clients who self-harm. *Journal of Advanced Nursing*, 40(5), 578–86.

NICE (2004) *CG16: Self-harm: The short-term physical and psychological management and secondary prevention of intentional self-harm in primary and secondary care*. London: National Institute for Health and Clinical Excellence.

NICE (2011) *CG133: Self-harm: Longer-term management*. London: National Institute for Health and Clinical Excellence.

Pembroke, LR (2007) Harm minimisation: Limiting the damage of self-injury. In H Spandler & S Warner (Eds) *Beyond Fear and Control*. Ross-on-Wye: PCCS Books.

Richardson, C (2004) Self-harm: Understanding the causes and treatment options. *Nursing Times*, 100(15), 24–6.

Tantum, D & Huband, N (2009) *Understanding Repeated Self-Injury: A multidisciplinary approach*. Basingstoke: Palgrave Macmillan.

The need behind the urge

Y. K.

My own 'lived experience' of self-harm dates back to adolescence, when I started to cut and burn myself in response to mind states and outer conditions that I had no other way to cope with at the time. Although this behaviour abated for a number of years towards the end of high school and through my first university degree, for much of that time I coped instead by binge drinking, sleeping around and heavily using cannabis, all more socially accepted forms of self-harm than cutting or burning. In the summer of 2003, I made my first in a series of suicide attempts, through large overdoses of over-the-counter medications. I needed two weeks in hospital for medical treatment, and was eventually admitted as an informal patient to a psychiatric hospital for six weeks. This was one of my darkest periods, but it was also a turning point. After being discharged, I began psychotherapy in earnest, determined to understand myself better and to ensure that this kind of crisis never happened again. I have worked hard in therapy (psychosynthesis therapy) ever since. There have been more overdoses since that time, more cutting, burning, drug taking, risky sex, chaotic relationships, depression and other difficult mind states. There have also been repeated hospital admissions, many different medications, stigmatising diagnoses, and mixed experiences of good treatment and mistreatment in the hands of countless mental health professionals, as well as staff in general hospitals, following acts of self-harm. However, I have also made great progress in understanding and changing my self-defeating patterns, I have found some meaning in my suffering, and I have created a good life for myself.

In 2006 I began training as a mental health nurse. Throughout the course I found myself coming into conflict with mentors, managers and colleagues because I could not help vehemently challenging what I saw to be, at best, unhelpful practice and, at worst, gross infringements of human rights. I spent a lot of the course studying and getting involved in alternative approaches in mental health (e.g. the work of organisations like Soteria, Windhorse, Open Dialogue, the Hearing Voices Network, the Spiritual Crisis Network, Icarus, MindFreedom International, etc.), which I thought should be on the curriculum but weren't. (I now teach these subjects on the same course I studied on, having been invited back as a visiting lecturer.) The training gave my life a purpose and a just cause to fight for. Having 'been there' myself, as a service user as well as a carer of numerous partners and friends, I couldn't simply jump the hoops and follow the status quo. The university was largely supportive of my efforts, despite the trouble I always seemed to be in, and in 2009 I qualified as a Registered Mental Nurse (RMN) and was given the School of Nursing and Midwifery's Award for Excellence. The greatest part of this achievement was, I felt, in having qualified without compromising my values and principles, something which working in the mental health system seems to do to a great many people whom I have encountered (though not all – I have also, at times, been extremely well cared for, and have witnessed inspiring practice from many practitioners too).

On qualifying, I found a job in a local third-sector organisation, working as an independent mental health advocate (IMHA). My job is to speak out for people detained (and usually medicated) against their will, and to ensure that they know their rights and can use them. This post suited me, but after a year and a half, I burnt out, and was off work for five weeks. A year or so later, I burnt out again, this time leading to a more serious breakdown, and seven months off work, with four suicide attempts and two psychiatric hospitalisations. I returned to work part-time a few months ago and am doing well now.

Throughout my nurse training and the years of working as an advocate, I spent probably more time than not 'surfing the urge' to harm myself in one way or another. Although I was 'functioning' and experienced many peaceful and happy times as well, there was a constant undertow of self-destructive energy that I had to work consciously not to be dragged down by. Every day, I felt a pull towards doing myself harm; daily, I would turn my head and heart away from it and towards something more wholesome, or at least less harmful. This repeated digging-out of new grooves, of new ways of being, has paid off. Although there were overdoses during the most recent crisis, I can see that a lot has changed since the early days in terms of my relationship with myself. Throughout the most recent period of suicidal despair, despite endless weeks of strong self-harming ideation, I found that I could not bring myself to cut or burn myself, take drugs, drink or sleep around. There was also much ambivalence around each overdose I took, with a part of me resisting and not wanting to do myself harm, even as I swallowed the pills.

Since coming through the worst of it all last summer, I have gradually found my feet and a new sense of self-appreciation that I don't think was ever there before. For the first time in years, I don't feel suicidal most of the time. Mostly, I don't feel like hurting myself at all. The urge pops up every now and then, but only for a few hours at a time at the most, and in connection to very specific triggers, which I can now recognise if not yet fully avoid. But most of the time, rather than making the most of a bad situation, I enjoy what feels like a good situation instead: spending time with a strong and supportive circle of friends, a warm home life, a meaningful occupation, a spiritual path, contact with family and a trusted therapist on board helping me steer a healthy course for myself. Best of all is the absence of wanting to hurt or kill myself all the time. It feels like a new chapter in my life – one that comes after 'living with the urge' – which I will tentatively call, 'life without the urge'.

I am going to describe a model that focuses on the idea of 'choice' with self-harm, which I developed during my mental health nurse training, based on both my personal and professional experiences. Anyone can use the model, not only people who are officially 'self-harmers', and I'd encourage all those working in the field to try it for themselves – doing so can break down deeply held 'us and them' separative notions often held by those who consider themselves to be 'not-self-harmers'. The model is illustrated in Figure 1.

The model comprises three concentric circles. In the inner circle, you write all the ways in which you might self-harm. This can range from forms of self-harm that are generally considered 'pathological', such as cutting, overdosing and burning, to more socially acceptable or invisible methods – like over-exercising, over-working, smoking, drinking, isolating yourself, sleeping around and pushing people away. In my own history, there were several years where I did not intentionally harm myself through methods like cutting, but where I did take a lot of drugs, drank a lot and had a lot of risky sex with strangers. I would put these inside my inner circle of self-harming behaviours along with cutting, burning and overdosing, as well as working too hard, drinking too much coffee and eating too much sugar. What does and does not

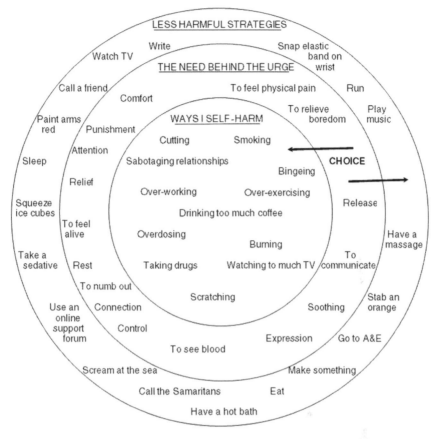

Figure 1: An example of the choice model

constitute 'self-harm' is, I believe, both relative and subjective, and is for each person to discern for themselves.

In the next layer, you try to name the reasons you might do any of the things in the inner circle. I call this layer, 'the need behind the urge'. Try and think of needs that all human beings share. The thinking behind this comes from the work of Marshall Rosenberg on 'Nonviolent Communication', and is echoed in the 'Human Givens' approach (Griffin & Tyrell, 2003). This layer identifies the deeper level of experience behind the act in the inner circle, which I see as simply the strategies an individual commonly uses for meeting their needs. For example, the 'needs' layer may include the need for comfort: over-eating might meet this need for some people, as may unsafe sex, or cutting or burning (the act of cutting or burning may be associated with having to patch yourself up afterwards, cleaning your own wounds and applying dressings, or having someone else do it) – these strategies would belong in the inner circle. Other examples for the 'needs' layer might be the need for expression, attention, control, rest or soothing. Sometimes I have cut myself to feel my body when I've gone numb (to meet the need to feel I exist), other times to vent my rage (for expression), other times to stop feeling so many conflicting emotions so intensely (for peace and rest).

The degree to which a person can identify these needs will vary, depending on their level of self-awareness. But the person in the helping role may in any case obtain a sense of them, through deep intuitive empathy, and be able to help the person work it out. Even if you can't get down to the level of shared human needs at first, the helper can ask (or the person can ask themselves) questions like 'What would self-harming in this way give you?', 'What would it actually feel like to do it?' or 'Imagine following through with the act; what would it feel like at the end of it?' Whatever responses to this kind of inquiry come up, you can put these into the second layer. Often these may be things like 'I feel I need punishment', 'Seeing my own blood', 'Feeling real' or 'Numbing myself from overwhelming emotions'.

In the third circle, around the edge, you identify some less harmful things you could do instead, to meet any of the underlying needs in the 'needs' circle. Some of these might be the same as the ones in the 'self-harm' circle. For example, if you know you self-harm by cutting but also by drinking too much coffee (cutting and drinking coffee would both go in the inner, self-harm circle), you might also put drinking coffee into the outer layer, as a safer strategy for dealing with one of the possible needs behind the urge to cut, for example, the need to 'feel a rush'. The outer circle could be seen as 'healthier or less harmful coping strategies' – things like:

- watch TV (to 'numb out for a while')
- squeeze ice cubes (to feel pain)
- paint red marks on your skin (to 'see blood')
- take a sleeping tablet and go to sleep (to 'disappear')
- phone a friend (to feel more connected, as a distraction or to vent)
- smoke a nicotine inhaler (instead of a cigarette)
- scream or break things (instead of your body) etc.

The final piece of the model consists of two arrows: one from the 'needs' layer, pointing inwards towards the 'self-harm' layer, and one from the 'needs' layer, pointing out towards the 'less harmful strategies' layer, showing that there may be a choice between more destructive and healthier strategies for meeting any of those needs.

I have found that people I've worked with have generally been very responsive to being asked, with kindness, questions about what the lived experience is like for them. They are immersed in the experience, often trapped inside it, and simply having another person gently inquiring in this way can give them a sense of being a little less alone, which can in itself be a relief. The kind of inquiry I am suggesting is very different from demanding, 'Why do you want to self-harm?', as if it's up to the person in distress to give an explanation for the sake of making it understandable to you. It's more like helping the person to find words to describe the texture of their experience.

On one occasion, I was sitting with a young woman on an acute ward who was fighting the urge to slash her arms. She had reported this to the staff, who were using 'behavioural' techniques to deal with her, and simply kept reminding her that if she harmed herself she would lose her leave. The more she went to talk to them about her urges, the less they paid attention to her, believing that this was the only way to break the cycle of her behaviour. Since (they believed) she self-harmed 'for attention', they thought they should starve her of attention whenever she mentioned it. Although she had regular dedicated one-to-one time with her named nurse 'to talk about her feelings', this did not include talking about what it was like to want to self-harm. It was as if talking about her urges was taboo, and I felt nervous about following my impulses in working with her, for fear of being told off for 'colluding' with her pathology. However, I was genuinely curious, and I was unimpressed with the team's conclusions that 'it was all behavioural'. That phrase does not help to get inside the skin of the person in distress; 'it's behavioural' is one of the many shortcuts that are taken precisely to avoid really knowing a patient's experience, a way of bypassing real human connection by settling for a poor, pseudo-understanding of what is going on for them.

Fortunately, I was able to get some time alone with this young woman. I asked her what was happening in her world. When she said she was feeling like slashing her arms, I asked her what that felt like to her. She described the pictures that were in her head, of what she felt like doing to herself, of things she'd done before, the way the images kept coming up and swirling round and round in her mind, and the way none of her distraction techniques were working. I asked how she was feeling in her body, and mirrored holding my stomach, as she was doing. She described a tight knot in her belly, which hadn't shifted for hours, and she said her skin felt hot and prickly all over. She said she felt disgusting. As she described how it felt, she started to cry, and she said she wanted to cut the bad feeling out from inside of her. I noticed myself feeling a lot more empathy with her than I had at the start, when she had simply been saying she wanted to slash her arms; now I had some idea of how she felt inside. With this increased empathic connection, further questions came – I asked what happened to the bad feeling when she imagined slashing herself. She visibly relaxed as she let herself imagine going through with the act, and she said she'd feel clean and relieved. I echoed, 'You need to feel clean, and relieved.' She said she needed 'cleaning out', then she'd feel relieved. I wondered aloud, whether there was a less harmful way we could help her feel 'cleaned out' and relieved. I wondered about a hot shower and a scrubbing brush. She agreed to do this, saying she thought cutting herself would be more effective, but that she may as well try.

This was not a substitute for long-term psychotherapy, nor a solution for every instance in which she would feel like slashing her arms. We didn't even know if the shower and scrubbing would help. But I could see that, momentarily at least, some new possibilities had opened up in her, other than the previous certainty that slashing her arms was her only course of action, and together we had gained a glimmer of insight into the feelings of self-disgust and the needs for purging – or 'cleaning out' – and for relief, that were expressing themselves through her urge to slash her arms. She had a very hot shower and scrubbed her skin raw, and said she cried hard whilst showering. She had succeeded in getting a sense of the needs behind her urge, and had discovered one new, slightly less harmful alternative to cutting, which might or might not be helpful to her on another occasion when those needs are asserting themselves again.

As in the above example, the needs-behind-the-urge model can be used at the time the urges arise (this is more or less how I have worked with my own self-destructive urges). It is important that the person is helped to 'feel in to' what's behind the urge that's arising, and that it's not assumed that, just because the person, for example, 'feels like burning', it means that they are angry and in need of 'a more creative form of expression'. It's not as simple as, when someone wants to cut, it's always to get attention or to deal with feeling overwhelmed; it's much more subtle than that. At each moment when a self-destructive urge is coming up, a part of the psyche is communicating something about how it is and what it needs at that very moment. The urge to cut (or voices telling the person to cut) can symbolise different needs at different times. The person can learn to get better at decoding and understanding the language their psyche is using, by being asked (or asking themselves) questions like 'What would self-harming achieve for you, right now?' or 'What's it like to be feeling like self-harming?' It's a process of being encouraged to come down from the spinning mind and grounding in the reality of the present moment, to the realisation that: 'I'm a person, feeling human feelings and looking for a way to fulfil my very ordinary human needs.'

I was helped to do this by therapists and meditation teachers early on in my journey, until it became something which a part of me would naturally and spontaneously do for myself. Whenever I was feeling strong urges to cut, my teacher or therapist would hold me with a steady gaze and a strong, gentle presence, no matter how ugly, unacceptable or overpowering the experience was for me. They kept helping me to explore the feelings that were arising, sense into the energy of the urge and listen to what was behind it. I failed to hear my own needs, or to meet them, many times, and often heard them but hurt myself anyway, as the habit of reacting to the urges was so strong. But gradually, I learned to sit with my own experiences, wrapping them inside the same cloak of stillness and mindfulness that my teachers and therapists had, and I became more and more skilful at responding to them, with increasing kindness. I got to know my inner world really well, and to understand, deeply, that even though my mind tells me I want to hurt myself, more fundamentally, my being wants to be well; the self-destructive part is only communicating something it needs through a particular metaphor, or language, that it's learned in early life. I don't have to do what my mind tells me to do. There is a gap between the urge and the action, a gap that's widened over the years, in which I get to choose.

The model can also be used to debrief with the person after an incident of self-harm. Too often, I see a lack of response to episodes of self-harm, other than a behavioural, 'This is how it's affected the people around you', punitive or dismissive kind of reaction. The individual hasn't been helped to unpick the incident, to think about what led to it or what could change in the future, and they haven't had any real empathy shown for the feelings and needs that precipitated the incident. Instead, they have been shamed or dismissed for having 'made the choice' they have, either in a very hard 'You need to learn to take responsibility for yourself', or else in a 'You're too ill to control what you do' kind of way.

One time when I was in hospital, I was in pain and panicking, as I reported to staff that I had swallowed a hard piece of plastic which had become lodged in my throat. One staff nurse said, accusingly, 'Why didn't you come to us first?' then rolled her eyes and muttered, 'I've got better things to do', as she walked out of the room. Then the ward manager came in and the first thing he said was, 'Can you give me your belt please?' (Belts were not allowed on the ward due to the ligature risk, but it seemed an odd moment to ask me for it!) I was finally taken to A&E, transferred to another hospital and, two operations later, the plastic was removed. The staff back on the psychiatric ward didn't talk to me about what led up to the swallowing at all until my next ward review; it was as though everyone was embarrassed about it or something. I needed to be invited to explore what had actually happened, what had led up to the incident, how it felt, and to have a sense that the listener was truly interested in hearing these thoughts. Unfortunately, I did not get this sense during my hospital stay at all and was only able to reflect meaningfully on the swallowing episode later in therapy.

Finally, the model can also be used more generally, beyond times when the person is in or right after a crisis, to help reflect on these kinds of needs-meeting mechanisms and open them to the possibility of having more of a choice in the future. I have sat with people I have been working with and, together, we have drawn up personalised versions of the model, which they have been able to refer back to when needed, and refine as their own inquiry into their self-destructive urges progresses. However, people differ in their ability or desire to partake in this kind of structured, written reflection and planning. Whereas some people may leave with the three concentric circles filled in, others may still benefit from a less explicit use of the model. If the helper can embody the spirit of the model in their interactions with the person, then hopefully the person will develop their understanding of the fact that there are hidden meanings and needs behind their urges, and that there is sometimes a choice as to how they meet those needs.

Thoughts

There are some key points from my piece that I would hope readers will take away, although I also hope that each person will take from it what they need.

- The way that others respond to someone who wants to self-harm or who has self-harmed can make a massive difference.

- No two 'self-harmers' are the same. No two incidents of self-harm and no two self-harm urges are exactly the same. The conditions, the feelings, the texture of the experience, the needs behind the urges and the response that's needed will all be at least subtly different from one incident to the next.

- There are deeper messages from parts of the psyche that are trying to express themselves through the metaphor of self-destructive urges and behaviour. Each person can be helped to learn the language of their psyche, to sit with their own feelings, and to respond in a better way to their own needs.

- There is always a choice available to us, between a more or less harmful way of responding to the needs behind self-harm urges. It doesn't feel that way at first, when the gap between the urge and the reaction is really tight, but with practice that gap can be widened, and the sense of having a choice will increase.

- It is unhelpful and cruel to shame someone who has self-harmed (or to shame oneself) for 'making the wrong choice'. They/you will have made the only choice they/you could at the time, given all the present conditions.

- There will be a story behind every urge and act of self-harm, which will not be heard unless it is inquired about, with curiosity, kindness and care. It is worth getting interested.

About the author

I am someone who has experienced self-harm from a number of different angles: as someone who has self-harmed myself; as a partner, friend and carer of others who've self-harmed; as a nurse; and as a mental health advocate. My personal experiences with self-harm have been informed by professional practice, and my nurse training and subsequent employment as a mental health advocate have formed part of my recovery story. I am pleased to be able to share some of my experience with others here in my writing and hope that it might make some small difference for others in their encounters with self-harm.

Reference

Griffin, J & Tyrell, I (2003) *Human Givens*. Chalvington: Human Givens Publishing.

25

Self-harm: An intelligent language for subjugation and stigma

Peter Dargan

The attitudes toward self-harm have always fascinated me: the theories, assumptions, narratives and stories we have that permeate our hospitals, our therapy rooms, our playgrounds, schools, televisions and newspapers. Thinking back over my own experiences, I think there is great merit in unpicking some of the ideas we have about self-harm, and, I would hope, also a great deal of potential to do good through greater curiosity and understanding.

I first began to self-injure around the age of nine or 10. I was very aware of what I was doing. The process developed during my early teens when I found a method that consistently worked for me, and I continued secretly until my mid-twenties, sometimes several times a month, sometimes daily. It felt like a long and complicated relationship, and although I may not currently be self-harming, it is still a part of my identity. For that reason I continue to take an active interest in the phenomenon of self-injury, and the attitudes and approaches of others persist in affecting me, whether it is currently an active part of my life or not.

Like many others who have self-harmed, I also had contact with several different professionals and services throughout this time in my life – GPs, psychologists, psychiatrists, nurses and so on. It was a period where I was much more naive about how professionals are encouraged (or not) to approach self-harm, and what the dominant stereotypes might say about me as a 'self-harmer'. Later in my adult life I have become more aware of some of these attitudes and have been exposed to the other side of the healthcare fence so to speak, which has made for an interesting comparison of experiences.

An 'emotional language'

When I think about attitudes towards self-harm, I am often reminded of an experience when I was at work several years ago. I have a very clear visual image of being sat with a colleague – a psychiatrist – in his office and watching as he sketched a large 'ladder' structure onto a flipchart. We had begun a conversation about self-harm and out of curiosity I had asked him a general question about how he understood the act of deliberately harming oneself. He numbered each step on the ladder nought to 10, and explained that this represented a scale of 'negative emotions', with a greater intensity of emotions increasing from nought up to 10. He went on to describe how (for him) this was the fundamental difference between 'you and I' and 'self-harmers'.

It made what came next equally more interesting and unsettling as he directed my attention to the ladder he had drawn out: 'You see, whereas, say, if I get to a four I might have a Diet Coke and a 10-minute break, or if I get to an eight where I become quite stressed or upset I might go for a walk and phone a friend, people who self-harm don't have these strategies. They don't have ways to "deal with" their feelings and they don't have a "language" to describe their feelings.'

As I sat uncomfortably listening to what I perceived to be a global oversimplification of a complex and highly personal behaviour, I can remember becoming increasingly preoccupied with some of the themes from this conversation, not least of which concerned 'Why Diet Coke!?' and 'This isn't the first time I've heard this from a professional.' It reminded me of a similar event several years previously when I had attended some work-based training, where a projected slide with the huge words: 'People who harm themselves do not have an intelligent language for emotions' was presented to the group prior to a discussion about how those who self-injure struggle to understand and regulate their inner feelings.

As I have worked more in healthcare (particularly mental health), I have become aware that this seems to be a rather prevalent idea – that is, that people who self-injure are deficient in some fundamental way in being able to identify, tolerate and communicate internal emotional states. This often seems to be taken as a *de facto* assumption, and self-harm seems to have become synonymous with 'poor emotional skills'. My sense, from my own experiences, is that many of the professional discourses that inform the way we approach self-harm can encourage unhelpful, assumptive and neglectful practice: practice that ultimately precludes people from attempting to form a relationship with someone and to understand what underlies their self-harm.

This idea of an 'emotional language' made me think about the real life stories where self-harm takes a prominent role, stories that are all too often laden with pain and suffering. Give it whatever label you want – 'trauma' that is physical, psychological, emotional or spiritual – there is a deep, personal, existential pain. It struck me that surely emotional literacy is one thing, but finding a language for trauma, or abuse, or suffering, is something entirely different.

Consider this: have you ever noticed how people can define the power of certain positive experiences in their lives simply by their 'indescribable' nature?

'Words cannot describe how I felt at the birth of my son. It was the most intense moment of my life, like beams of light were shooting from my chest.'

'When my partner asked me to marry them I felt like I was going to explode. "Happy" just doesn't do it justice, I just couldn't stop shaking and crying.'

I would hope that all of us have some of these indescribable positive experiences in our lives, where the power of our emotions seems to exceed the scale of language, and no words seem to fit. If anything, I'm sure we've at least seen others experience this difficulty in trying to find the right words, the right language, for something that is so powerful and overwhelming. But hang on – 'beams of light', 'wanting to explode'? – these aren't feelings! Does that then make these people emotionally illiterate? Or rather does it reflect the power of their experiences?

With that in mind, consider then the other side of this coin, when we have severely negative experiences:

'Over the years I watched as my father slowly killed himself, putting that poison into his body every day. I'd find him passed out on the floor or the sofa, not knowing if he was unconscious or dead. I never understood it and I never got used to it. Every time he drank and passed out and I had to feel for a heartbeat or a breath. It was like I felt everything in my body simultaneously and intensely realise how much I loved him and hated him at the same time.'

'My partner beat me for years. He would say that he loved me so much, and if you could see his face … how upset he got, and when he promised that it wouldn't happen again … he really did seem so sorry and so sad himself. He said that I made him do it, and I suppose on some level I believed him. I felt worthless in so many different ways. There are so many feelings inside my body I just don't understand them; I don't know what's real anymore.'

Are these experiences adequately describable? Would it not be normal for someone in these situations to feel incredibly overwhelmed and confused, with equally intense conflicting emotions? Is there a normal pathway or predefined process for dealing with and coping with these things? Why then do we assume that it is these people who are inherently flawed, rather than validating and exploring the complicated pain in their lives?

Of course, I'm not suggesting that everyone who self-harms was neglected as a child or experiences an abusive relationship. Nor am I suggesting that these examples are typical. But it does seem that a myriad of traumatic experiences can accompany self-harm, and I refuse to see that as a coincidence. I believe we all have our own pain. I cannot imagine the complexity of an emotional reaction to many of these traumas, and the subsequent transition required to make sense of these experiences and to convalesce and survive them. Equally, I cannot imagine how self-harm in the context of processing such traumatic life experiences isn't 'normal' or understandable, or even part of the transition into recovery. Perhaps rather than self-harm being seen as evidence of 'poor emotional skills', it may indicate that someone is experiencing an intense and complex reaction to a particular period in their life, and that they need to be understood and listened to, that a way needs to be found for their story to be told, so that it can be made sense of and heard.

There is such a hopeless rigidity about viewing people as globally incapacitated emotionally in this way. It discourages us from getting to know someone, and it clips our creativity for forming a relationship and working with them. Behind the scars, the cigarette burns and the bruises, there is a person who feels, who experiences life, who is moved by things that are important to them, and who has a sense of humour and laughs until they can't breathe. But our approach to self-harm encourages us to view people as emotionally disturbed, manipulative and, of course, attention seeking.

Attention: Superficial pain or a cry for help?

The concept of 'attention' is another powerful discourse I have encountered again and again, in both my personal and professional life, and as someone with experience of self-harm, I just don't understand it. Automatically assuming that people harm themselves to gain attention is incredibly thoughtless. 'Attention' by itself as a reward is completely meaningless – it's like saying people go to sleep because they enjoy being horizontal.

I find it staggering that whilst the majority of self-injury takes place in secret, most often in the community, hidden from the rest of society, with only the tip of the proverbial iceberg presenting to health services, this theme of 'attention' still prevails.

In fact, when I was actively self-harming I always felt caught in a bit of a 'Catch-22' situation, because the way society responds to self-harm can create a somewhat impossible scenario, particularly through the language we use to conceptualise self-harm and in the way we respond to it. I was always very careful when I cut myself, as I feared that if I needed medical attention then people would likely discover my self-harm. If they discovered it they might try and make me stop, and if I stopped then I wouldn't be able to function. It was a secret relationship I didn't want anyone to know about, and I didn't want to give it up. However, despite this, on select rare occasions, I did require medical attention, either because a wound wasn't healing properly or the bleeding wouldn't stop. Luckily, I have very few experiences of direct medical care for self-harm, but the ones I have had were so profoundly negative (and beyond the scope of this section) that I am relieved such contact was so rare. I can remember being sat on the edge of an examination table and hearing a doctor speak into her Dictaphone: 'Lacerations are predominantly superficial.' 'Superficial' – I hated that word; it made me squirm inside.

I can recall how trapped I felt. I would think: 'I can't win. It's bad enough I already felt embarrassed and degraded about needing medical attention, but not only have I just experienced something more akin to a veterinary examination, it also feels that if I harm safely in a way that does not put me at risk and which meets my needs then it is "superficial", whereas if I were to harm with greater severity then it would be an "attention tactic" or a "cry for help".'

I'm still not sure which is preferable. I abhorred those labels.

Furthermore, I feel that these responses to self-harm have the potential to create a self-fulfilling prophecy, because (perhaps mirroring these labels) the intervention you receive from healthcare services often depends on the severity of harm inflicted. Healthcare services unwittingly reinforce the idea that if you physically harm yourself more, you receive more input. With incredibly long waiting lists for outpatient services, you can often be waiting a long time to access any support you may need. Verbal accounts of suffering and pain are certainly not responded to as seriously as physical acts that reflect these themes, and are often not listened to or taken seriously at all.

Perhaps then, it is also important to recognise that, by its nature, self-harm does command attention. It can be visually shocking to see self-inflicted wounds upon someone's body. 'Why would someone do that to themselves?', we ask, 'Why do they want us to see?' However, I also think it is important to recognise that if wounds are on display, it still might not be with a view to receiving your attention.

For me, self-injury came into my life at a time where I wasn't able to talk to anyone about things that were happening around me – I was encouraged to hide problems from others and so I also had to hide my feelings about them. At times self-harm was about the only thing that I felt provided stability. I became an expert at concealment, because I was so scared that someone would try to make me stop and then I would have nothing. The idea of someone 'finding me out' was my worst nightmare.

However, it was very important that I could in some way see the impact of my self-harm. That felt almost essential. The blood, the wounds, the scars, to me they were important metaphors of what I was feeling inside and what I wasn't allowed to talk about. They were a personal rebellion against control, against imposed silence and subjugation. For me, anyone else seeing this wasn't important; it was a deep and meaningful relationship with myself. The marks on my body allowed me to give validation to what everyone else ignored. It was my way of saying 'fuck you' to the world. I could tell myself: 'This existential pain is real, this is happening, and it's happening to me.'

Because of this, I often wonder if – for me at least – self-harm was very much about self-care. I would harm safely and secretly, and afterwards I would clean and dress my wounds myself. Eventually the wounds would heal and turn into scars, and I used to fantasise that maybe all the crap I felt inside was leaving my body, and maybe I was developing scar tissue on the inside too, getting stronger somehow.

I once heard a speaker talk about the word 'convalescence' from the Latin 'to grow stronger', in the context of recovery and adjustment in returning to health after illness, and how this was a term that had largely fallen out of use in our language. I certainly think self-harm helped me to convalesce during one of the most difficult periods of my life. Without it, I do not think I would be here today, living a happy fulfilling life for which I am eternally grateful.

Stopping: So much more than a 'coping mechanism'

As I went through this convalescence, there were times when I was encouraged or instructed to stop self-harming. And as my life circumstances gained more stability, I became more motivated to stop. Of course, professionals and other people that cared for me were concerned for my wellbeing, and I'm certain had the best of intentions at heart. However, in my opinion, many people go about this encouragement in a way that represents the cardinal sin of self-harm interventions: assuming you can just 'swap' self-harm for something else, without exploring or understanding it, because it is 'just a coping mechanism'.

For me, self-harm was so hard to stop and went on for so long because it is so multifaceted and personal. Self-harm felt far deeper than just having one function – that of 'regulating feelings' – it is much more complex, which is why it is so difficult to end, and can on some levels feel impossible to replace. The act has meaning. Deep personal meaning. The ultimate insult is to instruct someone to try and 'swap' self-harm for an alternative strategy, without first attempting to gain an enhanced individual understanding of the phenomenology and meaning of the act. How dare you assume, without even having a conversation with me, that you can swap self-harm for a red pen, or an elastic band or squeezing ice cubes, when you know nothing of its importance.

Of course self-harm helped me to deal with overwhelming feelings, and of course the sensation of the act was reinforcing, but it also helped me in so many other ways that were just as influential. It helped me to feel more independent, through feeling more in control of my internal world. It allowed me to feel 'more normal' so I could fit in more, so I could socialise, so I could go to work, so I could take care of my family. It made me feel like all the shit in my life was leaving my body, like I felt cleansed and renewed somehow. The marks on my body gave me validation that all the crap in my life everyone else ignored was actually happening; these wounds were real and tangible and I couldn't pretend they weren't there. Monitoring healing wounds helped me to feel stronger as they faded, and provided evidence that things could get better. Using steri-strips and first aid kits helped me to find a way to be self-compassionate and caring in an environment where I didn't experience this from others. Self-harm contributed to my identity as someone who was self-sufficient and was surviving. Scribbling on my body with a red pen, flicking an elastic band, or holding ice cubes isn't going to replace any of that.

Get to know the person behind the self-harm; help them to make sense of and to be able to tell their story. Get creative – through music, art, literature, whatever is important to them. As Viktor Frankl once wrote in *Man's Search for Meaning*: 'To live is to suffer, to survive is to find meaning in the suffering.' That is how I have been able to live at peace with my own self-harm. I found my meaning; I began to understand why it came into my life and why it was important. Then, and only then, could I begin to find new ways of meeting the needs self-harm had met for so long.

Thoughts

- The presence of self-harm doesn't necessarily indicate that someone is 'emotionally illiterate' or lacks the capacity to understand their internal feelings. Rather, it may reflect the complexity of their lived experience.

- Professionals need to think more inquisitively about the language they use and the discourses that exist for those who self-harm. What does 'attention' really mean? How might it feel to be labelled as a 'superficial cutter' or a 'help seeker'? And how might these labels affect someone's relationship with their self-harm?

- Everyone who self-harms is an individual, so everyone's self-harm has individual meaning. Such 'meanings' need to be established before an intervention is attempted or it is unlikely to be helpful.

- It may not be realistic to 'swap' self-harm for something else. It may be better to take an individual approach than use an 'off-the-shelf' technique that applies assumptions of meaning and function to a person's self-harm.

About the author
Peter Dargan is a clinical psychologist currently based in the UK. He has an interest in happiness, mental health stigma within healthcare, and supporting those who experience health inequalities to have a voice. He enjoys black-and-white films, the jokes of Tommy Cooper, and has a love/hate relationship with football verging on the unhealthy. He hopes that through the personal stories in this book, self-harm can become a concept that is more understandable, relatable, and individual, so that people's experiences of services and support can become more humane, caring and compassionate.

CARING FOR AND WITH PEOPLE

26

Self-harm and suicide: Doubts and dilemmas

Lesley Foster

I think of myself as an expert on self-harm, and in particular, on caring for a family member or friend who self-harms. I've read and researched and considered evidence. I've talked with younger and older friends who self-harm. I've asked carers about their views and their experiences. I know the guidelines and the debates. And yet, when it comes down to it, I still don't feel that, really, I know very much that is directly useful to service users, families or mental health practitioners. There are so many difficulties and contradictions, so many unanswered questions. But at least the questions are being asked and the voices of experts – people who self-harm and those who care about them – are being heard.

My daughter Marianne, with her friend Laura, helped to formulate a considered, well-appreciated approach to self-harm some years ago when they were students in Liverpool. She had felt quite alone as a teenager, when she began to rely on cutting to try to maintain some kind of equilibrium. She kept her self-harm a secret until she was able to come to terms with it herself as a young woman. Then she explained it to me, with gentleness and consideration. So I thought I knew what to do, what to say and what not to say, how to support her and try to avoid making her feel even worse than she already did.

Through the next 10 years or so, Marianne made heroic efforts to deal with her distress. She was diagnosed with depression and anxiety, then OCD (obsessive compulsive disorder), and later on a smorgasbord of other maladies. These included personality disorder (a diagnosis that was later overturned by the personality disorder specialist) and autistic spectrum disorder (in spite of the fact that Marianne met almost none of the diagnostic criteria). Sometimes she made good progress and appreciated the therapy available to her, sporadic and ineffective though much of it was. She wrote poetry and stories, studied, took part in conferences and debates. She was sure that self-harm helped her, indeed that it was her only means of coping and saving her from suicide. She drew strength from her involvement with self-help groups, including a physical peer support group (until funding ceased, with dire consequences) and a number of virtual groups. She was active online whenever she was able, and she both gave and received support on forums that she had researched and that she trusted. She was sensitive to the dangers of acceptance or potential advocacy of self-harm, and she appreciated that self-harm was at best a short-term and unsatisfactory response to overwhelming distress.

But in spite of her knowledge, skill, sensitivity and determination, Marianne had periods of deep despair. There was no clear explanation for this, no particular trauma or childhood event she was prepared to accept as the cause of her near-constant, overwhelming distress – though it is possible of course that there were things she couldn't admit to me, to others, or perhaps even to herself. She tried to take her own life, and she was admitted to an NHS inpatient ward for a stay that was supposed to be short-term. Eventually she spent over two of her final three years confined to hospital because she was judged to be a danger to herself. Expert intensive treatment for OCD helped her to return home and resume her studies; but then a dismissive rejection by local mental health practitioners undermined her recovery. A deep self-inflicted cut damaged a nerve in her hand permanently, and she worried that the self-harm was becoming out of control. In early 2009 she took an overdose of prescribed medication, intending to die. She was found (I found her, calling in earlier than expected), and she came round in hospital, before being re-admitted to a mental health inpatient ward. She overdosed on hidden paracetamol whilst still there six weeks later, and this time she did succeed (if that is the right word); this time, she died.

Marianne had a great deal of insight into self-harm. A few years before she died, she wrote: 'I have spent arguably too much time thinking about self-injury – both generally and personally. I agree with the theory that it is a coping mechanism, comparable to smoking. I accept that it can be linked with issues around control – my body is easier to alter than the world. Personally I do not see my body as an object of hatred separate to my self – it is myself that I want to hurt, and my outer-self is the most accessible.'

She was convinced at that time that self-harm was quite distinct from suicide: 'I do not want to be a self-harmer, but I would rather be that than a suicide victim.'

It may be that being prevented from cutting while an inpatient made Marianne's distress even worse. In practice, in hospital she found ways to hurt herself every day, several times a day, by burning or ligatures or whatever she could manage, in spite of prohibitions and strict control of her possessions. She needed self-harm, to the extent that it seemed to dominate every moment. Honest to a fault in every other way, she lied and schemed to gain access to a razor blade, a knife, a paperclip – anything she could cut with. She craved the release that self-harm brought, sometimes to the exclusion of everything else. The distinction between self-harm and suicide appeared to have broken down by the time she died. She had said that life was too hard. Apparently she just wanted to get away from it, temporarily or permanently.

Marianne's attachment to self-harm seems to me to have been an addiction as powerful as any other; but much of the official advice available to her about dealing with it could be described as superficial or even trivial. Only other people who self-harmed appeared to 'get it'. She was so relieved to find a community of people who understood her need to self-harm. Her sense of belonging and contributing, her very identity, seemed to depend upon it. But did a strong supportive community of committed self-harmers make her dependency stronger, even more damaging? Did the associated imagery, the romance of doom and death, the black humour and knowing irony, help drive her towards her own personal tragedy?

One of Marianne's early poems asks similar questions, though the emphasis is very much on loneliness, rather than community.

How did I get into it?
This world of black and blue hearts
Black and blue bruises
Black and blue life
How did I get into it?
How did it get into me?
How did I get into it?
Sad music late at night
Late at night with razors
Late at night alone, on my own
How did I get into it?
How did it get into me?
Did I think [I could] bear it, control it or beat it?
Did I think I could live again after I died?

In some ways, self-harm prevented Marianne from accessing effective psychiatric treatment. Help was denied to her on a number of occasions because she was too 'high risk'. I also wonder whether the control self-harm gave her, the comfort it evoked and the all-encompassing neurological effect prevented her from benefitting fully from the drugs provided for her, in bulk and variety, by the mental health system. Self-harm promised an escape into delirious nirvana, however difficult that was to achieve in practice. It made dealing with painful emotions comparatively easy to avoid – in the short term.

In hospital, some ward staff appeared to condemn both self-harm and the mutual support of self-harmers. There was an intimation that people who self-harmed wilfully distracted staff from paying attention to patients who were 'genuinely' ill. A few days before she died, two fellow patients were discharged from the ward specifically because they self-harmed, and this certainly didn't help Marianne. I wonder whether a tolerant, enabling approach would have been possible, realistic and more manageable. Over the longer term, I'm convinced that careful, caring, expert therapy could have saved my daughter, and I'm still amazed and appalled that, in spite of her best efforts, and the enormous NHS resources spent on hospital stays and medication, this was not provided. Dreadful blunders were made at times, though at other times kind mental health professionals did their very best to help in very difficult circumstances.

I know that most people who self-harm do recover or simply move on – but also that some don't, and for these people, a new approach is needed. With the right treatment and support, would Marianne eventually have been able to give up hurting herself? Yes, I think so, and I hope so. Much, much more progress needs to be made on understanding recalcitrant self-harm in the context of the complexity of mental health conditions. At present, it seems as if the chances of effective treatment for someone like Marianne within the cash-strapped NHS are almost nil – but the consequences of not addressing the issues are surely unacceptable, on grounds of saving lives and also basic cost-effectiveness. In the end, for Marianne, I think that even the idea of having to give up self-harm became impossible, terrifying, much worse than any alternative up to and including suicide. I have spoken to many people in the last few years who imply that her death was inevitable, but I don't believe that. For women and men in a similar situation in future, and for the people who care about them, there has to be hope – and help.

Thoughts

- There is a need for much better understanding of self-harm and the complexities of the relationship between self-harm and suicide.

- Treatment of people with complex mental health issues, including self-harm and suicide risk, needs to be very much improved across mental health services.

About the author

The author of this piece of writing is the mother of Marianne – a pseudonym – who died by suicide when she was 29, after struggling with years of mental distress, which she tried to alleviate by self-harm. She (the author) is also a health service researcher.

27

From ignorance to understanding

Terri Shaw

As someone who has been in a 'caring' role around self-harm, both in a personal and a professional capacity, I am going to write about the 'journey' I have been on in terms of understanding the issue. I will reflect on the distance I have travelled and the strategies that have helped me shift from being someone who really struggled to know how to support someone who self-harmed, to where I am now: totally committed to bringing about an improvement in the way that self-harm is understood and responded to, and a firm advocate of the harm minimisation approach.

The start of my journey

On a professional level, I used to work as a nurse on a busy medical admissions unit. Self-harm was an issue I dealt with regularly, although I don't remember ever being given any training or help to understand what self-harm was about. As a consequence, it was an issue I found really difficult and I started to believe the general assumptions made by other staff on the unit, for example, the assumption that self-harm is 'attention seeking' and 'manipulative'. These negative and damaging assumptions inevitably impacted on the quality of care I gave to people who self-harmed.

On a personal level, I didn't know about my sister Sarah's self-harm until after her first admission when she was 20 years old. I got a phone call to say that Sarah had taken an overdose and had been admitted to a psychiatric ward; it was only then that I found out that she had been self-harming for a number of years. Despite the initial shock and worry I felt,

I did get some relief from thinking, 'At least Sarah is now in hospital where she will be kept safe and will be given some help.'

How wrong I was! Over the following years, when Sarah was in hospital she not only continued harming herself, but the injuries she was inflicting on herself were far worse than those she had done when at home. I can vividly remember the phone call that told me that Sarah needed surgery because she had cut through the tendons in her arm.

I still had no understanding of what self-harm was about and thought it meant that Sarah was trying to kill herself. Sarah's injuries frightened me and every day I lived in fear of the phone call that would tell me that she was dead. All I wanted was for Sarah to be kept safe and I couldn't understand how the hospital was failing her so badly. 'Safety' didn't seem much to ask – surely it was simply a case of keeping Sarah away from any means of harming herself?

I felt completely powerless in what I could do to help; I didn't know what to do or what to say and I was so scared of saying or doing the wrong thing. No one made any effort to tell me what was going on. I didn't know what was happening and I didn't know what was going to happen. All I knew was that Sarah was suffering and I didn't know how to help her.

I gave up hoping that it could ever get better. No one ever told me that things could get better and I had no reason to think that they would. I couldn't see anything that was being done to help Sarah, or anything that was being done to stop her from harming herself so badly. I'd even tried begging the consultant to 'section' Sarah – I was just so desperate to try and find some way of keeping her safe. Sectioning didn't help either – Sarah continued to self-harm even then.

What helped?

Desperate to understand and to help Sarah, I started to read about self-harm and learned that there are lots of different theories or models that offer explanations as to what self-harm is about. For example, I learned that Sarah might have a problem differentiating between her ego boundaries, or that she might have problems with 'attachment' to others. These theories didn't tell me anything that was of any use in terms of understanding Sarah or knowing how to help her. So, I decided to stop reading and I started to listen to the voices of people who self-harm. I listened to what they said about the reasons why they self-harmed and what they wanted in terms of help or support. It was only then that I started to learn.

For example, throughout Sarah's years of self-injury I had lived with the belief that she was suicidal. This had seemed to be the only possible explanation for why she was cutting herself and taking overdoses. It therefore came as a revelation when I discovered that, on the basis of what people who self-injure say about their own experiences, self-injury actually serves as a coping mechanism. More often than not, self-injury helps to avert suicidal feelings – it is a way to stay alive. I wish that somebody had explained this to me at the time.

However, this realisation still did not explain why Sarah's self-injury had worsened so dramatically whilst she was in the psychiatric environment. So, through conversations I had with Sarah, and through hearing accounts from other people who had spent time in hospital for their self-harm, I started to question the 'preventative' approach to self-injury that had been taken by the hospitals where Sarah was detained. This approach is typical of the dominant practice around self-harm and is aimed at trying to prevent people from self-harming. I had personally witnessed the failure of this approach and I found that I was not alone in this way of thinking. I became aware that there is a growing body of opinion that this emphasis on prevention simply does not work, and that a potential alternative is to support people to self-injure in a safer, more controlled way.

This approach is known as 'harm minimisation' or 'safer self-harm'. At the very core of a harm minimisation approach is the fact that, if someone really wants or needs to self-harm, then they will find a way, regardless of restrictions. It takes time, patience and support to help someone get to a place where they no longer need to self-harm, and a far more realistic way to ensure someone's 'safety' is to empower them to reduce the risk and damage involved in self-harm. For example, providing information about how to reduce the risk of infection or how to apply first aid, and informing the person about the potential consequences of their self-harm.

I spent a long time struggling with self-harm before I came to realise that it could be understood. With the benefit of hindsight, I know that the single most important thing that helped me in coming to this understanding was when I started to listen to the voices of people who self-harm. It was a long, slow, difficult journey, but I got there in the end.

Thoughts

- Self-harm can be understood.

- The voices of people who self-harm are the best source of knowledge.

- Lack of support and information can give rise to damaging misconceptions.

- An excessive focus on prevention can lead to unhelpful responses.

About the author

Terri Shaw, RGN, BSc (Hons), MA, PGCE, Co-director of *harm-ed*. My background is in nursing and whilst practising as a nurse I developed an awareness of the complexities involved in self-harm. However, my real interest and involvement in the issues stemmed from the experiences of my sister (Sarah) who self-harmed over a period of many years. Sarah's experiences prompted me to learn as much as I could about the issue and it didn't take long before I realised that self-harm was something that could be understood. Following on from those experiences, whilst studying for an MA in biography ethics and medical law, I undertook an in-depth research study, which focused primarily on the issue of 'harm minimisation' – an area in which I have a particular interest. Drawing from my experiences of caring for someone who self-harms, I am also very aware of the challenges that can result from trying to offer care and support – particularly from an emotional perspective – and I have spoken and published widely on this particular aspect of self-harm. I am committed to working towards improving understanding and responses to self-harm, which was the primary reason I co-founded *harm-ed*, a self-harm training and consultancy organisation, in 2006.

28

Experiencing self-harm: The observer

Fay Hunkins Walcott

I am a qualified social worker in mental health. I have worked for many years in this field and found that most of my experiences around self-harm involved learning on the job. I found that between 1995 and 2002 the training available in this area was sparse at best and vague. I think we, as professionals, were still trying to work out our understanding of this difficult area and how to best support someone managing such distress. Joining a multidisciplinary team helped, as we could discuss our various learning and theoretical backgrounds. I came across 'professional views' which ranged from direct hostility to the concept of self-harm with ideas of attention seeking and manipulative behaviour (which needed to be stamped out or ignored) through to ideas around illness and the need for hormonal rebalancing to achieve wellbeing.

However, one of my most valuable learning curves came when I encountered the individuals who self-harmed, and whom I had time to support practically and positively. I learned about the real dilemmas related to risk taking and risk management, for me as the practitioner and for the clients themselves. Helping the individuals to see their situation from this standpoint, and to navigate their way through what they felt could be their own personal journey between risk taking and risk management, was a powerful experience for me. I remember meeting a young woman who had experienced a lifetime of very unhappy parenting, struggling to parent her own children and manage self-harm, which was highly visible and thus, sadly, very difficult for many friends, family members and professionals around her to tolerate at that time. I remember her resilience in her parenting style, her commitment to ensuring her children did not see what she needed to do in times of distress, her commitment to working with the agencies (albeit sporadically), her ability to try new methods for managing her thoughts, as well as her current coping strategies. I don't know how she is now, but I am still in awe 10 years on from meeting her.

Experiences such as that of this young woman, helped me in my personal life when self-harm visited our household. One of my daughters found her early teenage years difficult to manage in terms of identity, isolation from peers and physical health difficulties. From a very young age she had always presented as anxious and would bite her hands and pull at her hair when angry. She is a highly intelligent young woman who found it difficult to get others to understand her perspective on matters. Her self-harm progressed on to cutting, high risk-taking behaviour in social situations, and food control. I think having prior experiences of self-harm through my job helped me to cope as a parent, and to develop a level of understanding to help her, both in her risk-taking methods and her risk management skills. We talked and cried a lot – together and in isolation. I think she is moving on now because she had the listening ear, the understanding, but more importantly, the time to get through her thoughts and learn to manage her illness, with others around her to shoulder some of the pain.

My current understanding of self-harm is that many individuals do change their coping techniques naturally with maturity, while others change with knowledge. I may be corrected on that.

I believe that peer support and a significant other actively listening when they can, and also being clear about their own abilities, are essential to the 'recovery' (whatever the person feels that should look like), for these seriously resilient individuals.

Thoughts

- Always seek the individual's own story.

- Always be open and transparent about your own knowledge and understanding.

- Whatever you learn, get it out there. You never know who may benefit from your own experiences.

- There is always hope for a better time ahead. Keep learning how to help others find that path.

About the author

Fay qualified as a mental health social worker in 1995 and practised for 14 years. She has also worked as the Head of the Mental Health Advisory Service to the University of Birmingham. Fay is currently managing her own professional mental health mentoring and training service, training large organisations and approved mental health professionals (AMHPs). She is an active supporter of the anti-stigma 'Time to Change' project. Fay is currently working primarily to support students in higher education with a special interest in international and ERASMUS student support away from home.

Embracing the self, holding the hurt: Self-harm in a survivor led service

Michelle Noad and Helen Butlin

Leeds Survivor Led Crisis Service (LSLCS) was set up as an alternative to statutory services in 1999. We deliver a non-medical approach to working with people who experience acute mental health crisis within a sanctuary environment and provide out-of-hours services to people in acute mental health crisis. We have three main services: Dial House, the Connect Helpline and group work. In contrast to many mainstream services, we use the person-centred therapeutic approach, which rejects psychiatric diagnosis. We prefer to acknowledge the person and their life experiences instead of any mental health label that they might have been given. As a service, we work extensively with self-harm: 47 per cent of our work in Dial House in 2011 was with individuals who had presented to us with issues relating to self-harm. We recognise that the term 'self-harm' can refer to a wide spectrum of behaviours that are harmful to the self or body. The staff here have also experienced their own periods of crisis. Helen's experience has included using self-harm as a way of coping, and her personal experiences will be interwoven throughout this chapter.

Dial House is a warm, colourful, detached house in Leeds. It is non-clinical and has a homely feel to it. The service presents itself as a place of sanctuary for those seeking solace away from difficult life experiences on a self-referral basis. We both work as crisis support workers and bring our own life experiences and who we are as individuals to the support we offer. In our feedback from visitors we often receive comments on how important the relaxing, comfortable space of the house is to their experience. The house itself acts as a barrier to the outside world, a robust sanctuary that holds the distress and offers a place to sit with and explore difficult feelings. Helen's experience of self-harm echoes the importance of the physical for her:

It started when I was small, that feeling – that feeling of floating free from everything real. Being a wisp, a trembling form, that had no place and did not belong. In the darkness, hot terror clawed at my throat, certain my body would evaporate and drift into the universe. I had to pinch hard to keep it here and stop the breath in my body galloping away ... The same feeling would return later. I was in the universe against its will and this intrusive physical matter that held me here needed to be destroyed, annihilated, sliced up into pieces to let the black thoughts ooze out. If the shell was shattered, the soft space inside that could not yet make a sound felt soothed. I quivered in the space between, desperate to be held.

Self-injury is defined by LSLCS' policy as: 'harm that is inflicted on the body with immediate effect', for instance, cutting, burning, inserting objects into the body, punching walls or overdosing. As a service, we respect self-harm as a coping mechanism, which acts as a creative way of surviving difficult life experiences and a means of communicating high levels of distress, to the self and others. The philosophy of the person-centred approach is based upon the 'self-actualising tendency' or the 'innate capacity in all human beings to move towards the fulfilment of their potential'. With this is mind, we practise in a way that gives each individual the respect and space to find and utilise their own resources. If part of that is self-harm, we do not judge this as 'destructive' or 'manipulative', but understand it as being a necessary act, which the person uses to survive. Furthermore, we will not encourage or try to force people to stop self-injuring if they are clear that it is a coping mechanism and they wish to continue doing it. We will provide a safe space for the individual, with a support worker by their side, to explore the distress that has led to them using self-harm as a way of coping. Helen describes the difficulty of expressing feelings that led to self-harm:

Another night and the silent dark surrounds me, suffocating in its cold indifference to what I'm feeling. I wish I could turn myself inside out. I wish I could explode into 1,000 searing white, painful stars. I wish I could curl up and fold myself into nothing. I wish I could burst all over this room. I wish I could disappear into the coldest reaches of space. But none of these things are possible. And none of them are feelings that could be put into words. Words that would make sense to anyone, not even myself. So I am gagged and bound to the feelings that overwhelm me, like an ocean. But the imagined towering waves, breaking over this tiny ship, are not here in this room. Here there is stillness and numbness and a silence and a nothingness that just does not feel right. And I would do anything to escape it. Anything to set free the boiling, angry ocean and give the space within somewhere – something – to feel.

Prior to Michelle's academic and professional life, she had limited experience or knowledge of self-injury, although she had a friend who self-injured:

In hindsight, I am embarrassed to say that I avoided the subject through fear and misunderstanding, as I couldn't understand why someone would want to deliberately inflict pain on themselves. However, during my studies and through working at LSLCS I came to understand self-injury as a way of coping; much of the work that I do is with young women who self-injure and do so in order to cope with unbearable and traumatic past and present life experiences. The defining moment was as a volunteer early on, speaking to a caller about their self-injury. I started to really accept that it is an individual choice and how we cope with what life throws at us. It's not weird or manipulative or strange to make scars on the outside of yourself rather than on the inside through using alcohol or drugs to cope with difficult feelings. Through reflecting on my own feelings of fear and misunderstanding, and looking at where they had come from and how they were influenced by social norms, I was able to come to a place of acceptance and offer unconditional positive regard to the people I support.

I have learnt from the visitors to Dial House that self-injury often helps to regulate and control difficult emotions or distressing memories. In particular, many of the young women that I work with have had horrific lives; quite often they have been sexually abused and it infuriates me that instead of being supported by the mental health system they are told that their personalities are fundamentally flawed and are diagnosed with borderline personality disorder. This is a diagnosis that has been criticised for applying particularly to females (Proctor, 2007). In 2011, the most usual gender/age profile for a Dial House visitor was a woman aged 35–44, although women under 25 made the highest number of visits. Additionally, where diagnosis was disclosed, this was personality disorder in 32 per cent of cases. This information has been collected purely for monitoring and evaluation purposes to provide to our funders, but demonstrates that young women who self-injure are on the margins of the mental health system.

LSLCS manages risk in relation to self-injury in an alternative way to the medical model. We often hear reports that mainstream dominant services are essentially aimed at preventing and stopping self-injury. However, self-injury is much more prevalent in mental health settings where people are disempowered due to lack of control. For instance, self-injury increases when people are inpatients in psychiatric units. At LSLCS people can safely, responsibly and discretely self-injure on our premises if they choose to do so. This is because we aim to provide an empowering service and, in keeping with the person-centred approach, we try to give people as much freedom, choice and control as possible in terms of managing their own risk. This seems logical, as many of the people who use our services have had very little experience of feeling in control in their lives.

Experience of working with those who self-injure has taught us that these are often people who are experienced in looking after themselves and their wounds. They do not necessarily want to end their lives; on the contrary, self-injury quite often helps them to stay alive. We have learnt the importance of boundaries whilst working with someone who self-injures. For instance, we would not be present whilst an individual injured themselves at Dial House, as this is a private act, nor would we assist with dressing any wounds, as this is the responsibility of the person. Instead, we would offer emotional support and unconditional positive regard in recognition that self-injury is a chosen coping mechanism for this particular person. However, in practice people actually rarely feel the need to self-injure at Dial House. We believe the reason for this is because we respect and accept self-injury as a coping mechanism and we are able to openly discuss it in a warm and welcoming environment.

Michelle reflects on her experience as a crisis support worker in Dial House and the support she needs in order to provide this safe and welcoming space for the visitors she supports:

Self-injury is a subject that is present in all of the work that I do and which is sometimes described to me in distressing and graphic detail. As a worker, it is extremely disturbing to hear such material, but when someone is incredibly distressed I think it is important that this distress is heard and acknowledged, regardless of how it is communicated.

As a team we are hugely supportive of one another and I feel completely supported by my colleagues when working with self-injury. For instance, I am able to debrief thoroughly with a colleague after a difficult support session or telephone call; this provides an immediate space for me to reflect upon and process any difficult thoughts or feelings. I also receive high-quality supervision. A defining aspect of the person-centred approach is the actualising tendency, and LSLCS believes in nurturing, developing and challenging its staff to help facilitate this process within themselves and support it in others. Supervision is part of this process and is provided by my line manager.

We also meet as a team once a month for reflective practice. This is a group process facilitated by the senior support staff where we are supported to reflect on our practice, and it is also a space in which risk can be 'held' and explored. Setting and maintaining appropriate boundaries in our practice helps with this process.

Helen recently facilitated a peer-led support group for women who used self-harm as a way of coping, and wanted to explore their feelings around it. Many of the women who attended had not previously found a safe space where they could discuss their experiences and feelings around self-harm without fear of judgement. We received feedback from group members that a self-directed, non-judgemental space was extremely helpful in allowing the women to identify and express their feelings around self-harm – positive or negative. They felt heard and held by the group, and less alone with their experiences and overwhelming feelings as a result. Helen's own experience of coming to terms with the distress that led to self-harm involved finding a space and a voice for those feelings:

In my own experience of moving away from self-harm as a way of coping, a space to explore the wordless wounds within gave me a new way of communicating, to myself and others. Exploring the feelings that overwhelmed me in a visual way, using imagery and metaphor, helped me feel that I had a language to communicate how I felt. This in turn made the feelings less intense. I remember very clearly a night where the panic I usually felt like a choking tide rising towards my throat was instead a huge lake of sadness. Instead of thrashing around in the dark, creeping shallows I was swimming in the calm of a deep, deep feeling. I felt in control of how far I swam and sensed that it was deep and wide but no longer infinite.

Thoughts

- Kindness, compassion and respect need to be more than just words – offer them to others as well as yourself.

- Don't let self-harm stop you seeing the person.

- Self-harm is very complex and individual – it means different things and has different functions for different people. Time and a safe space are vital for each person to unravel these complexities for themselves. A non-judgemental, calm, kind presence during this process can make it easier.

About the authors

Helen Butlin: I have volunteered and then worked for Leeds Survivor Led Crisis Service since 2007, and I am passionate about being part of a person-centred service with warmth, compassion and respect at its core. I studied English and American literature and philosophy and I love stories, green hills, loud music, sea breezes, train journeys, good conversation and puffins.

Michelle Noad: I started volunteering on the Connect helpline in September 2009 during my final year of studying BSc (Hons) Counselling and Therapeutic Studies. I have since gained employment at LSLCS as the Administrator and also as a Crisis Support Worker. Additionally, I co-facilitate a group for people who hear voices. I am passionate about challenging the stigma and shame associated with mental 'illness', and I am proud to work for a person-centred service that works 'alongside' people. I have many wonderful friends and family members whom I spend my free time with. I also enjoy R n'B music and the occasional brandy!

Reference

Proctor, G (2007) Disordered boundaries? A critique of 'borderline personality disorder'. In H Spandler & S Warner (Eds) *Beyond Fear and Control: Working with young people who self harm*. Ross-on-Wye: PCCS Books, pp. 105–20.

Self-injured therapists encountering self-harm

Gary Winship

Held in mind

I have always found Winnicott's (1960) idea of 'holding in mind' indispensable. In another of my favourite papers, McGregor Hepburn (1992) likewise describes the challenge in talking therapy of having to mentally hold on to the feelings that the client brings to therapy, that is, the therapist churns things over in their mind before presenting thoughts back to the client. We call it food for thought, and it's the art of therapy where the therapist finds a way of crafting meaningful words in a manner that the client can digest, allowing the client to experience some sense of being understood, and held in mind. The template for this emotional exchange, where one person holds on to the feelings that the other cannot manage, is the early exchange whereby Mother and Father do their best to try and make sense of the experience of the new baby. The task of parenting a small child, especially for Mother initially, is one of attempting to make the best sense of the riddle of baby's communications. An infant's communications can be muddled, ranging from gurgles and cries, or frantic scratching and tearing at themselves and others, to coos and inchoate language. Mother tries to find words and actions that make an appropriate response, which intentionally settles, stimulates or soothes, depending on the circumstances.

So it is often thus, when working with acutely disturbed clients whose communications are muddled, where anxieties, frustrations and distress are presented, that the practitioner needs to perform a similar act of thinking about the meaning behind confused communications. I have elsewhere described how mental health nurses more than any other psychiatric professional, by dint of their sustained and intimate contact with acutely disturbed clients, have to manage a good deal of holding the client in mind (Winship, 1995b). Sometimes this holding in mind can be accompanied by a procedure of physical holding – the occasions when physically holding a client to protect them from harm or from causing harm becomes an absolute human obligation (Winship, 1998). For mental health nurses working at the front line, there is a great deal of thought given to the professional obligation to hold, but there are controversies about how best to do it and legal precedents to observe. Physical restraint is often seen as a management regimen, sometimes as a protective procedure, but too rarely as therapeutic intervention (Winship, 2006).

However, the challenge, even where danger and harm are imminent, is to find a method that brings about a situation whereby the need for physical holding is superseded by mental holding. Most commonly, a client will be less likely to need holding if they are able to put into words and express what they are feeling and otherwise liable to act out. Put another way, this is words speaking louder than action: if a client can put into words that they feel like cutting themselves, then the words can replace the action. Jane Bunclark and Sally Hardy experimented with this idea on their inpatient ward. For several months, Jane and Sally's ward suffered what seemed to be a contagion of cutting and self-harm. In supervision, I suggested that the nursing staff try to predict when they felt that the patients were about to cut themselves, and then deliver this hunch to the patient. The outcome was highly effective in terms of a significant diminution of self-harming activity on the ward.

It is here that Winnicott's (1960) idea about 'holding in mind' starts to be useful. In my experience, especially with clients who have felt compelled to self-harm, the possibility that actions can be replaced by expression is made more likely when the client has a sense of being held in mind by their therapist. But what do I mean by 'held in mind'? It is not an insoluble idea, but it is difficult to describe exactly. I think of it in terms of having the capacity to be present with someone who is hurting, not shirking away from the client's mental distress, being able to think about the client in a concentrated manner and being curious even when the client seems to have lost the will to be interested in themselves. To hold a client in mind is about being resilient, even in the face of the client's hatred and attempts to push you away, to be sure enough of yourself that you can receive transference communications without getting too mixed up and losing track of who you really are. I would probably add that the capacity to be able to hold a client in mind is optimal if the therapist has had enough personal therapy to ensure that they are not helping the client because they are, in some measure, doing it to make themselves feel better – that they are not using the client to exercise their own desire to be needed. Bion (1970) has described this therapist disposition as being 'without desire'. In other words, the therapist is there for the client, and not themselves.

Perhaps I can best describe what I mean by holding a client in mind, by telling you about my work with a client where I failed to hold the patient in mind. It might seem a bit strange to try to explain something by describing the absence of the thing itself, but let's see. My client was in his late twenties. He presented as someone whose appearance would make most people curious, insofar as he was covered in tattoos and a large number of body piercings. His piercings ran around his eyebrows, several through his nose and lips, and all around his ears. He also had his nipples and naval pierced, so he informed me, which were permanently adorned with rings. Lately, it seemed, his tattooing and piercing has become almost an obsession, and by the time I saw him perhaps one-third of his body had been tattooed. He told me that he particularly enjoyed the sensation of pain, both for the tattooing and the piercings. He had been referred for psychotherapy because his general practitioner had become increasingly concerned about the client's low mood and an increase in thoughts of suicide. Pharmaceutical intervention had not corrected the client's mood, and his own attempts at self-medication with mind-altering substances didn't seem to work anymore – indeed drugs appeared to compound his misery. I learned that he'd experienced low moods since his adolescence, and even before his interest in tattoos and piercings, he had been prone to damaging his own skin with homemade tattoos and occasional self-cutting. There appeared to be some continuity between his earlier damage to his skin and his urge towards tattoos and piercings.

All of this background information taken together might have been less remarkable because, on the surface of his life at least, all seemed well enough: he had done okay at school, and he appeared to have a small circle of friends and a reasonably stable home life. He had lately moved back home with his parents, but that in itself was not so unusual in a day and age where living away from home was financially difficult for many young adults. He had enjoyed some success as a DJ playing rave music at festivals, and at first I found myself being curious as to what had gone out of kilter for him. However, after an initial flurry of clinical curiosity and the client going some way to detailing his history, our weekly sessions started to feel heavy and slow. By session six it started to feel like we were pushing a tractor around a treacle field. He would come into the room and sit quietly, seemingly waiting for me to speak. He didn't appear reticent to speak, but it seemed words were not something he found spontaneous or easy. He seemed anxious, so I was patient. I asked questions about his interests, found out a bit about his tattoos and piercings, enquired about his family and so on. Each time he would respond minimally, his elaboration frugal, and then he would drift off into silence. There would be little or no eye contact. I would sit and wait, meditating perhaps about what he had said, looking for clues and so on. I would break the silence and ask him what was happening for him, what he was feeling in the silence, what was going on in his mind, etc. His responses would be the same: 'I don't know what to say', or 'My mind is blank', or 'I don't know what I think'. My sense was that he wasn't being obstructive, rather there was a concerning deadness about him. I understood at least why the GP was worried.

After about three months, I noticed that the silences in the sessions were prolonged. In part I was struggling to find new ways of encouraging him to talk, but on the other hand, I wondered if the silent contemplative hour was, in some way, helping him. He was no longer saying he couldn't see the point of living, so I rationalised that there was some value in this silent contemplative treatment and I was prepared to let it go. And so we carried on like this for a while. I can't say exactly at what point I started to feel sleepy in the sessions, but I became aware that I had started to drift off in the silences. The silences might have been relaxed, or at least that was how I had figured it (some sort of overlapping therapeutic meditation) but the reality was that my mind had begun to wander. Our sessions were always on Tuesdays between 1.30 and 2.30pm, and being straight after my lunch break, I began to wonder if my sleepiness was some post-lunch digestive fugue. As our conversational exchanges lulled further into soporific reveries, and some several months down the line, I was struggling hard to remain alert and on task in sessions. This experience came into sharp distinction when one day I got halfway through a sentence and entirely lost track of the point I was trying to make. I felt rather uncannily that I had fallen asleep while I was speaking, or that I had been speaking while somehow half-asleep.

If being a sleep-talking therapist wasn't enough to concern me, at the end of another session around this time I recall standing up and being aware of a very sharp pain or cramp in my foot. Although I didn't think too much about it at the time, over the following weeks I noticed that I had taken to bending my toes very tightly inside my shoes. I also noticed that there was a trail of other activities that I might have adopted, such as bending my fingers back, pinching and scratching my skin, twisting and squeezing my ear lobes, all serving the purpose of making me feel suddenly awake. These activities all served to sharpen my alertness, awakening me in the sessions so that I could think about my client. I suspected that these activities had been going on for a while without me realising it.

Now, at this point you might well be forgiven for wondering which of us was the self-harming client in the piece? It occurred to me. In my defence, I noted that prior to the sessions I was perky enough, and then after my client had departed I would feel sprightly again. But during the sessions there could be no doubt that I had lost the plot. For the purpose of my vignette here, it is fair to say that this is an illustration of how not to hold your client in mind. Instead I was half-awake and preoccupied with my own personal challenge of being present. At best, I was only fifty per cent up to the job, for which I was being paid no small amount of recompense. I was in a state where my professional integrity was sorely left wanting.

Before I damn myself entirely, and you run off an email of complaint to the professional bodies that register my practice, you might wonder if there is anything that I was able to rescue from this wreckage? It didn't come to me quite in a flash, but there were sequential moments of realisation as I figured out what it was that I might understand about my client through my own demise. I have on occasions presented this case to my students, and while collecting myself to overcome the chagrin of my ineptitude, I have asked what they make of it all. And so I invite you to do likewise – to take a paragraph pause to ponder the same.

It occurred to me that my actions in inflicting my toe bending, skin pinching, ear-lobe-twisting pain, were to some extent mirrors to my client's propensity to use his piercings and his tattoos to make himself feel alive. Perhaps in the same way that I was experiencing a painful awakening in my mind to the presence of my client, so I was getting some sense of what it was that made him tick. In psychoanalytic terms, we call this process 'projective identification', whereby one person somehow manages to communicate their feelings to another person. While one can never rule out the possibility that the feelings evoked in the therapist simply belong to the therapist, in this case there was enough of a residue of competency on my part to be confident that to some extent my reactions in the session were something of my empathy with my client. And I gathered that his mind wasn't necessarily a pleasant place to be. I was able to glimpse some of the deadness that he brought to therapy, his leaning towards not feeling alive, that seemed manifest in a deep lack of attachment. I started to explore this dislocation between us, and I had a particular regard for his connection to his mother who I began to sense as a figure long dead in the water. I began to see his external decoration, with its colourful expressiveness, as cover for an inside that felt more dulled and vacant. My colleagues Shelley MacDonald and Lynn Johnston (who has done a dissertation on the topic) have explored this type of phenomenon in more detail, and have found other examples where we might advance the hypothesis of 'tattoo as body armour'. While this theory cannot be generalised – not all tattoos are a symptom of a self-harming mind – in my client's case, his tattoos and piercings were attempts to correct something on his body that was faulty in his mind. His mind was too isolated, poorly attached, and so in therapy my mind struggled to meet with his. In the end my capacity to hold him in mind, albeit falteringly, was hard won.

Stuck in mind

Having said something about the difficulty I had in holding my client in mind, I want to say something now about the other end of the spectrum, where psychiatric professionals can sometimes get so involved that they can't stop thinking about their client. Over the years, especially in the course of offering clinical supervision to mental health practitioners across a range of NHS settings, from acute units, to day hospitals and outpatient psychotherapy services, to high secure environments, I've been struck by how common it is for colleagues to report dreaming about their patients. And this would seem especially to be the case with patients who have self-harmed. You might say the work can get under your skin. This phenomenon is perhaps most pronounced among mental health nursing colleagues, who might find themselves still ruminating about a patient long after the shift has finished. There was one striking example of this from a supervision group some years ago, when a member of the group said she had dreamt that she had cut off the head of her patient. She said she was embarrassed to speak of it, but she was surprised because in her dream she felt no emotion. She said she felt guilty, but colleagues helpfully shared how difficult they too had found working with the same patient who was repeatedly self-lacerating and had even tried to set fire to herself. There had also been violent incidents where the patient had hit staff, and recently she had needed physical restraint. One of the nurses said that the patient 'surrounded herself with barbed wire', another member agreed and said he was frightened to make eye contact with her. One of the group remarked that a colleague had been brave holding the patient's head during the restraint because the patient was likely to bite. I said I thought that not only was it distressing to hold this patient physically, but also to hold this patient in mind. The dream of cutting the patient's head off, at least it seemed to me, might express something of not wanting to think about the pain of the work that belonged to the patient.

The phenomenon of practitioners dreaming about their self-harming clients – and I too count myself in this number – would seem to be an example of the way in which working with disturbed minds and damaged bodies can get inside you. My colleague Richard Wittington has done a lot of research looking at the way in which violent patients impact on staff. For two years or so, Richard and I worked together on the same psychiatric intensive care unit (PICU) at the Maudsley Hospital in London and we did indeed have to deal with a lot of violent 'acting out'. Richard's research looked at the management of violence as well as its impact on the staff, and from this research he developed a programme of doctoral study (Whittington & Wykes, 1994). There can be no doubting the usefulness of Richard's research, but I always felt that he had overlooked that impact of witnessing self-harm as a form of encountering violence. To some extent, being hit might be more easily processed because it is felt – pain is tangible and bruising visible. But what happens when a patient self-harms? The impact on the practitioner cannot be seen – there is no bruising – though might the self-harm still be experienced as an attack? I will try to illustrate this with a case account.

One of my patients on the PICU, for whom I was the key worker, made three serious suicide attempts: self-choking, cutting her wrists, and self-immolation. On each occasion I was on duty. At the time I was working with Murray Jackson, a psychiatrist and psychoanalyst who was seeing the patient for up to twice-weekly psychotherapy sessions. He said that he thought that it was no accident that on each occasion that I was on duty, there was a serious self-injury. He thought it possible that the patient was turning the rage she felt towards me, and whoever it was that I was in the transference (I had a beard like her husband!), back in on herself. He wrote about this in detail in a paper (Jackson, 1993, p.115). It made sense to me, and it was certainly the case that I experienced my patient's suicide attempts as an attack. On one occasion there was an investigation into the fire which led to my care plan being scrutinised externally to see if I had missed anything. The idea of rage turned back in on the self made sense to me. I have seen any number of patients emerge from a deep depression where self-injurious attacks are replaced by an outward turning of violence. Indeed, sometimes a violent outburst, where rage is vented away from the self, might be considered as some measure of progress.

In order to make sense of this experience of being attacked by an act of self-harm, I likened the mental activity as something I called 'unconscious bruising' (Winship, 1995b). That is to say, whereas in a physical attack the experience can be visualised, in response to an encounter with self-harm there may be a psychic equivalent. The idea of linking this bruising to an unconscious process was derived from the way in which the experience of the attack may become imprinted in dream work. Richard Wittington found that staff retained a painful memory of a violent incident long after the physical damage of the attack had been repaired, and years later a memory of an attack could still arouse distress (Whittington & Wykes, 1994). In some ways, the external bruises of an attack may heal much quicker than the internal bruises.

Thoughts

- Therapist self-maintenance and self-awareness are a necessary and core contingent when encountering clients who self-harm.

- There are subtle and sometimes unruly unconscious dynamics that may be transferred between client and therapist.

- Therapist wellbeing is an ongoing challenge and supervision is a helpful arena for tracking the psychodynamics of exchange.

About the author
Gary Winship is a United Kingdom Council for Psychotherapy (UKCP) psychoanalytic psychotherapist and registered mental health nurse (MHN). He has formerly worked as a lecturer at the Universities of Sheffield and Reading, and as Senior Adult Psychotherapist at Berkshire NHS Trust, Broadmoor Hospital and Maudsley Hospital. He has also been a visiting lecturer at University College London, University of Greenwich, University of East London and Goldsmiths. Winship's previous grants include Economic and Social Research Council funding, examining issues concerned with children and young people, such as arson, drugs, trauma and suicide.

Winship has worked in the field of substance misuse since 1980 when he began working on the inpatient drug unit at the Bethlem and Maudsley Hospital. In 1988 he took charge of one of the inpatient treatment wards where he developed an innovative therapeutic community ethos with an emphasis on democratic therapy. He later also worked in the outpatient service and co-authored the service protocols for the first dedicated methadone clinic in the UK based at the Maudsley. He has since been a supporter and advocate for East-West Detox, a UK charity which has worked closely with the famous addictions treatment offered at Thamkrabok Monastery in Thailand. Winship has published many papers and he is currently completing a book which will look at group and community-based treatments that are effective in harnessing recovery. He was described in an article in *The Times* (2009) as one of the two leading experts in arson in the UK. His website www.winship. info has received over two million hits in the last six years. Winship was formerly Associate Editor of the *Journal of Psychiatric Mental Health Nursing* (JPMHN) and editorial board member of *Perspectives in Psychiatric Care* (2002–2012) and the *International Journal of Therapeutic Communities* (1996–2000). His paper 'Further thoughts on the process of restraint' (2006) was cited by Amnesty International in a guidance document for human rights and was Blackwell's third most downloaded *JPMHN* paper in 2006–7.

References

Bion, WR (1970) *Attention and Interpretation: A scientific approach to insight in psycho-analysis and groups*. London: Maresfield Press.

Jackson, M (1993) Manic depressive psychosis: Psychopathology and individual psychotherapy within a psychodynamic milieu. *Psychoanalytic Psychotherapy,* 7(2), 103–33.

Mcgregor Hepburn, M (1992) Before and beyond projection? A discussion of the therapist's experience of holding the patient in mind. *British Journal of Psychotherapy*, 9(1), 24–32.

Whittington, R & Wykes, T (1994) Reactions to assault. In T Wykes (Ed) *Violence and Health Care Professionals* (pp. 105–26). London: Chapman and Hall.

Winnicott, DW (1960) The theory of the infant-parent relationship. *International Journal of Psycho-Analysis*, 41, 585–95. Reprinted in Winnicott, DW (1965) *The Maturational Processes and the Facilitating Environment*. London: Hogarth.

Winship, G (1995a) Nursing and psychoanalysis – uneasy alliances? *Psychoanalytic Psychotherapy*, 9(3), 289–99.

Winship, G (1995b) The unconscious impact of caring for acutely disturbed patients. *Journal of Psychiatric and Mental Health Nursing*, 2(2), 227–33.

Winship, G (1998) Intensive care psychiatric nursing. *Journal of Psychiatric and Mental Health Nursing*, 5, 361–5.

Winship, G (2006) Further thoughts on the process of restraint. *Journal of Psychiatric and Mental Health Nursing*, 13, 55–60.

31

With a hand on my arm

Emma Lamont

The inspiration behind writing the poem 'A hand on my arm' was around four years ago when I was working as a community mental health nurse. Often people I worked with had experience with self-harm or trauma in their past. These 62 'words of art' come from these people and the conversations we had. Writing the poem was a creative coping strategy for me to express my feelings without judgement. The poem, therefore, is for all the nurses who care (really care) for people every day, and for the everyday people who self-harm. I am glad it's found a home.

With a hand on my arm

Magical thoughts transcend my mind
Miles away from the usual kind
Estranged from myself and pressing down
I release demons and shadows, I've been trying to find
Destiny's time clock hurries me on
There's still time to repair the damage that's done
With a hand on my arm, now bandaged, intact
The demons fade for now, back into the dark

Lessons

- It's okay to talk about self-harm and the feelings behind it.
- People can and do recover.

- It is a myth that people who self-harm are attention seeking; some people I have met do not want anyone to know and go far to cover it up.

- People's views of self-harm are changing for the better. Student mental health nurses today judge less and think more about 'why?' and ask 'What can we do to help?'

About the author

I became a mental health nurse in 1990 when I was 19 years old, and over the years I have worked in both hospital and community settings for NHS Tayside. Nowadays I work as a Lecturer in Mental Health Nursing at the University of Abertay in Dundee, Scotland, teaching nurses of the future how to develop the knowledge and qualities required of a contemporary mental health nurse. A lot has changed since I became a nurse over 20 years ago, however, fundamentally people are still the same and I find life throws at us all many triumphs and tribulations to enjoy and learn from. As a young nurse I was probably quieter than many of my peers and that grew into being thoughtful about how I can make a difference. I understand through my own experiences that working with people who have experienced trauma, or who have high levels of distress, or have lost someone through suicide, can have a big impact on people working in the caring professions. During my nursing career I have become very interested in suicide prevention, working with risk, self-harm and recovery. I have been given the opportunity to study these in detail whilst undertaking a master's degree in mental health advanced practice, which I will complete this year.

32

A mental health nursing perspective on self-harm

Anthony John O'Brien

Introduction

Self-harm is an issue frequently encountered by mental health nurses in a range of practice settings, from primary care through to high care inpatient mental health units. Self-harm indicates a high-level of emotional distress. It can challenge nurses' sense of professional efficacy, and can be an indication of suicidality. The focus of this account is mental health nurses' perspectives on working with people who self-harm. The context for the discussion is my own clinical practice in a metropolitan emergency department in Auckland, New Zealand, where I am one of six mental health nurse specialists who provide a nurse-led service to people who present to the emergency department with self-harm or suicidality. In writing this I am aware that my perspective is filtered through the lens of my own practice context and will not represent the perspectives of nurses in other practice settings. Health service settings are also very different internationally, providing another filter for the views expressed here. Finally, I write as a Pakeha male professional, a position that represents a particular world view, and one that is very different to many of those I see in my clinical work. Although I hope that my personal and professional perspectives do not blind me to the perspectives of others, these interpretive filters must nevertheless be considered in providing this account.

Pakeha is a Maori language term for New Zealanders of European descent (King, 1999).

I begin with an outline of self-harm and suicidality in New Zealand, drawn from official reports. I then provide an account of my own practice setting, and the nurse-led service provided. I present the results of a six-month audit of that service and discuss some of the issues raised by the audit. The final section is a reflective discussion of self-harm, drawing on my own experience. Overall I have emphasised a narrative approach, but I have also attempted to show how such an approach can incorporate the more clinical aspects of assessment, such as risk assessment and diagnosis. I have presented this account as a personal reflection, although readers will notice the influence of narrative, recovery and other theory. I do not make recommendations for practice, preferring in this instance to leave it to readers to take what seems useful from the discussion and decide whether it has any application in their own contexts. I refer to both self-harm and suicidality because those terms refer to a continuum of responses. In my own practice I do not regard self-harm as necessarily implying suicidality. In this position I am influenced by research and theory about self-harm as a means of expressing and regulating distress. I regard the assessment process as critical in exploring the meaning and intent of self-harm. I am also mindful that an individual's previous self-harm may not explain a current episode, so the assessment process is an attempt, for both service user and nurse, to understand and make meaning of a unique event. I regard this meaning-making as carrying great potential for service users' future choices, safety and help seeking, alongside other strategies for support and mental health care.

Suicide and self-harm in New Zealand

Suicide and suicidal behaviours are regarded as major health and social issues in New Zealand (Ministry of Health, 2012). Although rates of suicide have declined since the mid-1990s, there are approximately 500 deaths from suicide each year. By international comparisons suicide rates in New Zealand are high, especially for the indigenous Maori population and for young people (aged 15–24). The rate for females aged 15–24 is the second highest among the states of the Organisation for Economic Co-operation and Development. Rates for Maori have been variable in recent years, but consistently higher than rates for non-Maori, as rates for non-Maori have decreased. In 2010 the Maori youth rate of suicide was 2.5 times the rate for non-Maori youth. There are also significant gender, rural/urban and socio-economic differences in rates of suicide and self-harm. Rates of suicide and self-harm vary across the country with the Auckland District Health Board region showing low rates of suicide by comparison with other DHBs. Rates of self-harm are difficult to establish as many incidents of self-harm do not come to the attention of healthcare providers or hospitals, and there is no mandatory reporting outside of hospitals. Suicide has been the target of specific prevention strategy (Associate Minister of Health, 2006) and action planning (Ministry of Health, 2008). In recognition of the high rates of Maori suicide, a specific prevention strategy for Maori has been produced (Ihimaera & MacDonald, 2009).

New Zealand mental health services

Mental health care in New Zealand is provided by the primary care sector in the first instance, with statutory providers, the 20 District Health Boards (DHBs) providing services for people with more severe or complex mental health problems. A range of non-governmental organisations provide mainly community care and support services (Ministry of Health, 2013). In addition to the adult mental health services there are a number of specialty services, including forensic, age-related, eating-disorders and addiction services. Mental health services are community based. All the standalone hospitals were closed in the mid-1990s and are now decommissioned or demolished. Service provision is relatively consistent throughout the country, with DHBs providing inpatient facilities and a range of community services including crisis assessment teams, home-based treatment, respite care and case management. All DHBs provide a mental health response to their local emergency departments – in some cases by calling in staff from mobile crisis teams – and in the case of Auckland, an on-site service. In addition to the services provided by DHBs, there is a large non-governmental sector in New Zealand and a number of services provided by voluntary organisations. Under the now-disestablished Mental Health Commission, mental health services were encouraged to develop a recovery focus to services, emphasising responsiveness and engagement (Mental Health Commission, 1998). Services are also expected to show responsiveness to ethnic minorities, especially Maori, in recognition of New Zealand's obligations under the Treaty of Waitangi.

Nurse-led service at Auckland City Hospital

The clinical service for people who present with self-harm to Auckland City Hospital is provided by a team of six nurse specialists, working within a liaison psychiatry service, who provide assessment and care planning either within the adult (16 years and over) emergency department, or on hospital wards for those whose injuries or medical consequences from self-harm require hospital admission. The service is provided seven days a week from 8am to 11pm, with a roster of a psychiatric registrar and crisis nurse providing cover after hours. Support for practice development and professional practice occurs through peer review, multidisciplinary team meetings (which include case reviews), and professional supervision.

The nurse specialists all have extensive clinical experience both in liaison psychiatry and in other areas of the mental health service. While most people seen by the service present with self-harm, we also respond to people who express suicidal thoughts when presenting to the emergency department or after being admitted to the hospital for other reasons. Prior to being referred to the nursing service, patients will be medically reviewed on presentation and treated for any injuries or medical conditions arising from their self-harm. These include lacerations, intoxication, ligature injuries and the effects of any toxicity caused by drug overdose. The nurse specialist will then provide an assessment and will work with the patient on a plan of care on discharge from the department.

The emergency department has a policy that all those presenting with self-harm are seen by the liaison psychiatry service before discharge. Referral is not a formal process. Because the emergency department is working to a government target to discharge, transfer or admit 95 per cent of patients within six hours, the liaison psychiatry service responds quickly, frequently having reviewed previous clinical records, liaised with health professionals and considered discharge options before referral.

Assessment is aimed at seeking engagement, exploring the issues contributing to the self-harm, developing a shared understanding of the event, and identifying priorities for managing identified issues. While the assessment process will cover areas such as screening for depression, risk assessment and assessment of mental state, these are allowed to emerge in conversational style rather than being assessed in a check-box manner. The model of assessment is psychosocial rather than psychiatric, with an emphasis on identifying issues that will promote safety, and on addressing skills in managing distress and crises. Education is provided on issues such as the role of alcohol in contributing to mental health problems and the disinhibiting effect of alcohol in precipitating self-harm is explored. Discharge plans reflect the findings of the assessment and are negotiated with the service user. They can include a range of responses, from support from family and friends with no health service follow-up, to hospital admission if there is sustained suicidality which cannot be contained within a community-based alternative.

A range of service referrals is utilised, including those to community mental health, age-related services, and alcohol and drug services. Use of the compulsory powers of mental health legislation is rare. In some cases assessments are carried out by a nurse working alone, in other cases by two nurses working together. Family and friends are included in the assessment process wherever possible, subject to the usual caveat of the patient's consent and the nurse's assessment of how any relationship conflict might influence the assessment process. The nurse specialists have access to a psychiatric registrar or consultant if they need another opinion prior to making a discharge decision. In practice, the nurse specialists make their own decisions in most cases, and few cases are reviewed with a registrar or consultant. All assessments are fully documented in the mental health service's electronic clinical record. A record of the assessments is also sent to general practitioners so that they are aware of the presentation and any implications for further treatment.

Audit at Auckland City Hospital

In 2010–11 the nurse specialists undertook an audit of the service in order to better understand the nature of the client population, its demographic characteristics, decisions made at discharge and other factors. While we felt we had a good experience-based understanding of our work, the audit was designed to test that understanding, and to establish the prevalence of emerging phenomena such as the use of text messaging to signal intent. In a series of group discussions we designed an audit form which recorded key variables for every presentation over a six-month period. The audit helped us to describe the volume and variability of our work, although it does not describe the clinical processes of assessment and decision making. It also does not tell us about outcomes for the patients seen.

The results of the audit showed that of the 337 patients seen, 75 per cent were assessed by the nurse specialists, including 69 per cent who were seen by the nurse specialists alone. Patients were predominantly single and female, and were living with a spouse, family or others. In terms of ethnicity, the group was representative of the Auckland population. A majority had had previous contact with mental health services. The median age was 28 years. The group was evenly divided between those who were employed or on a benefit, with the remainder being students. A small majority had a prior history of self-harm; however a significant minority did not. Self-poisoning was the most common form of self-harm, and 41 per cent of cases involved alcohol. Planning occurred in only 16 per cent of cases, but in 63 per cent of all cases there had been communication of intent. Text messaging was used to communicate intent in 13 per cent of cases. Patients were referred to a wide range of primary care and mental health or addiction services. Admission to a mental health unit was a rare occurrence. The cohort included significant numbers of people who had not previously self-harmed and who had not previously been seen by mental health services. This finding supports the suicide prevention strategy's focus on preventing new cases of self-harm (Associate Minister of Health, 2006). The use of alcohol is significant, and reflects the problematic role of alcohol in New Zealand society. Hospital admissions were relatively few, with fewer still needing compulsory admission. The limited role of hospital admission in discharge decisions is a reflection of the community focus of New Zealand mental health services (Ministry of Health, 2013) and perhaps that available services are configured to contain risk in a community setting.

Reflection

Self-harm is a potentially fraught area of mental health nursing practice. Services are frequently risk averse, and self-harm can challenge nurses' sense of professional efficacy. In the initial assessment of people presenting to emergency departments with self-harm, a wide range of factors can come into play. As the clinical audit showed, although people presenting with self-harm may conform to broad demographic patterns (for example in terms of age and gender), in other respects they represent a heterogeneous group. This heterogeneity is seen in the proportion of patients presenting for the first time and with no history of self-harm. The undifferentiated nature of such presentations requires that the nurse is able to engage readily, form an effective rapport, and work with the person in reviewing the circumstances of their self-harm.

This process is akin to inviting the person to 'tell their story' – however, I am cautious about the unqualified use of such an approach. For various reasons, including the residual effects of toxicity, sleep deprivation, and the clinical nature of the emergency department environment, patients may have difficulty in fully engaging in the assessment process. Also, patients may find their own narratives painful, distressing and not wholly accessible. In addition to any difficulties patients might have in engaging with the assessment process, nurses might be constrained by the need to meet service and professional imperatives in relation to risk and clinical assessment.

I like to think that the apparently conflicting requirements of narrative methods of assessment and the clinical imperatives identified above can be blended in the practice of the skilful nurse. I can't claim that I always feel I've been able to do that as well as I would like, but it is nevertheless important to have a commitment to a model of practice and to use that model as a basis for reflecting on practice. In an emergency department people are seen cross-sectionally; their primary relationships with health professionals lie outside the walls of the department, with families and friends, community mental health services, counsellors, primary care and other practitioners. Our role, as I see it, is to help the person develop and use their own resources, and to mindfully draw on the resources of others when necessary. Within the framework of recovery we are responsible for promoting hope – not the empty reassurance that all will be well, but the recognition that even in the face of apparently overwhelming difficulties there are steps that can be taken to build a future.

One of the challenging aspects of working with people who have self-harmed is the sheer variation in the range of people who have harmed themselves or contemplated suicide. On consecutive days I have been asked to see a young Pakistani woman, in fear of being forcibly returned to her homeland to face family retribution, and a middle-aged builder with significant alcohol dependence who was jealous of his partner's friendship with her male work colleagues. Both had at least briefly wanted to end their lives. On assessment, neither still wanted to die, but each needed support, information, problem solving and safety planning that was unique to their very different problems. In particular, each needed to feel that the nurse providing their assessment was able to empathise with their emotional state, even if they were unfamiliar with their individual life experiences. It is not always possible to match the age, gender and culture of the patient, and so clinicians must draw on all their life and clinical experience in order to understand the patient's experiential world. Even when individuals come from broadly similar demographic groups, their circumstances will be widely different, and often beyond the range of personal experience of the nurse carrying out the assessment. A narrative, conversational model of assessment certainly helps communication and to explore pertinent issues.

Sometimes as a clinician I have felt that despite my best efforts, the reasons, motives and meanings behind someone's episode of self-harm have escaped me. I might understand the circumstances of the event, and the background issues and stressors the person is experiencing. I may be able to write a mental state assessment that captures the behaviour, thoughts and feelings expressed at the interview. However, the essence of the self-harm may still elude me. At such time, I have to accept that as a clinician I operate within a particular interpretive framework, as much as I might attempt to extend that framework to understand another person's experience. It may be true, as John Donne said, that no man is an island. But it is not always given to us to fully understand each other, and there are times when it may be better, or at least necessary, to accept the limits of our understanding.

I have presented the above discussion as a personal reflection because as a practising mental health nurse, I am aware that as useful as theory is, it is best worn lightly in clinical encounters. Assessment methods, including those that rely on narrative traditions, need to be adapted to both the individual needs of patients, and to the clinical imperatives of service providers. I hope that my account will resonate with nurses in diverse practice settings.

Thoughts

- Each episode of self-harm is a unique event, even for people with long histories of self-harm.

- Very few people are unwilling to discuss self-harm; most people value the opportunity to 'make sense' of self-harm.

- In a conversational interview it is possible to cover risk assessment and mental state assessment.

- Self-harm provides an opportunity to identify successful coping strategies and to learn new coping behaviours.

- Sharing your formulation with the patient helps to normalise the process of assessment and clinical decision making.

About the author

Tony O'Brien is a mental health nurse who works as a lecturer in mental health nursing and a nurse specialist in liaison psychiatry. He is a member of the Centre for Mental Health Research at the University of Auckland. Tony is currently completing a PhD examining use of mental health legislation, especially factors associated with variation. He has published papers on compulsory community treatment, social deprivation and use of legislation, decision-making capacity, and the history of mental health legislation. Another current research project involves use of advance directives in mental health care. Tony's spare-time interests include fiction writing, poetry, writing book reviews and running.

References

Associate Minister of Health (2006) *The New Zealand Suicide Prevention Strategy 2006–2016*. Wellington: Ministry of Health.

Ihimaera, L & MacDonald, P (2009) *Te Whakauruora. Restoration of Health: Māori suicide prevention resource*. Wellington: Ministry of Health.

King, M (1999) *Being Pakeha Now: Reflections and recollections of a white native*. Auckland, NZ: Penguin Books.

Mental Health Commission (1998) *Blueprint for Mental Health Services in New Zealand: How things need to be*. Wellington: Mental Health Commission.

Ministry of Health (2008) *New Zealand Suicide Prevention Action Plan 2008– 2012: The summary for action*. Wellington: Ministry of Health.

Ministry of Health (2012) *Suicide Facts: Deaths and intentional self-harm hospitalisations 2010*. Wellington: Ministry of Health.

Ministry of Health (2013) *Mental Health and Addiction: Service use 2009/10*. Wellington: Ministry of Health.

YOUNG PEOPLE AND SELF-HARM

33

Hope fights the ongoing battle

Anon

Self-harm has been a part of me for a few years now. I had begun to struggle with my emotions and how I felt. Feeling low was becoming a common feeling for me, along with some other emotions (anger, anxiety, confusion). After a while I felt like feeling low was the only way I felt, and that this feeling was permanent. This made me feel that I had no control over how I felt. Self-harm started off for me as something that I could do to give me a sense of power and which enabled me to think that I had control over something. This helped me because, for a while, self-harming enabled me to feel better and more positive. I then felt like I was regaining and remaining in control of my emotions. I knew what I was doing wasn't right, but it gave me the tool to make myself feel happier, so I just tried to ignore the self-harm. After a while, I could no longer just ignore what I was doing and decided to tell someone. This was a big decision for me; one of my worries was what people would think of me, and I was afraid and fearful of how they may react. The person I told (a teacher) gave me some information and advised me to go to my GP. I thought I would be OK though and once again felt happier and in control of what I was doing, so I wasn't worried. However, this feeling didn't last for long and I increased how often I self-harmed.

I went to my GP and they referred me onto a specialist service where I began therapy. In these sessions I started to explore and address why I was still self-harming if it wasn't helping any longer, and I was given lots of information about self-harm. Although I was meeting with professionals (a specialist nurse and a psychiatrist) regularly, my mood and the way I was feeling continued to worsen, and I increased how frequently I was self-harming until it reached its worst level and I was doing it on a daily basis. This made me feel very scared and frightened; I felt very confused and unsure about what was happening. The control I thought I had seemed to be vanishing.

The child and adolescent mental health service (CAMHS) I was attending informed me about a self-harm group they were going to run and I decided to go. The group was really good, mainly because it made me realise that I wasn't alone. I met people who were similar to me, in the way that we were all self-harming. We were all provided with information and could discuss things between us and support each other. I think it was the friendly staff and other young people, and the fact that it wasn't serious all of the time, combined with the fact that it was non-judgemental, that gave the group such a good atmosphere and allowed us to be honest with and support each other. This enabled the group to work really well. We came up with lots of different techniques, from distraction (e.g. listening to music, tidying up, playing an instrument, writing, being with a pet, going on a walk, bubble wrap) and relaxation (e.g. having a bath, watching a film), to just making sure you are around someone. I tried some of these techniques when I had the urge to self-harm. Sometimes they worked, sometimes they didn't. I have found that using a combination of skills is the best approach, and to have a few so that you can vary which one you choose to use. Another set of skills that I learnt and practise now is mindfulness. This is where you focus on exactly what you are doing at the present moment and put everything else to the back of your mind. If anything does come into your head just try and refocus. This helped me as it gave me the opportunity to give my mind a rest and stop thinking. Some exercises that I have found useful and which help me practise mindfulness are: initially drawing something (preferably a simple outline) and just retracing it, looking at the back of your hand, picking out 10 sounds that you can hear, and focusing on your breathing.

When meeting with someone, the thing that helped me was having the opportunity to speak, and knowing that there was someone there when I felt like I really needed something/someone. Therapy has also helped me to recognise that self-harm is a coping strategy – not a healthy one, but still a method of coping, even if it doesn't feel like it. Another step that I've taken towards recovery is telling my parents about what I do. I wasn't sure about doing this at first and didn't really want to, but informing them and making them more aware was something that needed to be done. I felt extremely anxious about it and was paranoid that they would hate me, but they reacted really well and have been quite supportive; as time goes on, I think I will see it as more of a positive thing. Knowing more about self-harm will also help my recovery I think, as it will help you to understand and make more sense of what is happening.

When thinking about and trying to stop self-harming, I've found in my experience that you really have to want and be committed to stopping. Currently I don't feel that I am ready to stop, but I know that when I do choose to stop in the future, I have a wide range of skills and coping strategies to use to try and help myself.

If you haven't been able to relate or take anything from this, please try and take something from the thoughts that follow, especially the last point, if nothing else. Give most things a try – something may surprise you, like it did me. You are not alone. Don't give up hope.

Thoughts

One of the things that could have been better about the way I was treated is that the first person I told instructed me to stop. In my opinion, if you choose to stop, it must be your decision and only your decision – you must stop because you want to, not just because you are being told to. Linking to this point, if you tell someone and don't get a reaction you think is fair, tell someone else. I did and this led to me receiving much better treatment which will enable me to have a better recovery. However, what I have found good in my experience are the friendly, approachable people from CAMHS who listen and are there when I need someone. The group that I attended was particularly good as it made me feel less isolated and made me realise I wasn't alone. Not having people being judgemental of me is another positive part of my experience.

About the author
I am a 17-year-old, white British female and I am currently studying for my A-levels at sixth form. I am interested in science and would like to go to university to pursue this further. In my rare, spare time, I enjoy playing the piano and baking. I have several friends that I have known since school, some of whom I see at college, and we all go out, meet up together and socialise.

34

Mislead society

Chloe

You tell me that I'm selfish.
Then you tell me that I'm bad.
You scream and shout the house down.
Then you tell me that I'm mad.

You have a hard life too.
You struggle a lot you say.
But you don't hurt yourself like me.
Maybe, but then I cope a different way.

I know that you don't like it.
And I aren't saying that I do.
But all I know is I accept it.
And I'd like you to accept it too.

Shouting and screaming will not work.
I need love, not to feel more pain.
Look in my eyes, not at my scars.
I need your help, not your blatant disdain.

Now every time you glance at me,
You don't see me, you just see cuts.
And I know that when you think of me,
You just think, selfish, crazy, nuts.

I'm doing things to help myself.
Using elastic bands and ice.
I use writing, singing and scribbling down.
But your understanding would be nice.

I'm not mad and I'm not selfish
I don't do this to upset you I swear
I don't do it because of anything you did
And to ostracise me is not fair.

Sometimes I just feel empty
Sometimes I need something to bring me back
Sometimes I need to find myself
I need something to put me on track.

I'm not saying this is the best way
There are other ways to cope
But if you could just try to understand it
It might offer me some hope.

Just know I'm not the only one
So when you look down on me
There are thousands of others you look down on too
Its time you opened your eyes to see.

This is one hard habit to kick,
Because of the chemical change inside.
But I want to kick it and come out on top,
It's just that society makes me hide.

I don't talk about it because I'm scared,
You'll pin a million labels onto my head.
But I'm not a label, I'm a human being.
Society has been sorely misled.

Thoughts

I have learnt much from my encounters with self-harm. However, I
see the main lessons more in what I have learnt from others' reactions
to it than anything else. I have learnt that though there are potentially
more effective and safer ways of coping (such as holding ice, pinging
elastic bands around one's wrist, writing, singing and drawing), people
who have little experience with self-harm are usually very misled in
their interpretations of it. For example, I have learnt that shouting is
a reaction that many parents will turn to when they find out, but that

often, this is possibly the worst thing they could do as, in my experience and that of others I know of, what we need is reassurance and love, not hostility. I have learnt that you need not be ashamed of self-harm, and that while I am not saying it is the best way of going about things, I can accept that it is a way, just like any other way of coping, and that this is something that more people need to be educated about. Self-harm is a very taboo subject, making it very difficult to talk about it, and therefore more difficult to eradicate the stigmas that are already associated with it.

About the author

I am 18 years of age, female and have been dealing with self-harm now for six years. The lighter side to me really enjoys reading, writing, drawing/painting (anything that is likely to get me into a very colourful mess is usually what I go for) and singing (which I have had training in for five years now). In many ways I am thankful for my journey through self-harm, mainly because now I have the experience to see where the issues are lying not with self-harm itself but through others reactions to it. Knowing there is a problem is half of the battle to change it, so my experiences give me a better insight and understanding towards changing the stigmas.

35

Doing the small things right: Developing a young person's mental health liaison team

Laurence Baldwin and the Child and Adolescent Mental Health Liaison Team

Before we explain the issues that we worked on and how we changed our service, we should probably explain a bit about our personal motivations to change things and why it is important to us.

Laurence

I've worked in child and adolescent mental health (CAMHS) for a long time, but I have to admit I had always been a bit uncomfortable with self-harm. I'm a bit squeamish, which doesn't help, but I have also struggled over the years to understand why people self-harm, even though I feel I can relate to the distress that often underlies it. When I was asked to be part of the new team I was a bit apprehensive actually, and I think this is how a lot of people feel, even professionals with a lot of training. I'm glad I've been involved though, because through the experiences of being with young people in their acute distress, I feel I can relate better to all the young people that I meet – the ones who do self-harm, and the ones who don't.

Chris

I think what most professionals can sometimes forget is the significance for the young person and their family of the admission to a paediatric ward following self-harm, and the subsequent contact with the clinicians. As clinicians we perhaps have contact with 150 young people per year, and although we try to see their individual stories, I fear that sometimes the magnitude of their experience is lost. For many young people and their families we may be remembered for a number of years: 'That is the nurse who met with me when I was really struggling and helped me sort things.' I think that having the same worker on the ward and for follow-up sessions can help convey to the family and the young person how seriously 'the system' has taken the self-harm episode, as well as having very practical benefits in being able to monitor progress or otherwise.

Melissa

I think that any change that helps encourage the development of consistent therapeutic relationships with young people and their families at a time of crisis can only be a positive thing. Closer working with the ward staff has also highlighted to me what great care and support they provide at what can be a very difficult time for the young people.

Marie

When young people attend hospital following self-harm or attempted suicide, the event can hover over and around them like a huge scary monster. To be able to help them see it in the context of their life and the difficulties they are having, can relieve much of the anxiety and guilt they often feel. Having a professional there who is not afraid to talk about what has happened can help restore feelings of control.

Judy

Young people and their families have taught me that alongside self-harm lies complexity and misunderstanding. Sadly, it is the young person's experiences and meaning-making which is often lost within anxiety, chaos and confusion. As a member of a dedicated team I was fortunate to be granted the space and time to hear and to gain understanding. When we were able to facilitate the communication of the young person's experiences to those who had the willingness to truly hear and to value what they heard, a process ensued that exemplified human nature at its best. I saw people unifying and collaborating, the corollary of which was the young person experiencing communication, responses and relationships differently.

Introduction

In our young people's service (a specialist child and adolescent mental health service, usually known as CAMHS) we had, for a long time, worked to meet our commitment to providing a good service for young people who self-harm, and to meet the standards for best practice set by the NICE guidelines (NICE, 2004, 2011). The guidelines suggest that when someone under the age of 18 is admitted to the local casualty department or emergency department after a non-accidental injury, then they should also be admitted to a children's ward to allow a specially trained person to carry out a proper assessment to see if they need further services, to assess the level of risk they present (mostly to themselves, but sometimes to other people), and to make sure they are safe to go home.

Pressures on the service meant that in the past we had tried to do this in a variety of ways, originally by having a member of staff from each locality team available to go to the hospital if someone was admitted. The virtue of this was that they could pick up any follow-up work that needed to be organised in the local area and provide continuity of care for the young person. In practice, however, this tied up a lot of resources, so for a long while we had instead run a service-wide rota, which meant only one person was on standby to go to the children's ward. Whilst more efficient in terms of use of staff it had a couple of quite serious drawbacks. There was now a need for a handover of care from the person on call to a more locally based worker if any further care was needed, with all the issues of getting to know new people and learning to trust them before any more work could be done. It also led to times when there was more than one person who needed to be seen on the ward, and the person on call ended up being overwhelmed by the need.

Both of these systems also meant that the staff on the children's ward were never sure who they were going to see from CAMHS, and depending on the rota, may have only seen an individual CAMHS worker once every three months, which they found a bit confusing. Despite the fact that as a service we did have a standard assessment format, designed to ensure that every CAMHS worker covered the same essential areas when they saw people, there was some feeling that not everyone did the same thing when they came on the ward. Sadly, a while ago we had an unexpected child death in our area. Although this was not directly related to how we provided these services, the subsequent serious case review identified a need to change the service as part of its recommendations.

The changes we made

As part of a wider process of transformational change within the whole CAMHS service, we took the opportunity to reorganise how we delivered this part of our responsibilities. We changed an existing paediatric liaison team into a team that could focus on delivering a more consistent service to the paediatric ward for those young people who had been admitted for self-harm, and reduced the role that team had previously had in delivering CAMHS for children and young people with significant physical health problems. We kept an element of the previous paediatric liaison team's function by offering a consultation service to the hospital (e.g. to the diabetic clinic where a significant number of young people had poor management of their diabetes which was felt to have a psychological component). In the process of change there were some staff changes, but the net effect was to provide a small but stable group of well-trained and experienced staff who consistently delivered a service. By bringing in the consultant nurse to do two days per week within the team it was also made clear that this was a service which we had prioritised, and that we were making serious efforts to improve how we did things.

Another major change we instituted was that the new CAMH liaison team would offer the initial follow-ups after episodes of self-harm to maintain the continuity where possible. This could only be done on a short-term basis, for up to six sessions, in order to prevent the small team from developing a huge caseload and not being able to perform their primary function of urgently assessing new cases. Within the system that we use in the wider service – Choice and Partnership Approach (York & Kingsbury, 2009) – there is provision for a planned handover for longer-term work if this is necessary.

After a couple of months we also extended the team's remit to include the young people aged 16 and 17 who had previously been seen by the adult mental health liaison team (a consequence of older UK government policy). This increased the numbers of people we were seeing, but gave a better service in liaising with our young people's specialist services, which are set up for this age group.

What changed as a result?

The first and most obvious effect was within staff relationships between the specialist CAMHS staff and the ward staff at the hospital (which is run by a different NHS Trust). Initially there was some resentment about the changes we had made, mostly because some staff felt they had lost a valuable resource from the previous paediatric liaison team. However, the experience of seeing the same faces coming up to the ward to do the self-harm assessments, inevitably meant that individual relationships could form through familiarity in a way that hadn't happened so much when there was a rota and a wide variety of CAMHS staff visiting the ward on a less frequent basis. In human terms, it has meant that we know the key staff and they know us. This eases the to and fro of interactions, and means, for example, that the ward staff are much happier to let us use their photocopier, kettle, or whatever, without resenting it as an imposition.

In particular, the issue of safeguarding vulnerable children was highlighted as a major issue that was likely to keep children and young people on the ward, rather than them being there inappropriately because of a perceived mental health issue. We made a key ally early on in the named nurse for child protection (a senior paediatric nurse, working for the hospital, who was well known and respected by the ward staff). Once her role and ours were seen to be closely allied then it became easier for ward staff to understand why young people, originally admitted because of their self-harm, might have broader needs and be seen as vulnerable and in need of protection. This has reduced the feeling which is sadly sometimes still present, that these are 'our' patients rather than needy children and young people, and reduced the feeling that our primary aim should be to get 'our' patients off the ward. The other child protection bonus was that through the named nurse we increased interagency working. By calling planning meetings for young people when they were on the ward, the other agencies were more able to be involved quickly in the discharge planning and created a more collaborative approach to care planning.

It is harder to be able to explain what difference the changes made to the children and young people involved. We do have some young people who are admitted a number of times, and we could have asked them if they noticed a difference, but fortunately there are only a few of them. Most people will only receive a service once, so they couldn't really comment on any difference. We know, however, that young people prefer continued contact with just one person with whom they can develop some trust, rather than being seen once and passed onto someone new.

The only staff who helped were those that knew self-harm was a positive thing – a way of staying alive ... A mental health liaison nurse or team is vital for A&E – I think the attitudes of the nurses in my local hospital arise from ignorance, fear and being overwhelmed with a situation they would do little about ... A quiet 10 minutes, decent out-of-hours help – not anonymous phone lines but shifts of staff you can get to know.
(Mental Health Foundation, 2006, p. 96)

There is still an element of this transition happening, but the handover can now be more fully planned, and can happen after a fuller assessment of what the young person wants and needs, hopefully leading to a smoother transition.

It is an important principle, and one we have tried to keep in mind at all times, that there is no typical young person who self-harms. McDougall, Armstrong and Trainor (2010) make this point very clearly from their experience in helping, and we agree that the most important thing in helping is to be there to listen, to try and understand, and not to make assumptions or judge.

Don't take our word for it – what the staff said

We conducted an initial evaluation to check that the changes we had made were making a difference. This was a simple survey which allowed the staff we were working with to anonymously respond and feed back their experience of the change.

The ward staff had not noticed, for example, that we tended to get to the ward earlier (usually in the morning, rather than the afternoon, as had been normal when there was a rota), and felt that the referral process was the same, which it was! In practice we had also adopted the practice of our colleagues in the adult mental health liaison team, of being proactive in accessing the Emergency Department records to see who had been admitted overnight and was likely to need attention.

What ward staff had noticed, and felt was 'better' or 'much better', was the continuity of seeing the same CAMHS staff:

Good to have the same members of staff, and makes working better as a team.

It is nice to get to know the team.

We asked specifically about communication between CAMHS staff and ward staff, and this was also felt by ward staff to be better than previously:

Much better, making discharge planning quicker.

And whilst there was still an element of there being a difference between 'our' (CAMHS) patients, and 'their' own patients, there seemed to be a general feeling that the changes were making things better from a staff perspective:

> *The new service enables us to manage the care of CAMHS patients much easier and quicker.*

Don't take our word for it – what the young people said

Despite the difficulty of sensitively approaching the young people who had used the new service, we did decide to try and get basic feedback from a selected sample. About a quarter of the people we wrote to answered, and only one of them felt that she had not been listened to, the others all being happy with how the service had been provided:

> *The worker was nice and listened to me and gave appropriate advice.*

> *I felt listened to and my problems understood.*

We also asked what we could do to improve the service, which only led to one (two-part) suggestion:

> *A specific emergency helpline, or unit for young people in crisis.*

We do not have a local inpatient unit, but can take this to our commissioners as part of our longer-term suggestions that more local services of this sort are needed for our young people. The emergency line suggestion is not one that we could provide locally, but we can make better efforts to publicise the national helplines, for example those run by PAPYRUS (www.papyrus-uk.org/contact) or by Childline (www.childline.org.uk).

We still need to work on some areas to continue to improve the service. One example is that 16- and 17-year-old young people are not admitted to the children's ward, as this would not usually be appropriate, so we are seeing this group often in the medical assessment unit, or on the assessment-unit part of the adult emergency department. This is appropriate for most of the young people, in that we are treating them in a more adult way, but it can also be difficult. We also need to work on publicising better the other sources of help available (such as the out-of-hours helplines), and extend the advice and consultation we are able to offer across other parts of the hospital where young people are admitted to 'adult' areas, such as medical and surgical wards.

Thoughts

We made some structural changes to the way we delivered self-harm follow-up services within our specialist CAMHS. This seems to have achieved the aims of:

- Improving consistency of therapeutic relationships with the young people by being able to follow them up and only hand over when a clearly identified longer piece of work has been identified for the locality team to do.

- Improving relationships with ward staff by having the same group of CAMHS staff on the children's ward regularly for self-harm follow-ups.

- Improved consistency of delivery of the type of assessment and service offered by this core of staff, and better relationships with the Safeguarding Children staff, therefore better outcomes for Child Protection.

About the authors

Laurence Baldwin is the Consultant Nurse for Child and Adolescent Mental Health Services with 25 years' experience in CAMHS and a research interest in a variety of young people's mental health issues.

Chris Kirk is the Clinical Team Leader of the CAMHS Liaison team which deals with self-harm and other mental health issues for young people in the local acute hospital.

Melissa Lynch and Marie Levesley are the CAMHS nurses on the team. They both work for Derbyshire Healthcare NHS Foundation Trust.

Liz Banahan and Judy Tansley are CAMHS nurses who were originally part of the team but are now working elsewhere in our service.

References

McDougall, T, Armstrong, M & Trainor, G (2010) *Helping Children and Young People Who Self-harm: An introduction to self-harming and suicidal behaviours for health professionals*. London: Routledge.

Mental Health Foundation (2006) *Truth Hurts: Report of the National Inquiry into Self-harm Among Young People*. London: Mental Health Foundation.

Available at http://www.mentalhealth.org.uk/publications/truth-hurts-report1/ (retrieved 3 July 2013).

NICE (2004) *CG16: Self-harm: the short-term physical and psychological management of self-harm in primary and secondary care.* London: National Institute for Health and Clinical Excellence.

NICE (2011) *CG133: Self-harm: longer-term management.* London: National Institute for Health and Clinical Excellence.

York, A & Kingsbury, S (2009) *The Choice and Partnership Approach: A guide to CAPA.* Bournemouth: Caric Press.

WOMEN'S SERVICES: THEN AND NOW

36

Taking over the asylum: Abuse, self-harm and survival in a high security mental hospital[1]

Sam Warner

It is Monday 10 December 1990 and I'm late for the annual clinical psychology party, which is happening somewhere in Liverpool city centre. I'm on the women's admission ward in Moss Side high security mental or 'special' hospital (as it is euphemistically called) counting forks and knives and locking them away. Having responsibility for securing sharp objects isn't a usual role for a trainee clinical psychologist, but these are exceptional times. There's a strike going on and the majority of nurses have left the hospital and the patients in it to fend for themselves. This is not necessarily a bad thing.

There are three high security mental hospitals serving England and Wales. These are Ashworth, Broadmoor and Rampton. In 1990 Ashworth, on Merseyside, was in fact two hospitals that were subsequently amalgamated: Moss Side housed (about 80) women patients and Park Lane housed male patients. The majority of nurses at Moss Side and Park Lane at that time were members of the Prison Officers' Association (POA) rather than a nurses' union, such as the Royal College of Nurses (RCN). The POA were in dispute with both hospitals because a discretionary travel allowance was being withdrawn from staff, and as a result the POA had started disruptive industrial action. The tipping point for the strike was when two POA nurses refused to take a patient to a mental health tribunal and were subsequently suspended for disobeying a 'reasonable' instruction. The majority of the workforce at Park Lane and Moss Side walked out – that is

---

1 The events referred to and most of the quotes used in this chapter are taken from contemporaneous records kept by myself and others in the form of diaries, reports and records of personal communications, as well as published data.

about 600 nurses. This left the small number of (mainly RCN) nurses who disagreed with the strike, and other professionals and administrative staff, to work on the wards and to care for the patients.[2] This is where I come in.

In 1990 I am in the second year of my clinical psychology training course. I come from a background of working in women-only community groups around the issue of sexual violence. I volunteered first at my local Rape Crisis Centre and then left to co-run Taboo, which was a support service in Manchester for women and girls who had been sexually abused in childhood. Groups like these were, in fact, much more than support services. They were campaigning, activist and survivor organisations. We didn't want to be a sticking plaster for a shitty world. We wanted to change the world. This is why I wanted to train as a clinical psychologist. I'd had enough of having no money, no power and no status (or very little). My quickest route to gaining all three was to use my BA degree in psychology to gain access to a training course in clinical psychology. So this is what I did.

It was probably inevitable that I would end up on a placement working with women patients in a special hospital. The vast majority of women[3] patients here have endured horrific experiences of sexual and other forms of abuse. These women have been excluded from society when community-based services fail to contain and address their distress. The end of the road for abused women, who are contained and controlled, but not heard and understood, are special hospitals. Women here experience visions, voices and flashbacks associated with abuse, which continue to frighten and torture them years after the original abuse has ceased. They are aggressive and violent, sometimes to others, but much, much more often they hurt themselves.

Almost all of these women turn their hurt, powerlessness, anger, despair and self-loathing inwards and self-harm. At the 1990 rehab Christmas party I look around and I can't see one woman who hasn't been abused and who doesn't self-injure. There is Jo,[4] who has just returned from A&E. 'How's it going?' I ask. 'Well the pen I swallowed is still stuck, which is OK as long as I don't sit down too quickly.' I stand and eat mince pies with Jess, who is struggling to hold her cup because

---

2 See Blom-Cooper et al, 1992, volume 1, pp. 187–9.
3 My focus in this chapter is on women because that is who I worked with in Moss Side/Ashworth hospital in 1990. I fully recognise that men are also sexually abused and that they also suffer when mistreated by services that misunderstand and misrepresent them.
4 All names have been changed and identifying histories meshed and blurred in order to protect anonymity.

her wrists are so damaged and painful from the many paper clips she has pushed into them. And across the room there is Lena, who is painfully thin because she is refusing most food, and who cannot smile because she has burnt her face with cigarettes.

These women have been hurt so much in their lives, and have come to hospital in need of care and compassion, which are not much in evidence in Moss Side Hospital. I'm not exaggerating much when I say walking into Moss Side Hospital is like walking through the gates of hell. On the gates going in (and on the wards and in the corridors) are British National Party stickers that state 'Love the white race: protect its future' and 'Outlaw homosexuality'.[5] These stickers have been put there – openly – by (POA) nurses. When I first went to work at the hospital I pulled the stickers down wherever I found them. In the end I stopped – there were just too many.

Moss Side Hospital is a terrifying place to live and work and it is no wonder that women patients here continue to use extreme methods of self-harm to cope with ongoing powerlessness and abuse. And there is ongoing abuse. There is Cathy, who was repeatedly raped by her father, who still visits her once a week – and the hospital does not intervene. Her father gives over proxy control to a nurse, who takes a 'special interest' in Cathy in exchange for the bottles of whisky Cathy's father buys him. This special interest extends to booting Cathy every so often – so she remembers her place. I saw her once and her face was smashed in and covered in blood. She defended the nurse saying, 'I mean, I've only ever been hit once when I didn't deserve it.' The incident was written up (in her notes) as 'head-banging in seclusion'. There is also Miriam who had her arm broken by another male member of staff; she feels acutely embarrassed that it happened to her. There is Georgie who was sexually assaulted by male patients on the 'gardening party'. She was removed, the men carried on gardening. There is Lena who talks about the male nurse who repeatedly sexually assaulted her a few years ago. There is Violet, the only black patient in the hospital, who faces endless racism. Some of the things said when I was present include: 'Oy, chocolate drop' (by another patient), and 'Alright nig, did you have a good day?', and 'You're alright really, you've got Marilyn Monroe skin underneath there' (both by nurses). And they cannot understand why she tries to scrape her skin off. At 'socials', there are the many women who make a positive choice not to sit and talk with male patients, particularly the sex

---

5 See Blom-Cooper et al, 1992, p. 169, for examples of BNP materials seen in and around the hospitals during 1990.

offenders. This is written up as 'problems with socialising'. And there is the casual use of other degrading and offensive language including, 'slag', 'slut', 'wop', 'mess-pot', 'muppet' and 'low-grade' by staff,[6] and sometimes patients. Any or all of this happens on an average day.

The verbal abuse, aggression and intimidation by some workers is not meted out solely to the patients, but is also directed at other members of staff. One of my fellow clinical psychologists removed an 'Outlaw homosexuality' sticker from a ward the other day and the day after a message was left on the psychology department phone warning, 'He'd better watch himself or he's going to get his face damaged.' Sue Hope, another clinical psychologist, also received offensive and abusive mail during the same period.[7] This included:

> *I regret to inform you that this time you will be getting a fatal stabbing, and will not be so lucky to survive this time you left-wing communist slut.*
> *All the best*
> *NF [National Front]*

And written on a 'stay fit in the office' poster, Sue received the following message:

> *Stay fit in the office – and away from the nurses or I will tear your fucking head off you cock sucking bastard.*

It got a lot worse than that during the strike. But for now let me thank God for the strike. For three glorious weeks the POA bullies are not here. And we – a skeleton staff of POA refuseniks (clinical psychologists, rebel nurses, secretaries and other like-minded mental health and ancillary workers) together with the patients themselves – have taken over the asylum. When the 600-odd POA nurses refused to work they left the wards empty of staff, and the patients, in both Moss Side and Park Lane Hospitals, without means of getting food, medication, freedom from their bedrooms or access to the bathroom. We open up the wards and let the patients out of their bedrooms. We don't want the POA to 'win'. We want to show them that the hospital can function better when they are away than when they are here. So workers and patients are having to help each other: to make sure patients and workers stay safe together. This means, for me, being guided about what to do by the patients. When

---

6 Ibid. p. 230.
7 Ibid. pp. 167–168.

I supervised my first mealtime, Lena reminded me to count the cutlery and put them in the locked drawer. 'You're supposed to lock that now', she said.

It was one giant act of good faith and mutual trust. Last week I was doing a day shift on the high dependency ward. This ward is reserved for some of the most dangerous 'mentally disordered' women in the country: the women the rest of the hospital cannot cope with. During the strike there was no 'high staff-to-patient' ratio. We trusted the patients not to 'go off' (lose control, get violent, hurt themselves) and they trusted us to treat them with respect, as fellow and equal travellers on this weird and wonderful, if unexpected, journey. Georgie and some of the other women on this ward have been baking cakes. This is a massive thing because women on the high dependency ward are not usually allowed in the kitchen where there are knives to cut with, tiles to break and also use as weapons, and fire to burn. They shared their cakes with me (very tasty), and I shared my cigarettes. Smoking cigarettes together is not unusual – you can smoke anywhere in the hospital, and a lot of us do – even in therapy. When I started working at Moss Side Hospital, we began running a women's group in the rehab department. I didn't take my cigarettes with me for the first session, it being 'therapy', I didn't think it was allowed. The patients very kindly shared their cigarettes with me during that first session. I paid them back the next time.

There are a lot of cigarettes smoked in psychiatric hospitals and we relied on our cigarettes during the strike. This was particularly so for the women patients who, as a collective act of defiance, had decided not to 'cut up' or kick off whilst the POA were out. This is huge and hard work, and liberating and terrifying. This means that we have to pull together even more now because self-injury is a daily event for the majority of women here and someone kicks off somewhere most days too. Women might not be facing the same levels of control and punishment during the strike, but the strain of keeping going without the back-up of self-injury is showing. Nevertheless, women are supporting each other in ways I have not seen before. Cathy, who sometimes copes with her ongoing experiences of abuse by winding other patients up so that they kick off (it's then them who get jumped on and hurt and removed to seclusion), is helping calm people down. Six days into the strike and she is sat with Miriam, playing 'snakes and ladders'. Miriam usually gets secluded, albeit briefly, most days. Miriam has learning difficulties and she gets frustrated when people don't understand her. She then screams and shouts, and hurts herself and others by throwing or breaking things; staff have become used to placing her in seclusion to 'calm down'.

Cathy, who doesn't have a lot of patience herself, is using snakes and ladders as a pacifier instead, and I overhear her saying, through gritted teeth, 'No Miriam, one, two, three gets you to that square, which means you go down the snake, not up the ladder.'

Although the POA are not on the wards they are still wandering through the hospital grounds and they are still provoking women. The POA social club is next to the duck pond in the middle of Moss Side Hospital and many of the nursing staff live in staff homes near the main site. In some ways they are more trapped by the hospital than the patients because they work here all their lives, as their fathers did, and their fathers before them. One night during the strike, as the POA leave their club, they bang on the windows of the nearest women's ward, shouting, 'Cut up you fucking bitches!' It feels like a declaration of war. The POA are out to intimidate anyone who stands up to them and the verbal attacks that preceded the strike have transmuted and intensified into physical intimidation and aggression during the strike, the worst of which is directed at 'scab' nurses. Nurses who come in have had their cars damaged with paint thinners and their tyres let down. At least one nurse has skidded off the motorway as a result of this.

I have to admit that we haven't had a totally united front inside the hospital during the strike either. There is still conflict between staff and patients. Jess had a go at me for playing table tennis too long with a social worker last week: 'You're just as bad as the fucking nurses – no time for us.' In fact, no one wanted to talk to me and I felt self-conscious, like a spare part (I'm not used to eight-hour shifts). And there is still conflict between staff and a general negative attitude towards women. A couple of days after the strike began I'm sat in a side room on the admissions ward with six other women (all patients). Mary is fiddling with a television aerial, trying to get a picture. Mary had transferred to Moss Side Hospital the day before the strike began and had brought a TV with her. She can't have the TV in her bedroom here. (There are no plug sockets in women's bedrooms because 'they might stick their fingers in them'. I'm told the men in Park Lane Hospital can have TVs in their bedrooms – this is just one of many inequalities). We're saying, 'Down a bit. Up a bit. Yes that's better; I can see a picture now.' Suddenly, two psychiatrists I don't know walk in and one of them shouts, 'Get away from the TV. What are you doing? Are you trying to break it?' I reply, 'No actually we're trying to tune it in!' The psychiatrists take one look at me, with my nose stud, multiple earrings, shell-suit and curly perm and storm off to the nurses' station. They are checking out what medication I'm on and whether they can give me some more. A nurse explains,

'That's no patient. She's a psychologist.' One of the psychiatrists returns, 'It's Sam isn't it? How's it going? You must be very tired.'

It's the day after the clinical psychology party. I had a few drinks, but I wasn't really in the mood. I'm back at the hospital. A joint statement has been issued by the hospital and POA: the strike is over. I need to be here, to share these last moments of almost freedom with the patients. I'm having a final cigarette with Jo. We are sat away from the ward, on the floor of the bathroom on the high dependency ward (we wouldn't be allowed to do this usually). We are both desperately sad. Jo is also scared about retribution from returning nurses and I feel bad because I know I can't protect her. Neither of us wants to go back to the way it was.

Postscript

I thought there were more than 80 women patients at Moss Side Hospital. Maybe they simply remain a large presence in my heart. I also remember the strike being much shorter than the three weeks recorded in the Ashworth Inquiry (Blom-Cooper, 1992). Maybe that time just went too fast. The strike gave patients and staff a break from business as usual in the most brutal of environments. We showed how real care and respect can go further than control and restraint. My memory is that no woman cut up during that time. I know they did as soon as the POA came back. My memory is also that no woman patient was put in seclusion during the strike. They were afterwards. And what happened to us all? Well, the nurse who beat Cathy was removed from the female wards, after I complained. Cathy returned to prison sometime later. I wrote a report that recommended that Violet was moved to a less abusive, less racist institution – where she subsequently started to flourish. Georgie was sexually assaulted by male patients a few years later on her first attempt to rejoin the garden party. She was again removed. Mary didn't stay long. She went back to the medium secure unit she had come from. Georgie and Jess also subsequently transferred to other, less secure facilities. Miriam and Lena were still in Ashworth when they closed the female estate in late 2003 and were moved, with all of the remaining women patients, to other secure psychiatric hospitals. Jo never left Ashworth. She died there.

Thoughts

- Service users need safe services.
- Service users do better when respected and when we aim for collaboration.
- Too much control and constraint undermines progress.
- Self-harm is meaningful.
- It is more helpful to understand the journeys that lead people to self-harm than to organise them into diagnostic categories.
- We need to stop name-calling – psychiatric labels are too often negative, reductive and divisive.
- We need to build mental health services around need not diagnosis.
- In the most desperate situations, people find ways to survive.

About the author

I still work with women who have been sexually abused and who self-harm. I still don't want to be a sticking plaster for a shitty world and I still want to change things. Psychiatric care in the UK may not be as abusive or brutal as it was in 1990, but women still get mistreated and misunderstood, and too many women like Jo still die because of institutional failure, abuse and neglect. It is still necessary, therefore, to come together, to make common cause, to tell our stories and to fight for more hopeful relationships, kinder mental health services, and safer, more equal worlds.

Reference

Blom-Cooper, Sir L, Brown, M, Dolan, R & Murphy, E (1992) *Report of the Committee of Inquiry into Complaints about Ashworth Hospital.* London: HMSO.

37

Our encounters with self-harm

*Nichola Christiansen,
Sarah Shuttleworth, Della Rachel Smith
and The Women's Group*

The process of writing this chapter

After discussions with the women we work with, we decided to run a number of group session to discuss self-harm and to enable us to co-write this book chapter together. We were keen to have an honest dialogue with the women we work with to enable us to understand how they have experienced services. Discussing the topic of self-harm with those who have personal experience appealed to us because we have always been very touched by the stories that people tell about their lives. Their words stay with us in a way that information presented in a textbook does not. They bring the topic to life. Some women declined to join our discussions as they felt that the topic was too raw and painful. Those who chose to join us spoke honestly and candidly. Their stories both saddened and shocked us, but also inspired and encouraged us. They prompted us to scrutinise our own practice and that of others within the mental health profession. To explore the experience from the other side of this interaction has been immensely helpful in increasing our empathy and motivation to continue working with this complex group of individuals. We accompany people through some of their darkest times, and the way we respond to their pain can compound it or make it easier to bear. Our reactions matter.

Unless you self-harm you can never understand ... remember that we are all different.

What does help?

It helps if people don't make a big fuss when we self-harm, but if they try to be understanding and patient instead, so we know they are there to talk to afterwards if we need them, and that they will listen to the reasons why we self-harmed. Although attention isn't a particular reason for self-harm, sometimes it's nice to know that people have acknowledged that we are upset. It helps when people are being sympathetic and caring, and when they ask us, 'Do you want to talk?'

It also helps if we have some form of distraction, which could be a physical activity such as knitting or smoking, or practising mindfulness to try and calm down and take our mind off things.

What doesn't help?

In any instance of self-harming there are several things that are not helpful to us. If someone is laughing, shouting or saying it's silly/attention seeking, it can make the situation worse. Making wrong assumptions as to the reason why someone has self-harmed can be frustrating. It is also not helpful if certain privileges are stopped, such as Section 17 leave* and cigarette breaks, as this is seen as punishment and takes away things that may be useful distractions or ways of coping. Similarly, it isn't nice to use family or children as a way to make us stop, as this feels like emotional blackmail and doesn't help. What people say can make the situation worse, especially calling us 'attention seekers' or 'time wasters'.

Why do people do it?

There are many reasons why someone might self-harm. First, it is a way of coping and can be an obsessional and addictive way to let out particular emotions. It could be a way to gain relief from thoughts, voices or pain in the head. Or it might be that the person feels they deserve to be hurt and self-harming is the only way they know to let people know they need care. Some people might do it to 'destroy' or punish themselves or others for something they have done, using self-harming as a way to 'let the evil out'. In other cases, people may self-harm as a way to

---

* A type of authorised leave from the hospital given to someone who is recovering but still detained formally under the Mental Health Act.

fulfil stereotypes – they may think, 'People already think this about me', and believe they may as well confirm what people think. Sometimes, if someone sees other people self-harming as a way of coping, they may then try this strategy out and become 'addicted' themselves. Severe self-harming can also be a way for someone to acquire a disability, perhaps perceiving that they will be treated differently or that they deserve it. A lot of the time it is impulsive, and the self-harmer is not totally aware of what they are doing. Similarly, it may be a way to get out of a dissociative state and back to reality.

How does it feel?

It feels different for every person, on each occasion, and it can depend on what you have done as to how it feels afterwards. It may feel as if you are now free 'like an angel' and that you have escaped whatever situation it was that you were in – giving you a sense of relief. There may also be a need to try again if it didn't feel good enough the first time, and 'it is just another scar so doesn't matter'. It's important to point out that self-harm pain feels different to physical pain, such as needles.

What is the effect on other people?

We don't like it when we see other people self-harm but we don't always think of the effect and the consequences it has on people whilst we do it. The effect it has may depend on the relationship we have with the person, for example, whether they are a close family member, a friend or a virtual stranger. Police and staff in A&E do not have the kind of relationship with us that staff who regularly support us and those closest to us do, so it may be hard for them to know what we want; we may want someone familiar to talk to. It may also depend on where you are. Being in hospital may desensitise you (and staff) to self-harm, as you get used to seeing it every day, so it isn't paid as much attention as it would be if someone was openly self-harming in the community.

How can we help staff understand?

First of all, self-harm isn't funny and we think it should always be taken seriously. Staff can go home at the end of the day but we remain in hospital, which can be frustrating for us. It isn't always deliberate and isn't done to attention seek; neither is it enjoyable. We may self-harm to try and let staff know what is going on in our heads and that we can't cope with something. When there is a situation we need to be listened to, as we are trying to show how we feel. If we are in 'hot mind' we can't always easily fight the urge to self-harm, and sometimes it is impulsive and we are not quite sure how to stop it. The way that people react and what they say is important and can make a big difference, both good and bad. Before you make any comments think to yourself: 'Would I say this to someone in the community?' Don't be judgemental.

Challenging myths

One common belief about self-harm is that it is attention seeking, but it is not true that we only self-harm to get attention. Sometimes attention isn't a bad thing and we use self-harm to communicate our feelings – particularly if we don't feel we are being listened to. Sometimes staff, other patients or health professionals say we are self-harming for attention, which is upsetting and makes us reluctant to go back for help. Some of us have had experiences where we have been stereotyped and looked down on in A&E, so now we do not want to seek help there anymore. This makes us feel unimportant and dismissed, and is also dangerous if we are not getting the help we need! It is not attention seeking, but a cry for help and demonstrating emotional pain physically. Another important point to make is that not all self-harm is done publicly; it can be a private thing, which challenges the misconception that self-harm is always done for attention. There is a fine line between self-harming and suicide attempts, and they are very different for some people. Someone attempting suicide intends to kill themselves, whereas self-harm is done to hurt and/or scar.

How do we manage self-harm?
Lessons we've learnt – staff perspective

When a service user is self-harming on our inpatient unit, there is no specific overall procedure for dealing with self-harm, although we might be guided by general principles. We understand (and women we support have confirmed to us) that self-harm is an intensely individual process and should be managed as such. Our overriding principles include:

always maintaining dignity, being empathic and non-judgemental, and physically intervening only as a last resort if the self-harm is likely to cause significant damage to the person. We assess the particular situation and what works best for the person and base our actions on that. Interventions range from something as simple as bringing the person a soft toy to provide comfort, to physical restraint – always using the least invasive techniques that we can. We understand that physical restraint may be re-traumatising, however, at times it is necessary to keep people safe. It is important to try and develop an understanding of the reasoning behind what triggered the specific self-harm, as well as to take time to reflect on and discuss it with the individual after it has happened. We have tailored our dialectical behavioural therapy (DBT) to provide ways of coping with distress, other than self-harm, and have trained all of the staff on the ward in an adapted, simplified version of DBT, so they too can work with service users to manage their self-harm.

Our Encounters with Madness
Alec Grant, Fran Biley and
Hannah Walker (eds)
ISBN 978 1 906254 38 4 (2011)
rrp £18.00, website £17.00

A collection of user, carer and survivor narratives, this book is grouped under five themes: On diagnosis; Stories of experience; Experiencing the system; On being a carer; Abuse and survival.

The book will be of great benefit to students of mental health and narrative inquiry, users and carers, and to those generally interested in the pedagogy of suffering. Unlike most other books in this genre, the narratives are unmediated. Written by experts by experience, there are no professional biomedical or psychotherapeutic commentaries, which often serve to capture and tame, or sanitise, such stories of direct experience.

Our Encounters with Suicide
Alec Grant, Judith Haire, Fran Biley
and Brendan Stone (eds)
ISBN 978 1 906254 62 9 (2013)
rrp £18.00, website £17.00

Too often the rhetoric of 'suicidology' is occupied only by those who have never had personal experience of suicidality. The first-person voice is strangely absent. These frank accounts go some way to correcting the balance.

We hope that these narratives will be helpful for people who may have had similar encounters, or are harbouring future suicidal intentions, and for those who care for them personally or professionally; that readers can use the stories in the book to make better sense of their own experiences and decisions.

Thinking About Suicide: Contemplating and comprehending the urge to die
David Webb
ISBN 978 1 906254 28 5 (2010)
rrp £14.00, website £13.00

The literature of suicidology has studiously ignored the voice of those who actually experience suicidal feelings. David Webb suggests this is no accidental oversight but a very deliberate and systematic exclusion of this critically important first-person knowledge. The only thing that is banished with even more vigour from suicidology is mention of the spiritual wisdom that set the author free of his persistent urge to die.

Webb rejects the dominant medical model that claims suicide is caused by some notional mental illness. Thinking About Suicide calls for broad community conversation on suicide that is required to bring it out of the closet as a public health issue.